Using Computers in History

Using Computers in History: A Practical Guide is designed to introduce students to historical computing through practical workshop exercises. Utilising topics such as the performance of the American and German economies in the 1930s, the working-class pattern of nineteenth-century emigration and the cotton industry, the authors explain and illustrate the range of computing possibilities available to the contemporary historian.

Using Computers in History:

- raises awareness of the use of the computer as an important tool for the historian
- provides a practical introduction to basic computer terminology and the different software available
- examines the use of spreadsheets and how to design and work with them
- includes spreadsheet exercises based around a range of historical data sets
- explores the use of databases and shows how to construct them
- prompts students to apply the skills they have learnt to a number of examples
- offers guidelines for further study.

M. J. Lewis is Senior Lecturer in Business History and History and Computing at Sheffield Hallam University. **Roger Lloyd-Jones** is Reader in Economic and Business History, also at Sheffield Hallam University. The authors have run a course on history and computing at the university for several years.

Using Computers in History

A practical guide

M. J. Lewis and Roger Lloyd-Jones

London and New York

First published 1996
by Routledge
11 New Fetter Lane, London EC4P 4EE

Simultaneously published in the USA and Canada
by Routledge
29 West 35th Street, New York, NY 10001

Routledge is an International Thomson Publishing company

© 1996 M. J. Lewis and Roger Lloyd-Jones

Typeset in Plantin and Helvetica by
Florencetype Ltd, Stoodleigh, Devon

Printed and bound in Great Britain by
TJ Press (Padstow) Ltd, Padstow, Cornwall

British Library Cataloguing in Publication Data
A catalogue record for this book is available from the British Library

Library of Congress Cataloguing in Publication Data
Lewis, M. J. (Myrddin John).
    Using computers in history: a practical guide/M. J. Lewis and
  Roger Lloyd-Jones.
        p.   cm.
    Includes bibliographical references and index.
    1. History – Data processing.   I. Lloyd-Jones, Roger.   II. Title
  D16.12.L49   1996
  902.85–dc20   95–20050

ISBN 0–415–10311–8 (hbk)
        0–415–10312–6 (pbk)

Contents

Appendices

Figures

Tables

Acknowledgements

The genesis of this book began in 1989 when we introduced the first run of a course in History and Computing at the then Sheffield City Polytechnic. From the outset it was obvious that students required a text which could guide them through the exercises undertaken in the computer workshop. We hope this book will provide such a text and that it will promote interest in the relationship between history and computing and encourage students to use a History and Computing approach in their independent studies. Our ultimate aim is that the book will help you, the student, to become a practitioner yourself.

In producing this book we have accumulated a number of debts. We would like to acknowledge the following people. Dr Peter Wardley of the University of the West of England read and commented on the first draft and provided invaluable advice on technical issues. Professor John Benson, University of Wolverhampton, gave comments on the examples used in Chapter 6 on the material conditions of the working class, and Dr Brian Bradfield gave advice on the political history exercise used in Chapter 7. Alison Oram and Dr Michael Cronin, Historical Studies at Sheffield Hallam University, provided examples of data from their own respective research areas of Women's History and Irish History. Steve Thorpe and Carl gave technical advice which ultimately made this book possible. Claire L'Enfant of Routledge perceived the potential of a book in this area and encouraged us to go ahead with it. Finally, we give our thanks to the present and past students on the BA Historical Studies degree at Sheffield Hallam University. It was from them that we learnt a great deal about the needs of students in developing computer skills.

Part

Introduction

How To Use This Book and Getting Started

The majority of students doing history in higher education now have the opportunity to participate in historical computing. In 1981 there were few courses in higher education offering computing to history students, but 'now there is scarcely a History degree . . . in the United Kingdom that does not contain some element of computation' (Speck 1994: 28–29). This is a book for history students. It is designed to introduce you to historical computing through learning by doing. To examine the historical exercises contained in this book you will actually use a computer and in turn acquire important computer skills as well as learning how to apply these skills to the study of history. These skills are not only specific to your degree in history, but in addition they are applicable to the world of work: 'students perceive that their new computer skills . . . are marketable and capable of capitalisation, not just when they graduate but in term-time and vacation employment' (Middleton 1989: 35).

As you work through this book you will learn how to use two software applications which, alongside word processing software, are now recognised as important additions to the tool kit of the historian: spreadsheets and graphs, and database management systems. 'Software application' is the term used for such pieces of computer software that you will be using: they include word-processing, spreadsheet and database management software. 'Software' is the generic term that covers all the programs that run on a computer system, as opposed to 'hardware' which is the actual physical components of the computer. This book will show you how to access the software applications and help you to use them effectively. A spreadsheet is a software application of particular use for the historian in handling statistical information, and most software packages come with a graphics capability which allows you to convert statistical information and present it in graph form. Database management systems have also become of increasing importance to the historian. A database is a collection of information which is structured in a particular way. For example a database might contain information from the nineteenth-century census which would look at the various attributes of people, i.e. their age, gender, occupation, address, etc. To study this information you use a database management program. You will learn more about the uses of these applications to the historian as you move through the book. To run software you use a microcomputer: the PC (personal computer). The PC is the 'hardware' which allows you to use the software applications. For the historian the development of the PC has been a major breakthrough and the corresponding design of new software has meant that you no longer need to take a course in computer science to operate a computer nor learn the language of computer programming. Indeed, 'one no more needs to know how to program a computer to get results from one than to learn how a washing machine works in order to do the weekly wash. In both cases it's more a matter of knowing which buttons to press' (Speck 1994: 29).

This opening chapter is simply designed to get you started. The first section of this chapter provides a brief outline of the organisation of the book and some comments on how it may be most effectively used. Do not worry if your knowledge of computers and software applications is rudimentary: the book caters for students with different levels of computing skills, starting with the absolute beginner. The second section of this chapter provides guidance on getting started with computers, and the third section introduces you to Microsoft Windows. This is a commercial software package which allows you to organise and run programs such as spreadsheets and databases. If you are an absolute beginner, or have not used Windows before, then it is important that you read these sections carefully. If you are a more advanced computer user then you can skip these sections and proceed to Chapter 2.

1.1 How this Book is Organised

The book is organised into three parts. The first part introduces you to some of the basic principles of History and Computing and discusses their value to the historian. If you are a beginner, or relatively inexperienced in applying computers to history, then you should familiarise yourself with these basic ideas before moving on to Part 2.

In Part 2 (Chapters 3–7) the focus is on the use of spreadsheets and graphs in the study and presentation of historical information. Chapter 3 provides a discussion of the functions (i.e. uses) of spreadsheets and graphs and how they can be used by the historian. Spreadsheets are an ideal tool for the organisation and processing of historical statistics, and this necessarily raises the question of the role of quantification in historical studies. To accommodate this, Chapter 3 introduces you to the different types of historical data commonly used by historians, explains some of the basic statistical terms used, and confronts the problems and issues necessarily associated with using statistics to study the past.

Chapters 4 and 5 are companions. You learn a set of basic techniques for building your own spreadsheets in Chapter 4, and then proceed in Chapter 5 to construct a set of graphs to display the information. These chapters also introduce you to the software application we have selected to demonstrate how spreadsheets work in this book. Commercial spreadsheet software is now readily available, and there are a number of industry-standard software packages in general use. Amongst the most common are Microsoft's Excel IV, Lotus 1-2-3 and Quattro Pro. We have chosen the first of these as the exemplar for this book, and it runs on the Windows system. This software was chosen because:

- It is a commonly used commercial package in both higher education and the business world.
- It is regarded as user-friendly. You can learn quickly the basic tasks required to operate the application, and then progress to more advanced tasks.
- It forms part of an integrated package of software for the historian. Microsoft produces compatible software for word processing (Microsoft Word Version 2 and now Version 6), and also Microsoft Access, a powerful database management system which is used in this book. It therefore provides part of a workstation containing the main software applications used by historians.

- There are numerous supplementary software manuals which can be used to guide you through the techniques of using Excel.

Before we proceed further, there is a need for a point of clarification concerning the terminology used by the software designers of Excel. They refer to a spreadsheet as a 'worksheet', and a graph as a 'chart'. When we explore the use of Excel in this book, we will use the terminology specific to the Excel software to describe spreadsheets and graphs.

You learn how to use this software by undertaking a series of workshop exercises. These take you step-by-step through the techniques of building historical worksheets and creating charts. The workshops are task-oriented; each specifies a limited number of tasks to work through at your own pace. It should be emphasised that there is no time limit on completing these tasks, the important thing being to work through them and build up your confidence as you proceed. By undertaking these task you will learn about the structure of the Excel worksheet, how to build small worksheets and perform calculations, and finally to create and design to your specifications a variety of different charts. Three sets of historical information are used to demonstrate the use of spreadsheets and graphs to the historian: changes in the gender balance of the British labour force, 1841–1931, the state of the political parties in the House of Commons, 1900–1910, and public expenditure on defence and education, 1870–1914. Chapters 4 and 5 should be worked through by beginners and those more experienced users who are not familiar with Excel. These chapters provide the foundation for Chapters 6 and 7 where you use worksheets and charts to examine a number of historical themes.

Chapter 6 focuses on the debate over the conditions of the British working class in the second half of the nineteenth century. Historical data is provided, and by using worksheets and charts you are invited to explore a specific question: did the working class gain from the process of industrialisation during 1850–1914, and was this reflected in higher wages and earnings? This chapter is again based on a series of workshops which take you through a number of tasks with the aims both of extending your technical competence in handling historical material and of enhancing your understanding of the historical theme. This chapter finishes with a worksheet exercise using the major industrial city of Sheffield as a case study. You are provided with information reflecting the different types of historical data discussed in Chapter 3, and asked to produce a report on living standards in that city for 1850–1914.

Chapter 7 aims to enhance your progress towards more independent study. Rather than working through task-oriented workshops, this chapter allows you to practice your accumulating skills in worksheets and charts in a series of exercises drawn from a range of historical disciplines. The themes are based on political, economic, social and demographic history. You are provided with data relevant to each specific theme, and recommended to build appropriate worksheets and charts, and then to examine a number of historical questions. The aim is to give you the confidence to become more independent in the way you use computers to examine historical material. As one historian has recently remarked: the outcome of teaching history and computing must be to provide students with 'the ability to control the process, rather than seeking to control it ourselves' (Hitchcock 1993: 197).

Building from the earlier chapters, Part 3 (Chapters 8–10) of the book increasingly shifts the focus of history and computing to independent study. By independent study we mean student project work, research methods, dissertation work, etc., which are not class-based but where the student sets the initial questions, decides on the sources and methodology to be used, and is responsible for the academic content and presentation. In this part of the book you will be shown how to use a database management system. This allows you to organise raw historical data and then use the functions of the application to structure the information. The outcome is a database of structured historical information. Chapter 8 explores the properties of a database and the potential uses of a database management system, and provides suggestions on how you might develop independent study work. Chapters 9 and 10 are companions. Historical projects are used as examples, taken from a range of historical disciplines, to show how databases can help in assisting and developing your own work. In Chapter 9 you are taken through the various stages of using a database in independent study and an historical example is used to facilitate your learning. There are a number of commercial database management packages available, amongst the most popular are Paradox, Dbase, and the more recent Microsoft Access, which is used as the exemplar in this book. It is a powerful database management system, is operated by a mouse, and the basic techniques you learn from Excel are transferable to the operation of this program. Finally, Chapter 10 examines the potential of three further examples of using databases in independent study.

By the end of this book you will have gained hands-on experience in a range of computer skills applicable to the field of historical studies. It also follows, of course, that the skills learnt are applicable to other areas than historical studies; an important spin-off of History and Computing is the acquisition of transferable skills. Transferable skills have always been part of the process of teaching and learning in history, but they tend to remain implicit rather than explicit. We maintain that a key principle of History and Computing is that it allows you, the student, to identify clearly a range of skills which can be applied directly to your historical studies as well as making a positive contribution to your career development. But, at this stage, your main concern may be simply: how do I get started?

1.2 Getting Started

This section contains a short introduction to some of the common terminology used in computing. It is not our intention to elaborate technical terms in this book, rather to provide you with the necessary knowledge for you to progress to actually getting started quickly with using a computer (for a further elaboration of these issues see Mawdsley and Munck 1993: 13–26).

If you are a new user of computers, then you will want to know about the basic parts which make up a computer package. This package consists of the computer software and the computer hardware. Computer software is the generic title given to all programs which you can run on a computer. An application is a pre-written computer program such as word processors, spreadsheets, or database management systems. By running these

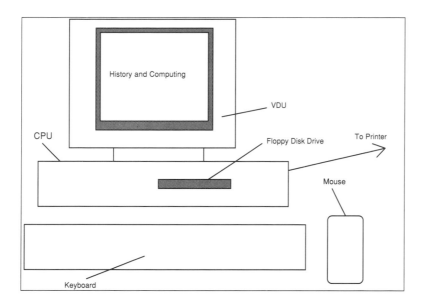

Figure 1.1 Components of a computer system

applications, the functions that they provide are opened up to you. The computer hardware is the actual computer itself. This is the microcomputer or PC. The two most common types of PC used by institutes of higher education are the IBM computer and other machines compatible with it, and the Apple Macintosh computer (Wardley 1990: 673). The difference between the two types of machines is that they use different operating systems. An operating system is a program which manages the communication between other programs and the computer itself and which handles the filing of documents and data (Spaeth 1989: 61). There is considerable disagreement concerning the merits of the two machines, but recent developments in computer operating systems have seen a narrowing in the distinction between the two types (Wardley 1990: 673). The main components of a computer are shown in Figure 1.1, and are described as follows.

- *VDU (visual display unit)*. This is a screen which allows you to view what is happening. VDUs come in colour or monochrome (black and white.)
- *CPU (central processing unit)*. This contains the electronic heart of the computer: the microprocessor chip. The chip is a piece of silicon on which has been printed a complex circuit that processes the instructions to the computer. The chip also determines the amount of memory available to the machine. The computer memory (or RAM) 'holds the operating system, software and documents in use while you work' (Spaeth 1989: 60–62; Mawdsley and Munck 1993: 14). This may sound highly technical, but with modern computers you do not need to understand the intricacies of how they work. Working with a computer is like driving a car: you do not need to know how the internal combustion engine works to be a proficient driver.

● *Keyboard.* This is one of the ways you communicate with the machine, i.e. it is the interface between you and the computer. The keyboard provides two basic functions:

(a) It allows you to type information into the machine.
(b) It allows you to type commands to tell the computer what to do.

It is not our intention here to discuss the components of the keyboard. In this book you will use the keyboard mainly to type information using the alphabet and number keys. When you are required to use command keys on the keyboard they will be described and explained to you. Expertise with the keyboard comes with practice, but your university or college may well offer advice or a course in keyboard skills.

● *Mouse.* This is an alternative to the keyboard for giving commands to the computer. The mouse is used to move a pointer which is displayed on the screen, and you use this to select objects and select commands when working with a computer application. When you work with this book, the mouse will be the main instrument you will use, and instruction on using the mouse is given in Section 1.3. With practice you will quickly gain confidence in using the mouse.

● *Disks.* It is important that you have some basic understanding of computer disks. There are two types of disk:

(a) Removable disks. These can be put in or taken out of the computer as necessary. These are more often referred to as 'floppy disks' because the early versions were flexible. However, the most common floppy disks used today are hard-cased to give added protection. It is on a floppy disk that you store your work, and you need to acquire a disk before you start working through this book. Two types of floppy disk are available: 3.5 inch double-sided double-density and 3.5 inch double-sided high-density. We recommend that you acquire the latter because they have greater capacity and you can store a greater volume of information. Floppy disks are inserted into the disk drive of the computer (see Figure 1.1). The disk drive is a recorder which records your work to disk. Most modern computers have one disk drive for floppy disks and this is called the A: drive. You will learn more about storing and saving your work on disk in Chapter 4. Before you can use a floppy disk it must be *formatted*. Formatting refers to the preparation of your disk so that it can be read by your computer. Formatting is a simple operation, and your computer services will provide instruction on how to format a disk. Be careful of how you handle your disks: they are durable but should be looked after with care.

(b) Fixed disk. This is a disk which is set into your computer case. It is referred to as the hard disk drive, and a light appears on your computer to show when it is operating. This drive is called the C: drive and stores the software, data and documents permanently, so that you can select them and use them when required (Spaeth 1989: 62–63). There is no need for you to know more than this basic information about the hard disk drive.

- *Printer*. The printer is connected to your computer and is the machine for producing the final output which is referred to as 'hard copy'.

The key technical advance in hardware has been the development of the microcomputer (PC). The first successful commercial PC was introduced in 1981 by IBM (Spaeth 1989: 60), and since then technology has advanced considerably, both in terms of the capacity of the machines to store complex software and large files of information, and in the speed at which they operate. The advance of the PC allowed computing to spread outside the realm of computer laboratories using large and complex mainframe computers, and 'Now without leaving their book lined studies historians can manipulate data on a PC' (Speck 1994: 29). When you are introduced on your course to History and Computing you will use either a free-standing PC or a networked PC. The former is a single PC not connected to any other PC, while the latter is one of a number of PCs linked to a master computer called a 'file server' (Mawdsley and Munck 1993: 20–21). The network allows you to access software applications which are common to all users of the network. Your computer network will be serviced by technicians who will be able to provide you with help and further instruction. Having familiarised yourself with the basics, you can now go on to the next section and learn about the Windows system used in this book. It is now time to turn on your computer.

1.3 The Windows System

Loading Windows

Windows software, which is produced by Microsoft, is a system that allows you to work with the software applications in this book by providing the interface between you and the applications you use. For example, it allows you to run applications such as word processors, spreadsheets and database management systems. When you open the program you see a screen which is designed as a window, and the window contains icons (graphical images). These denote the software applications you will use. You use the mouse to display the contents of the icon and also open a series of pull-down menus from which you can select a number of options. This type of program design is known as WIMP. That is, the program uses a window (W) design for the screen, icons (I) to represent the software, and a mouse (M) to select applications and pull-down (P) menus (Wardley 1990: 637; Mawdsley and Munck 1993: 21–22). You will become familiar with the WIMP environment shortly, but first you need to load the Windows program.

To load the Windows program follow these instructions:

1 Turn on the computer and the VDU. If you have problems with this then seek help from your tutor or a member of the technical staff.
2 Not all computers have the same starting procedures for Windows, but the following cover the various possibilities:

(a) Your computer starts up and the Windows program loads automatically. If this is the case then you are set up to work with Windows.

(b) Your computer displays DOS, the Disk Operating System. Windows is not a disk operating system, but rather it is a program which augments DOS by creating a user-friendly environment for you to work in. It is known as a graphical user interface (GUI) because it allows you 'to select files and programs by clicking on icons (graphical images) with a mouse' (Mawdsley and Munck 1993: 21). Before the introduction of the Windows program you would need to have learnt DOS commands. This is now no longer necessary. You will see on screen the symbol C>. This is known as the C drive prompt, and you are being prompted to type in a command. Type WIN and the Windows program will load.

(c) You are using a networked computer with a main menu displayed on the screen. See your computer network instructions for starting Windows.

The Program Manager

When you start Windows the first thing you see is the Windows Program Manager shown in Figure 1.2. The Program Manager organises software and allows you to start applications. Before examining how this works, there are a few basic terms in Figure 1.2 you need to become familiar with:

- *Window*. The rectangular area of the screen where you do your work
- *Desktop*. The background on which the window or windows appear

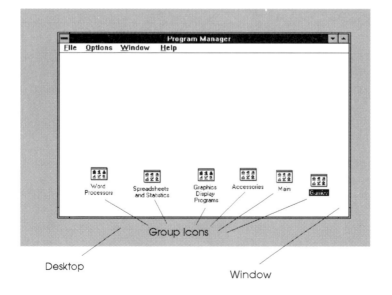

Figure 1.2 Windows Program Manager

● *Icon/group icon.* The applications you work with, such as your worksheet or database programs, are represented in Windows by small graphical symbols called 'icons'. A 'group icon' represents a collection of associated programs. For example, the group icon labelled 'Spreadsheets and Statistics' in Figure 1.2 contains Programs relating to these applications. Note: the names of the icons displayed on your screen may be different from those shown in Figure 1.2, but the principles of group icons are the same, and by opening these group icons you can determine what applications they contain.

Using the Mouse in Windows

The fastest way to work with Windows is to use the mouse. The cursor that appears on the screen as a white arrow is moved by the mouse. The mouse is shown on your screen and is the tool for navigating around the Windows screen. A mouse can have one, two, or three buttons. Normally you will use only one button, the left button, which from now on we will refer to as the 'mouse button'. Locate this button on your mouse. If you move the mouse across the flat surface of your desk then the mouse pointer (the arrow on the screen) also moves. Practice moving the mouse as follows:

1 Cup the mouse: the buttons should be under your fingers with the cord leading away from you.
2 Move the mouse to the right, without pressing the mouse button, and watch the pointer move to the right of the screen.
3 Move the mouse to the left and watch the pointer move to the left of the screen.

You select menus or icons with the cursor (the white arrow) which is moved by the mouse. When the cursor is pointing at a menu or icon you click on the left button of the mouse. You can learn quickly how to use the mouse by undertaking the mouse lesson which comes with the Windows program. This is an ideal way to learn for students who have never used a mouse. There are a number of pull-down menus at the top of the program manager window: **File**, **Options**, **Window**, **Help** (see Figure 1.2). To use the mouse lesson follow these instructions:

1 Take the mouse pointer to the **Help** menu, i.e. point the arrow at this menu option.

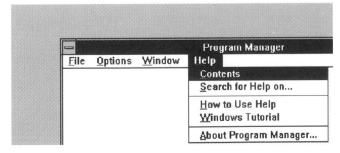

Figure 1.3 The Windows Help menu

This Tutorial has two lessons.

- If you want to learn how to use the mouse, or if you need to brush up on your mouse skills, type **M** to begin the Mouse lesson.

- If you are already a skilled mouse user, type **W** to begin the Windows Basics lesson.

Or, if you want to run the Tutorial at another time:

- Press the **ESC** key to exit the Tutorial.

Press the ESC key to exit the Tutorial

Figure 1.4 The Windows Tutorial

2   Click once with the left mouse button. The options contained in the menu appear as shown in Figure 1.3.

3   Select the option **Windows Tutorial**. Point the arrow at this option and click once on the mouse button. The Windows Tutorial opens as shown in Figure 1.4. Type **M** to begin the mouse lesson, and follow the instructions which are displayed on the screen.

Opening a Group Icon Window

You can open any group icon by pointing to it with the mouse and double-clicking (pressing and releasing in rapid succession) the mouse button. To demonstrate this, open the group icon labelled **Main** displayed in your window. Another window appears: the **Main** group window, similar to that shown in Figure 1.5. The **Main** group window contains the application programs contained in this group, and each application is represented by an icon as shown in Figure 1.5. You can run these applications by double-clicking on the selected icon.

Closing a Group Icon Window

To close the **Main** group window follow these instructions:

1   Point to the **Main** group window control box shown in Figure 1.5, and click once with the mouse button.

2   A menu appears with a number of options. Point to the **Close** option and click once with the mouse button. The window will close and the group icon will be restored.

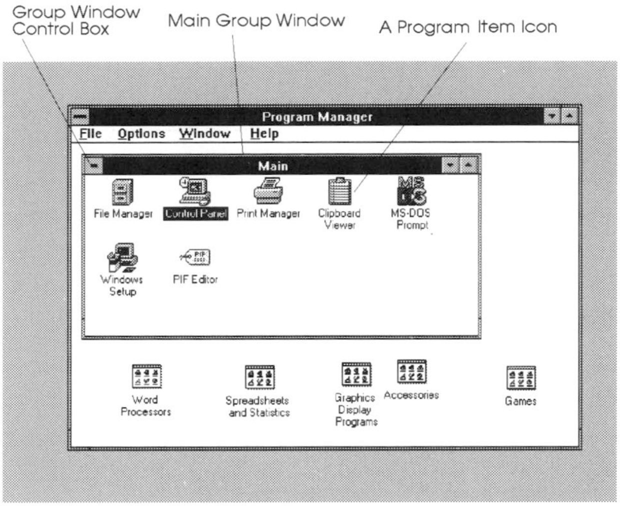

Figure 1.5 Group window

Opening Other Group Icon Windows

Find the main group icon that contains the Microsoft Excel applications program. In our example it is contained in the group icon labelled **Spreadsheets and Statistics**. It may well be different on the screen facing you. For example, there may be a main group icon labelled **Microsoft Excel**. When you have located the main group containing this application, double click on the icon and open the window. The **Microsoft Excel** program icon appears as shown in Figure 1.6. By double clicking on this icon you will be able to start the Excel program which is used in Part 2 of this book. Now close this window by clicking on the control box and selecting **Close**.

Learning More About Windows

In this section you have learnt the necessary things you will need to know to use the Windows applications in this book. If, as you progress, you want to learn more about the functions of the Windows operating system then there are a number of manuals on the market which examine the features of the system. You can also use the Windows Basic Lesson contained in the **Help** menu. To access this lesson click on the **Help** menu and select **Windows Tutorial**. The Windows Tutorial appears on screen as shown in Figure 1.4. Type **W** to start the Windows Tutorial.

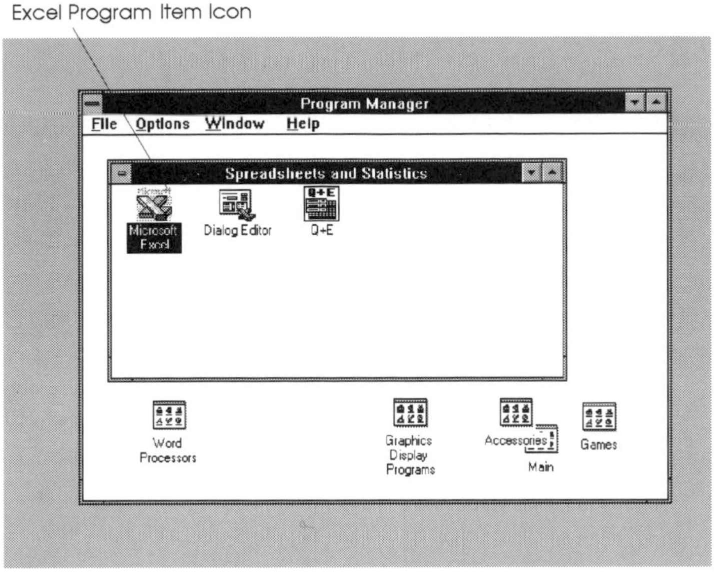

Excel Program Item Icon

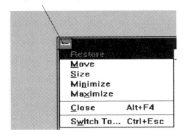

Figure 1.6 Microsoft Excel program icon contained in group window

Program Manager text box

Figure 1.7 Program Manager text box

Quitting Windows

To quit Windows follow these instructions:

1 Click on the Program Manager text box, shown in Figure 1.7.
2 Select **Close**. A message box appears: **This will end your Windows Session**.
3 You have two option buttons to choose from: **OK** or **Cancel**. Point to the **OK** button with the mouse and click on the mouse button. Your Windows session will now end.

You should now have gained the basic skills of using Windows, and can proceed to Chapter 2 which examines some of the advantages of using a History and Computing approach.

Introduction to History and Computing

2.1 Introduction

The use of computers by historians is not a new phenomenon. As a leading advocate of historical computing recently claimed: 'Historians have used computers for over thirty years in their research' (Greenstein 1994: 1). In the 1960s a small group of historical researchers with access to mainframe computers in their universities deployed them to construct large historical databases. These historians employed sophisticated statistical techniques and the theoretical models of the social sciences. The emphasis was on quantification (measurement) as the cornerstone of historical analysis (Mawdsley and Munck 1993: 3). In particular, economic historians, especially in the United States, were at the forefront of this 'new history' and, using computers to formulate their statistical models, they presented a number of revisionist interpretations of historical events (sometimes referred to as 'cliometrics'). Although these studies opened up new lines of debate and enquiry, they were not well received by the majority of professional historians who saw historical enquiry being relegated to a statistical exercise and thus foreclosing on a range of historical questions which were non-quantifiable. There is little doubt that this controversy delayed the acceptance of the computer as a tool in the study of history. However, the 1980s witnessed a revival of interest in the computer by historical researchers which was facilitated by the development of the PC and sophisticated software packages. This opened up a new window of opportunity for historians (Mawdsley and Munck 1993: 5; Greenstein 1994: 33–34).

The developments in History and Computing have been reinforced by a growing literature on the topic. In 1989 the first edition of the journal *History and Computing* was published to provide a medium for promoting 'information exchange on the use of computers in the practice of history both in teaching and research' (Morris 1989: iii). This has been reinforced by institutional developments, in particular the work of the Computers in Teaching Initiative (CTI) which promotes the spread of knowledge across the humanities and encourages the development of computing as a transferable skill. One of the main initiatives of the CTI was the establishment of the DISH (Design and Implementation of Software for Historians) project located at the University of Glasgow. This project has been further expanded into CTICH (Computers in Teaching Initiative Centre for History) which disseminates information and produces a newsletter, *Craft*. Further, at the University of Southampton, the HiDES (Historical Document Expert System) project develops software packages to bring historical sources directly to students and support interactive learning (Wardley 1990: 672; Speck 1994: 29). Such initiatives have been important in developing historical computing in the teaching curriculum, but the literature on History and Computing is still not sufficiently receptive to the needs of students. For example, it is problematic how easily understandable it is to undergraduate history students, and there remain question marks concerning its status as a valid approach to historical studies. Two recent books have attempted to address these issues: Daniel Greenstein's *A Historian's Guide to Computing*, and *Computing for Historians* by Evan Mawdsley and Thomas Munck (Greenstein 1994; Mawdsley and Munck 1993). These two works are different in their scope. The former provides a useful introduction to the potential of computers for the historian, and attempts to dispel myths surrounding History and Computing. The latter adopts a more text-book approach providing numerous examples of how the historian can put into operation computer software. Our approach focuses on the practical use of computers by developing a task oriented approach. That is, you learn by doing and acquire an understanding of the opportunities that the computer offers for historical enquiry.

Nevertheless, it is probably true to say that the majority of professional historians remain sceptical of an approach to history using a computer:

> the profession is still divided between the small minority of historians who use computers as tools for analysing historical data and the vast majority who, while they might use a PC for word-processing, remain unconvinced of the case that it can become a method-ological asset.

> (Speck 1994: 29)

This controversy is fuelled by the debate over the nature of history itself: is it to be driven by quantification or the more traditional techniques of historical investigation relying on the interpretation of non-quantifiable sources of information? This controversy is misleading for two reasons. First, measurement is fundamental to the process of historical interpreta-tion 'irrespective of whether or not the sources on which the interpretation are based contain any numbers': simply open an historical text book and count the number of quantitative statements made (Greenstein 1994: 7). Indeed, historical documents often contain implied quantification. Take the example of a woman giving evidence on housing in South Wales to the Royal Commission on the Coal Industry of 1919:

> Women acquiesce in bad housing in Wales because they have no alternative, under the present circumstances due to the *extreme shortage* of houses, *a shortage* which was *very acute* in industrial areas long before the war. The statement made that they acquiesce in bad housing because they like *low rent* I strongly resent on behalf of the women, as they have had to pay a *very big increase* in rent this last *ten years* for the *same* houses and conditions.

> (Cited in Beddoe 1988: 145, our emphasis)

The witness is clearly making quantitative statements (in italics): she condemns the condi-tion of housing, and suggests that these conditions have deteriorated over a 10-year period. A legitimate task of the historian is to test such statements, i.e. how extreme was the shortage of houses, how long had it continued, and how much had rents increased over the 10-year period referred to?

The second reason that the controvsersy misleads is that computing has been associated with economic history because it appears to lend itself more easily to a quantifiable approach than other historical fields. In this book, whatever your historical interest – political, social, cultural, science and medicine, or women's history – we maintain that the computer offers a tool for your study. It is 'a tool which, like many other tools, has some general utility in the study of history' (Greenstein 1989: 9). The computer is not a 'magic box' that will solve all your problems, any more than using it in your historical study is simply an exercise in 'number crunching'. Consequently, we will show how, for example, spreadsheets and databases can be used across a range of historical studies. We now turn to an examination of how computers can aid the historian in his or her work, and in particular explore the use of spreadsheets and databases.

2.2 The Historian and the Computer – Spreadsheets and Databases

Let us start with a basic proposition: historians are concerned with building a record of the past relating to a specific historical subject. To build up the record historians select from the available supply of facts those which are considered to be of historical significance (Carr 1990: 105). For example, a business historian may be interested in building up a record of the number of firms in a town, the number of people they employed and the type of business they were engaged in. Similarly, a social historian may gather facts on the family life, wages, employment conditions and cultural attributes of workers in the nineteenth century. Whatever the area of interest the historian is initially concerned with collecting information directed at the aims of their specific investigation.

But how do historians organise the facts they collect? In other words how do they manage information? Historians 'by necessity, are constantly developing systems for collecting, organising, and selectively retrieving information' (Greenstein 1994: 61). Historians have, of course, as long as the subject has existed, been managing information without the aid of a computer. For example, you can store information alphabetically in an index card box or in a filing cabinet. Similarly, lists of statistics can be arranged in tables manually and a pocket calculator used to process the statistics. However, it is in the area of information management where a computer provides a valuable tool for the historian, especially when the historian deals with information that is extensive or complex. In particular, spreadsheets and database management systems provide tools for the historian to manage their information more efficiently and quickly. This can best be shown by exploring some of the possibilities and advantages of using spreadsheets and databases.

Spreadsheets

A spreadsheet allows you to arrange information in a tabular form: it is an electronic table displayed on the computer screen and consists of rows and columns. It is an ideal tool for managing numerical data (statistics). Often statistical information comes in a structured format, i.e. you collect information from historical sources which contain lists or tables of data. The information you collect is therefore already categorised by the original compilers of the historical source. For example, assume you are interested in examining housing conditions during the Industrial Revolution; you might wish to concentrate your research on a key industrial town such as Manchester. In 1815 the Classification Committee of the Special Board of Health in Manchester instructed investigators to examine the state of housing in the 14 rating districts of the town. Their findings were presented in a tabular form under the following headings (Lloyd-Jones and Lewis 1993a: 33–36; Shuttle-worth 1832: 31):

District	No. of Houses Inspected	No. of Houses Reported as Requiring Whitewashing	No. of Houses Reported as Requiring Repair	Number of Houses in which the Soughs Wanted Repair	Number of Houses Damp	Number of Houses Reported as Ill-ventilated	Number of Houses Wanting Privies

This is clearly an example of a structured data source, i.e. the data form a table broken down into clearly defined categories. This provides an ideal source of information for entering into a spreadsheet, and Figure 2.1 shows an illustration of how the data will look when entered. Each category of information is contained in the columns in the spreadsheet identified by a column heading, and each row contains the associated statistics.

Having set up the spreadsheet you can then use the statistical functions of a spreadsheet, discussed in Chapter 3, to process and re-work the information. For example, you can calculate:

- The totals for each of the categories in the table
- Each category as a percentage of the total number of houses inspected for each district: for example, the number of houses damp as a percentage of the number of houses inspected.

Figure 2.2 shows the above calculations on a spreadsheet. A spreadsheet is thus a quick and efficient tool for reorganising your information and presenting it in different ways.

In terms of presentation most modern spreadsheet packages come with a graphics capability which allows you to display information in a variety of graphical forms. Figure 2.3 shows a three-dimensional column chart displaying the totals for the categories of information in

1	2	3	4	5	6	7	8
District	No. of Houses Inspected	No. of Houses Reported as Requiring Whitewashing	No. of Houses Reported as Requiring Repair	No. of Houses in which the Soughs Wanted Repair	No. of Houses Damp	No. of Houses Reported as Ill-ventilated	No. of Houses Wanting Privies
1	850	399	128	112	177	70	326
2	2489	898	282	145	497	109	755
3	213	145	104	41	61	52	96
4	650	279	106	105	134	69	250
5	413	176	82	70	101	11	66
6	12	3	5	5	0	0	5
7	343	76	59	57	86	21	79
8	132	35	30	39	48	22	20
9	128	34	32	24	39	19	25
10	370	195	53	123	54	2	232
11	N/A	N/A	N/A	N/A	N/A	N/A	N/A
12	113	33	23	27	24	16	52
13	757	218	44	108	146	54	177
14	481	74	13	83	68	7	138

Figure 2.1 Manchester housing data in spreadsheet table

District	No. of Houses Inspected	No. of Houses Damp	% of Houses Damp
1	850	177	21
2	2489	497	20
3	213	61	29
4	650	134	21
5	413	101	24
6	12	0	0
7	343	86	25
8	132	48	36
9	128	39	30
10	370	54	15
11	N/A	N/A	N/A
12	113	24	21
13	757	146	19
14	481	68	14
Total	6951	1435	21

Figure 2.2 Manchester housing by rating district – percentage recorded as damp

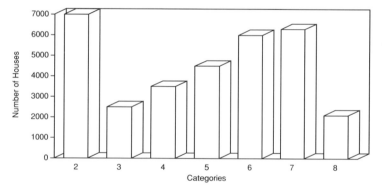

Figure 2.3 3-D column chart showing totals for each housing category

Figure 2.1 (categories 2–8). Graphs are an ideal way of presenting data and visually presenting information to the reader.

So far we have dealt with data that is structured in the original historical source, but sometimes historians will have to handle unstructured statistical data. An example of this can be taken from Women's History: a study of the changing role of women in the teaching profession between 1900 and the Second World War (Oram 1995). In this example the historian is concerned with examining the changing gender balance between male and female teachers and their levels of qualifications. For example, did female teachers enhance their status by gaining formal qualifications? Information on these issues were provided in the annual reports from the Board of Education, but the evidence needs to be pieced together, i.e. it is not presented in a structured format. The historian needs to select the

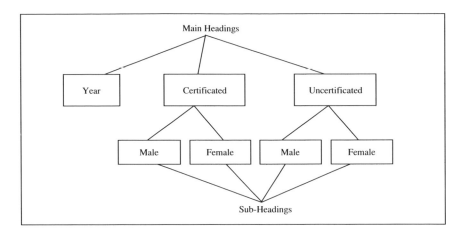

Figure 2.4 Categorisation of data in spreadsheet

Date	Certificated		Uncertificated	
	Male	Female	Male	Female
1920	34435	79668	2659	33113
1921	34241	81830	2177	33281
1922	35460	82611	2219	32598
1923	36430	80278	2063	30819
1924	36886	80091	1975	30210
1925	37162	81390	2134	31593

Figure 2.5 Data on teachers in spreadsheet: public elementary schools, England and Wales

relevant information from the source and give the data a formal structure by developing a set of categories (Igartua 1991: 78).

For the purposes of this study information was extracted from each of the annual reports from 1920 to 1938 using the following categories:

- Number of male teachers
- Number of female teachers
- Number of certificated male teachers (i.e. possessing a formal certificate for teaching)
- Number of certificated female teachers
- Number of uncertificated male teachers (without formal certificate for teaching)
- Number of uncertificated female teachers.

Having collected the data under the above categories the information was entered into a spreadsheet table using the headings shown in Figure 2.4. The spreadsheet now represents a table of structured information and includes three main headings and four sub-headings.

Date	Certificated				Uncertificated				Total
	Male	% Male	Female	% Female	Male	% Male	Female	% Female	
1920	34435	30.2	79668	69.8	2659	7.4	33113	92.6	149875
1921	34241	29.5	81830	70.5	2177	6.1	33281	93.9	151529
1922	35460	30.0	82611	70.0	2219	6.3	32958	93.7	153248
1923	36430	31.2	80278	68.8	2063	6.3	30819	93.7	149590
1924	36886	31.5	80091	68.5	1975	6.1	30210	93.9	149162
1925	37162	31.3	81390	68.7	2134	6.3	31593	93.7	152279

Figure 2.6 Calculated data in spreadsheet: teachers in public elementary schools, England and Wales

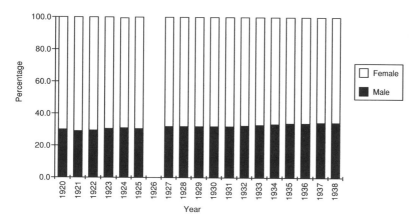

Figure 2.7 Proportions of female and male certificated teachers, 1920–1938

Note: There is no information available for 1926

The table also includes a heading for the year, and thus the data represents a time series, that is it is structured in a chronological order allowing you to examine change over time. A partial view of the completed spreadsheet is shown in Figure 2.5.

Having constructed the spreadsheet you can then process the information. Figure 2.6 shows a partial view of the processed data. We have calculated the total number of teachers for each year and the proportional distribution between males and females by type of qualification. By processing the data, you generate a new main category of information: Total Number of Teachers, and four new sub-categories (% Male, Female, etc.). Figure 2.7 shows a column chart which shows the proportions of certificated female and male teachers for 1920–1938. Clearly spreadsheets can be put to a number of potential uses and these will be explored in detail in subsequent chapters. We now turn to a preliminary examination of historical databases.

Databases

Like a spreadsheet, a database is an electronic table, but more importantly it is an electronic filing system which allows you to organise and systematically retrieve information. Let us assume you are interested in demographic history and you have been given a topic on nineteenth-century emigration and asked to look at some primary sources. You have fifty records taken from the 1889 *Select Committee on Colonisation* (Parliamentary Papers 1889) which provides information on British emigrants moving to Saltcoats, a district of the Canadian province of Manitoba. A sample of Scottish and English emigrants as recorded in the original source is as follows:

> Henry Meil from Orkney, a farmer aged 37, married with 3 children and a capital sum of £60.
>
> William Wilson from Renfrewshire, a farm servant (labourer), aged 20, single with no children, and a capital sum of £10.
>
> George Scott from Yorkshire, a businessman aged 39, married with 2 children, and a capital sum of £80.

The information is unstructured and we will need to give it a formal structure. Figure 2.8 shows the various categories of information identified from the original source and describes each category. These categories relate to the attributes of individual emigrants, i.e. their

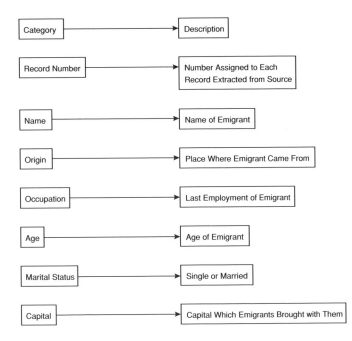

Figure 2.8 Categories of information on emigrants

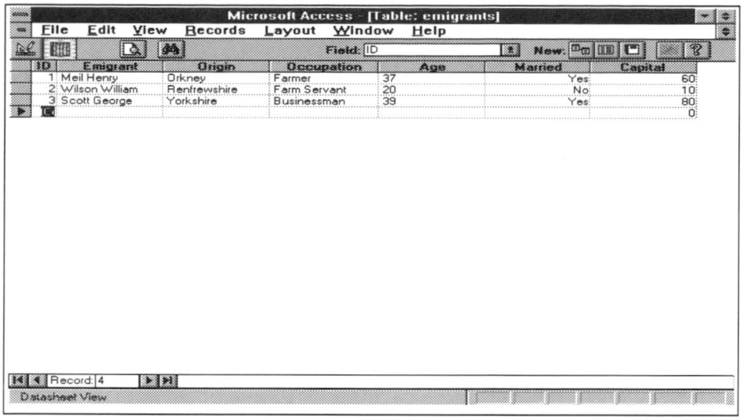

Figure 2.9 Structured data in database table – emigrants to Saltcoats, Manitoba

age, occupation, etc. Having defined the categories we can now decide on the appropriate application to use. You could, of course, enter this information into a spreadsheet and create a table using the categories in Figure 2.8. However, for this data a more appropriate application to use is a database management system which creates a table of information and allows you to selectively retrieve information. Both a spreadsheet and a database allow you to enter numerical and textual information, but a database is far more convenient for the deposit and retrieval of textual information. Figure 2.9 shows the first three records on emigrants entered into a database table. Each row of the database table (i.e. reading from left to right) constitutes the record for each individual emigrant. Each column (reading from top to bottom) is called a 'database field' and contains information on a specific attribute of the individual emigrant, i.e. information relating to the categories defined in Figure 2.8.

The advantages of a database over a spreadsheet become obvious when you attempt to retrieve information. If you had used a spreadsheet to capture the information on emigrants then it would be cumbersome to selectively retrieve information. For example, you might want to list all the records of farm servants who emigrated out of the total number of emigrants. Using a spreadsheet this would be a time-consuming operation. You could perform this operation using a spreadsheet by listing all the occupations alphabetically and then trawling through the data manually. However, using a database management system you can filter (select) the appropriate information quickly, and it will automatically give you a list of the relevant information. This would clearly be less of a problem with the example of 50 records, but in larger databases, containing hundreds or even thousands of records, the ability to selectively retrieve information quickly is paramount. Further, a database management system allows you to undertake a more complex filtering of information than a spreadsheet and relate different categories of information. For example, you can select all records of farm servants within a certain age group, e.g. between 15 and 30. You can therefore develop different categories of information from the original data source.

A database management system is thus an ideal tool for organising and selectively retrieving information. It provides the means to manage data and thus as historians we can search for trends and patterns which will provide the basis for making an historical interpretation of information and examine well-known propositions made by historians. For example, the general literature on nineteenth-century British emigration suggests that the typical British emigrant was aged between 15 and 30 years of age. The bulk of British emigrants (approximately 60 per cent) went to the USA, and you might want to ask: did the age structure of British emigrants to Canada fit the general pattern? We can use the database to test this assumption. A database is the aggregation of the total number of records you have accessed. What we want to do now is to disaggregate the information, that is, search in a specific field for that attribute we want to study. We can use the functions of a database, which are discussed in Chapter 8, to focus on the field named 'Age' and request it to list, or to count, the field records by age category. We can then determine how many of our 50 emigrants fall into the age category of 15 to 30 years. We have used this example for illustrative purposes, a realistic test of the hypothesis would require significantly more than 50 records, but of course a historical database has the capacity to handle high volumes of data.

Further, our example has focused on just one attribute; you can of course use the database to inquire across the range of fields and attempt to build a picture of the typical emigrant. What you are doing with a database is defining the relationship between data categories in a structured format. 'It means creating units of analysis pertinent to the question we are asking, either by aggregation' (our initial accessing of the records) 'or by breaking down the information into separate relations [disaggregation], and joining them in an order different from that obtaining in the sources' (ready for interpretation) (Igartua 1991:76). There is, however, a controversy amongst historians who use historical databases concerning the integrity of the historical source (see Thaler 1989). That is, should the data be structured or coded before input into a database or should it be entered in its original form (see Higgs 1990; Schurer 1990). This issue will be touched upon in later chapters when you examine the use of database management systems in your own independent studies.

We hope that this first section of the book has excited your interest in the benefits that computer applications have for the historian. They can open up new types of inquiry as well as providing you with a tool of analysis and inviting a critical evaluation of historical data. The following chapters will help to equip you with the means of applying computer techniques to the study of history.

Part

2

Spreadsheets and Graphs

Spreadsheets, Graphs and the Historian

3.1 Introduction

This chapter examines how the historian can use spreadsheets and graphics in the study of history. It is important that you read this chapter carefully. It provides a basic understanding of the advantages of spreadsheets to the historian, and explains their application to the study of history as examined in detail in the workshop exercises in Chapters 4 to 7. You will learn about:

- The functions (purposes) of a spreadsheet
- The capability of spreadsheets to handle different types of data
- The application of spreadsheet and graphics technology to the study of history.

Section 3.2 defines the functions of a spreadsheet and illustrates the use of a variety of different types of data. The term 'data' describes the materials on which the historian works (Floud 1977: 16). In Section 3.3 the application of this technology to the study of history is explored and there is a discussion of some of the problems in using historical data.

3.2 Functions of a Spreadsheet

A spreadsheet is a computer application which is used to store numerical information in a tabular form. A spreadsheet can best be thought of as a table split into rows and columns. The columns are denoted sequentially as A, B, C, etc. and the rows sequentially as 1, 2, 3, etc. Where a column and row intersect is called a 'cell' and is where you type in the information. An example of a spreadsheet table is shown in Figure 3.1.

Each cell in the spreadsheet has a unique label to identify it. For example, the number 50 is located in cell A1 and the number 89 is located in cell C1. The spreadsheet represents a data matrix. The matrix is made up of individual cells which contain numbers and is the way you arrange data in the spreadsheet. For example, Figure 3.1 is a data matrix with three columns and four rows and is made up of twelve individual cells. You will learn more about the layout of a spreadsheet in Chapter 4.

A spreadsheet is a tool which allows you to store, organise and perform calculations using numerical data, referred to as 'statistics', and you can then proceed to display the final data in a variety of graphical forms. Thus, a spreadsheet is a computer application for the processing and display of statistical information. Spreadsheets are widely used in business for processing and disseminating large volumes of information and this is one of the significant developments of the information technology revolution. But spreadsheets are not

	A	B	C
1	50	56	89
2	60	80	90
3	80	90	100
4	100	80	190

Figure 3.1 Spreadsheet table

confined to the world of business and are increasingly used by historians for both research and teaching purposes.

For the historian, a spreadsheet serves a number of purposes or what we will refer to as functions. These functions, which are explained in more detail below are as follows:

1   To store and allow the retrieval and flexible use of data
2   To create calculations from the original data
3   To ensure a high degree of accuracy in calculating large amounts of data
4   To enhance the presentation of data
5   To organise data in a specific way
6   To study the changes in the data over time
7   To study comparisons between similar data types
8   To study the relationship between different sets of data.

To illustrate these functions we will use the different historical data types shown in Table 3.1. A basic understanding of these data types is important at this stage because they are used in subsequent chapters to demonstrate the use of spreadsheets to the historian.

Table 3.1 Historical data types

Historical data type	Explanation
Calculated data	Data which is calculated from the original data by typing in a formula
Aggregate data	Data which produces a total
Disaggregated data	Data which breaks down the aggregate data into categories
Proportional data	Data recorded as a percentage of the aggregate data, producing a proportional distribution
Comparative data	Data which allows a comparison of trends from similar types of data
Time series data	Data which is arranged chronologically to study change over time
Relational data	Data arranged to establish the relationship between two or more variables

Function 1

On a spreadsheet you can build up what are known as 'data sets', which often contain a large volume of statistical information. For the historian, a data set contains a selection of information relevant to a specific historical theme (Floud 1977: 17). For example, in Chapter 6 we use a number of data sets to explore trends in the standard of living from

1850 to 1914, and when you see the term 'data set' it will refer to a selection of information relating to a particular historical theme. Data sets are stored on files on a floppy disk, producing a permanent store of data in machine-readable form. You can easily retrieve the data by accessing your file and you have a degree of flexibility in the way the data is presented. You can edit (change) the stored data to include additional information, delete information and perform new calculations. The advantages of these functions will become obvious when you undertake the workshop exercises in subsequent chapters.

Function 2

A spreadsheet is a useful device in the process of number-crunching and performs calculations far more rapidly than manual processes. Input the right formula, press the correct button, and it will display the calculation. By using this function you can summarise your data and produce, for example, totals. You can also re-organise the original information and present the data in a different form, as demonstrated below under Function 5. This type of data we will refer to as 'calculated data'. To illustrate calculated data consider the spreadsheet in Figure 3.2 which contains a data set on the number of livestock in British agriculture for selected years between 1867 and 1939. An obvious calculation you would wish to perform is to calculate the total number of livestock for each year. Column F contains the calculated data and was compiled by typing a simple formula into the spreadsheet. For example, the total in cell F1 is 36,319: the sum of rows B1 to E1 on the spreadsheet. You will learn how to create your own formulas and calculations in subsequent chapters.

	A	B	C	D	E	F
1	Year	Cattle	Sheep	Pigs	Horses	Total
2	1872	5625	27922	2772	1258	36319
3	1895	6354	25792	2884	1545	35030
4	1913	6964	23931	2234	1324	33129
5	1918	7410	23353	1825	1337	32588
6	1939	8119	25993	3767	987	37879

Figure 3.2 Numbers of livestock in British agriculture (in thousands)

Source: Mathias 1969: 477

Function 3

A major advantage of a spreadsheet is that it allows the accurate calculation of data at high speed. The structure of a spreadsheet and its edit function facilitate the accurate entry of data. Where large volumes of statistical data are concerned it is more accurate than a pocket calculator. However, you should still check the results of the data you enter and the calculations you make.

1	A	B	C
2	Sector	No. (million)	%
3	Agriculture, Forestry	1539	24
4	Manufacturing, Mining	3057	48
5	Commerce, Transport, Public Services	297	5
6	Public Admin., Forces, Domestic Service	1500	23
7	Total	6393	100

Figure 3.3 Occupational groups in Britain, 1841

Source: Mathias 1969: 478
Note: The figures in column B represent millions, reducing entry time

Function 4

So far, you have been concerned with the presentation of historical data in tabular form. However, a spreadsheet has a variety of components for displaying information, and of particular use to the historian is the use of graphics. Graphics allow you to present historical information in an easy-to-understand format and also aid the process of analysis by highlighting the basic trends (patterns) in the data. You can produce bar charts, column charts, line charts, pie charts and scatter charts; these charts are illustrated in this chapter and will be explored in more detail in later chapters.

Function 5

The organisation of data is a key function of a spreadsheet. You can sort (arrange) data in either ascending (0–100) or descending (100–0) order, or find the minimum and maximum values contained in a given set of statistics. You can also work with disaggregated data and display the data as a proportion of the aggregate or total data. Disaggregated data is data which is broken down into selected categories. An example of disaggregated data on a spreadsheet is given in Figure 3.3 which shows the breakdown of the British labour force into four general occupation categories for 1841. The total (aggregate) labour force in 1841 was 6,393,000 and the numbers working in each category are shown in column B of the spreadsheet. Column C contains calculated data which shows the proportional distribution (share) of each category to the total. The percentage working in manufacturing and mining, for example, is calculated by dividing the number of workers in this category (3,057) by the total number of workers (6,393) and then multiplying by 100. Figure 3.4 shows how this data can be displayed in graphical form. The bar graph shows the numbers in each category and the pie graph shows their proportional shares. You will learn how to work with disaggregated data in subsequent chapters.

Function 6

Using a spreadsheet you can arrange your data to study changes over time and analyse trends. This is known as a 'time series' because the data is ordered chronologically. Chronological ordering often occurs naturally in the process of collecting the data, e.g.

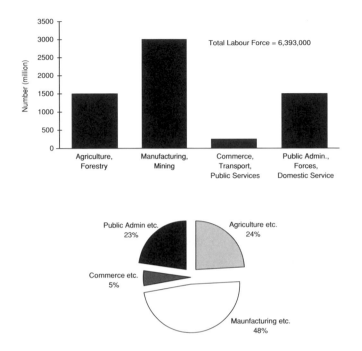

Figure 3.4 Numbers and percentages employed in different occupational groups, 1841

	A	B	C	D	E	F	G	H
1	Year							
2	1920	1929	1937	1951	1964	1973	1979	1986
3	2	9.7	10.1	1.3	1.7	2.0	4.7	11.3

Figure 3.5 Unemployment rates in Britain, 1920–1986 (percentage of workforce)

Source: Calculated from Broadberry 1991: 217

daily, monthly, or yearly (Floud 1977: 85). For example, business historians will want time series data on a firm's profit and loss, costs, sales revenue, investment outlay, etc. But such information is not just the province of business history for 'almost all data on individual people will contain chronological information, such as date of marriage or death, which may be used to construct time series data' (Floud 1977: 86).

Figure 3.5 shows a time series for rates of unemployment in Britain for selected years between 1920 and 1986. To highlight the trends in unemployment the data is converted to a line graph which is shown in Figure 3.6. The trend in the data refers to the magnitude of change, in other words the increase or decrease in the unemployment rate. Using a spreadsheet you can also calculate the proportional change over time.

Figure 3.7 shows population change in England and Wales by decade between 1801 and 1841. Cells A3 to E3 contain the population figures for each date, and cells F3 to I3 contain the calculated data for percentage change. For example, to calculate the percentage change between

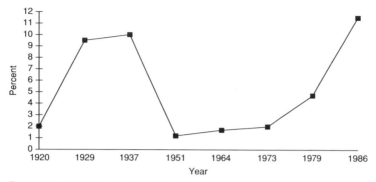

Figure 3.6 Unemployment rates, 1920–1986

Source: Compiled from data in Figure 3.5

	A	B	C	D	E	F	G	H	I
1	Population (000)					Percentage Change			
2	1801	1811	1821	1831	1841	1801–11	1811–21	1821–31	1831–41
3	9061	10322	12106	13994	15929	13.9	17.3	15.6	13.8

Figure 3.7 Population change in England and Wales, 1801–1841

Source: Mitchell and Deane 1962: 8

	A	B	C
1		Universities	
2	Date		
3		Germany	England
4	1870	2346	397
5	1900	12313	2012
6	1914	26360	6340

Figure 3.8 Expenditure on science and technology in universities: Germany and England (thousands of marks)

Source: Pollard 1990: 155

1801 and 1811 subtract 9,061 from 10,322, divide by 9,061 and multiply by 100: (10,322–9,061)/9,061*100. We shall return to a discussion of time series trends in Section 3.3.

Function 7

You can use information that compares trends and a spreadsheet will highlight the comparisons between the data. This type of data is known as 'comparative data'. An example of comparative data is given in Figure 3.8 which provides evidence for examining the provision of scientific and technical education in German and English universities in the late nineteenth century. Using this data we can compare the trends across the two countries and gauge the extent to which resources were being devoted to a crucial area of education provision. To allow you to draw trends from the data Figure 3.9 shows a bar chart illustrating the comparative expenditures for the university sector.

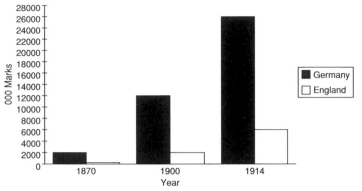

Figure 3.9 Expenditure on science and technology in English and German universities

Source: Compiled from data in Figure 3.8

Function 8

Using a spreadsheet you can study the statistical relationship between two or more variables which may at least allow a tentative prediction of causal relations. This type of data is known as 'relational data'. You might, for example, want to explore the nature of the relationship between the following (see Rowntree 1991: 164):

- Rainfall and attendance at football matches
- The length of education and annual earnings
- The growth of urban population and the level of urban crime
- The size of capital investment and the size of firm in terms of employment.

Such relationships are often explored in their historical context by creating a time series. To demonstrate this, Figure 3.10 shows a hypothetical spreadsheet with two variables, the rate of urban growth and the rate of urban crime per thousand of the population. The data forms a time series as the variables are examined for 10-year periods. From this information you would want to know the statistical strength between these two variables. You can calculate this by using the spreadsheet to produce a scatter chart to calculate the correlation coefficient, which will be explored in Chapter 7. Figure 3.11 shows a scatter chart which has been produced from the information in Figure 3.10. The scatter chart plots the relationship between the two variables. For example, when the urban growth rate was 15 per cent the rate of crime was 18 per thousand.

1	A	B	C
2	Date	Rate of Urban Growth	Rate of Crime
3		(%)	(per 1,000 of Population)
4	1850s	15	18
5	1860s	22	24
6	1870s	21	25
7	1880s	18	23

Figure 3.10 Relationship between urban population growth and the rate of urban crime

Source: Rowntree 1991: 164

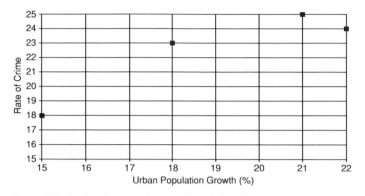

Figure 3.11 Scatter chart showing statistical relationships

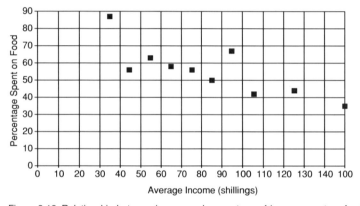

Figure 3.12 Relationship between income and percentage of income spent on food

Source: Fraser 1981: 34

A further example is shown in Figure 3.12 which plots the relationship between average yearly income and the amount of income spent on food in 1889. From the data plotted you might consider the following proposition: the higher the level of average income then the lower would be the percentage of income spent on food. In other words, we would expect lower income groups in the late nineteenth century to have to spend a larger propor-tion of their income on basic necessities such as food. Study Figure 3.12: is the above proposition supported by the data plotted in the chart?

This section has shown the range of functions that a spreadsheet can perform in dealing with historical data. The next section discusses explicitly the potential application of spread-sheets for historical studies. The great advantage of a spreadsheet is that it allows you to handle a large volume of statistical data, and in order to capture the advantages of spread-sheets to the historian we must address the issue of quantification. The functions need to be put to work if their potential is to be realised. That is, as historians, we can learn by doing.

3.3 Applying Spreadsheets to the Study of History

This section will examine how the historian can apply spreadsheet technology to facilitate the study of history and the ideas formulated here will be used in the workshop exercises in Chapters 6 and 7. We can identify two main applications of a spreadsheet to historical studies:

- The testing of historical propositions
- The analysis of statistical trends over time.

These two applications will now be explained with the use of historical examples.

The Historian and Testing

A spreadsheet is a tool or application which is concerned with problem solving. For example, a businessman may apply information technology to overcome the problems of calculating wages or costs. Similarly you can use spreadsheets to investigate the problems of the past which concern the historian. A task of the historian is to test historical propositions by analysing statistical data. In other words, the historian is concerned with investigating historical problems by using quantitative analysis. Quantification is part of the everyday activity of the historian and spreadsheets are a tool which facilitates the process of quantification. The historian, 'like other social scientists', uses 'quantitative concepts frequently and inevitably' (Floud 1977: 2). We could hardly study the process of urbanisation in the nineteenth century, for example, without asking a number of quantitative questions:

- How large were urban populations?
- How fast did they expand?
- What factors accounted for expansion, i.e. how many immigrants moved to the towns?
- What changes took place in the composition of the urban population (e.g. age structure, gender, occupation)?

The quantitative evidence you produce may confirm or falsify a given proposition and thus meet one of the requirements of scientific investigation. To illustrate the ideas introduced so far we will briefly consider a specific historical debate: the relationship between education and economic performance in the late nineteenth century.

Consider the following proposition:

> A central cause of the poor performance of the British economy compared to that of Germany in the late Victorian and early Edwardian period was the poor provision of education in science and technology.

To test this proposition you first should consider the quantitative evidence for education provision. One measurement which is commonly used is the amount of state support in the form of expenditure on science and technology. Comparative data for the universities

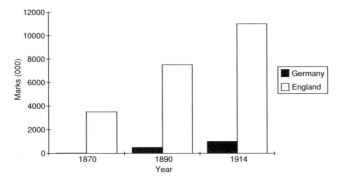

Figure 3.13 Expenditure on science and technology in non-university sectors: England and Germany

Source: Pollard 1990: 155

in England (not the whole of Britain) and Germany was shown earlier in Figures 3.8 and 3.10. Studying this data, you could conclude the following.

In quantitative terms, although expenditure increased over the period in England, the volume of expenditure was higher in Germany. Even in 1914 German expenditure was over four times that in England. Consequently you might argue that Germany's more rapid rate of economic growth, compared to Britain's, from 1870 to 1914, was a function of the former country's higher expenditure on science and technology. However, there are three points of caution which you should keep in mind when analysing this or any historical data produced on a spreadsheet:

● Historical statistics are often incomplete and thus the spreadsheet data may offer only a partial test of a proposition. In our example, the data covers only the university sector and this prompts the question of what other sources of information you may require to gain a fuller picture? The spreadsheet provides only partial evidence and this should signal to you the need to search for other sources. To facilitate the process of historical analysis additional data is required. As historians too frequently discover, this data may not be available; however, there is information on science and technology expenditure for the non-university sector and this is shown in the bar chart in Figure 3.13. The chart shows that state expenditure on the provision of science and technical training at the non-university level in England was at a far higher level than in Germany and in total England did not lag greatly behind (Pollard 1990: 156). You could also examine data for numbers of graduates in science and technology or numbers of teaching staff or students to develop a fuller picture. We would also have to explore further the costs and benefits of directing resources to the different sectors of education.

● Spreadsheets store and process quantitative information but as historians you will have to refer to qualitative evidence (contemporary writing, documents, etc.). Take the question of education again. Pollard, using a variety of qualitative sources, shows that the quality of education in the continuation schools, the flagship of the German education system, was sub-standard, and there was a high drop-out rate. Similarly, although contemporaries in Britain complained of the lack of science and technical training so did the Germans complain of inadequacies in their own provision. Historians thus need to support the quantitative evidence with a range of qualitative sources. The spreadsheet will only take you so far.

- The historian faces problems of causation in testing historical propositions. The proposition you started with contained an implied causation between the provision of science and technology and economic performance. Certainly the growth of the British economy slowed down after 1870 compared with that of Germany, and in the key new industries of the second Industrial Revolution such as chemicals and electrical engineering British business lagged well behind before 1914. But the link between the two variables, education and economic growth, is problematic. In the first place, it is difficult to measure the contribution of education to economic performance. Secondly, the lines of causation are indeterminate. Does a higher level of investment in education lead to faster rates of economic growth or vice versa? In other words, the spreadsheet will produce numbers, but you need your historical skills to interpret and critically assess these numbers. You must be careful not to assume that the final number produced by the spreadsheet provides a definite causal explanation. With these caveats in mind, let us explore further the use of spreadsheets.

The Historian and Trend Analysis

Working with spreadsheets historians can highlight the patterns of change over time. Trend analysis is part of the everyday activity of the historian. A time series, generated by a spreadsheet, allows the analysis of trend movements in both the long and the short run. For example, analysing birth rate data in the 1930s some contemporary experts projected the UK population of the 1950s to be less than 10 million. It is important therefore when working with your spreadsheet time series not to confuse short-run movements with long-run trends. At the same time, long-run trends may suggest a smooth process of change

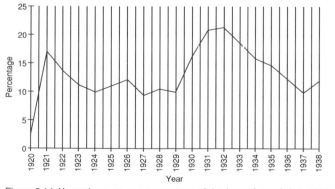

Figure 3.14 Unemployment as a percentage of the insured population, 1920–1938

Source: Aldcroft 1983: 108

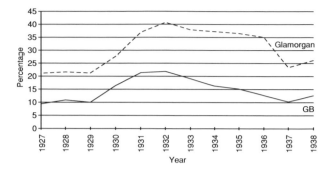

Figure 3.15 Percentage unemployment in Glamorgan and Great Britain, 1927–1938

Source: D. Thomas 1988: 31

but disguise quite dramatic short-run fluctuations which could be of interest to the historian. Take the example of unemployment shown in Figure 3.6. If you take the long-run trend from 1920 to 1986 you might infer that unemployment rose sharply between 1920 and 1929, rose marginally between 1929 and 1937, decreased sharply between 1937 and 1951, rose marginally from 1951 to 1973, and then increased significantly again to 1986. However, this smoothes out sharp short-run fluctuations in unemployment. This can be demonstrated if you take a snapshot of unemployment in the interwar years and look at an annual time series. Figure 3.14 shows such a time series and highlights the sharp short-run movements in unemployment associated with the interwar years.

There is another issue of concern to the historian in the data contained in Figure 3.14, and that is the question of representation. How representative is the data for the study of unemployment in Britain over the interwar years? Does the data capture adequately the historical event you wish to study? The trends in Figure 3.14 support the contention that the interwar years saw mass unemployment and were bleak years for the British working class. However, the data represents the national picture, and measures aggregate unemployment in the whole of the United Kingdom. This raises again the issue of aggregate and disaggregated data. You get a different picture of unemployment in the interwar years if you study unemployment on a regional level and disaggregate the data. Figure 3.15 compares the aggregate data for unemployment to that of the main coal-producing county of South Wales, Glamorgan, between 1927 and 1938. There are two basic trends in the data:

- The trends of unemployment in Glamorgan mirror those of the UK with a sharp rise at the height of the depression between 1929 and 1932, a gradual although slower recovery between 1932 and 1936, and a sharper fall between 1936 and 1937.
- The unemployment rate in Glamorgan was significantly higher than the national aggregate. At the peak of the depression in 1932 unemployment in Glamorgan was twice the national figure and in some areas within Glamorgan such as Merthyr and the Rhondda Valley unemployment was over three times the national figure.

The incidence of unemployment in the interwar years was not uniform: there were declining and prosperous regions. For example, although all regions in Britain suffered high rates of unemployment when the depression hit after 1929, the rates of unemployment in the South and Midlands, with the growth of new industrial sectors, were significantly lower than those experienced in the older industrial districts such as South Wales, Lancashire, Scotland and the North East. The historical concentration of these regions on the old staple industries which were in structural decline in the interwar years created severe problems of unemployment and regional deprivation.

This chapter has demonstrated the use of spreadsheets and their application to testing historical propositions by quantitative analysis. The historical workshop exercises in Chapters 6 and 7 will develop a number of propositions which you can test by applying spreadsheet techniques. For example, the workshops in Chapter 6 will test out propositions concerning the standard of living of the working class. But keep in mind the problems we have raised concerning the use of quantitative data. During the workshop sessions you will be encouraged to ask further questions of the data and develop a critical awareness of the data being used. When you work with spreadsheets you should think about the nature of historical evidence and this can only help to make you a better historian.

Having explored the use of spreadsheets to the historian, you can now proceed to learn how to use a spreadsheet in Chapters 4 and 5 and then to examine in detail the historical themes and data in Chapters 6 and 7.

Chapter 4

Presenting Historical Data with a Spreadsheet

4.1 Introduction

The program we have selected to demonstrate the use of spreadsheets is Microsoft Excel IV, a powerful spreadsheet and graphics package. This chapter will first guide you through the main components of Excel and the terms most frequently encountered when using the program. You will then undertake a series of workshops designed to give you hands-on experience in building and working with spreadsheets. In the next chapter you will then learn how to construct graphs from the information in your spreadsheets and highlight trends in the data. The best way to learn how to use a spreadsheet is to learn by doing. Both this chapter and the next are designed to prepare you for Chapters 6 and 7 where you will explore a number of historical themes. Here you will learn about:

- The Excel worksheet (the term used in Excel for a spreadsheet) and its components
- Terms used in Excel, and other spreadsheet programs, such as cell, range, active cell, etc.
- How to build a small historical spreadsheet and design it by using the menu and tool bar commands
- Entering formulas and performing calculations
- Printing spreadsheets.

What you learn in this chapter is very important and provides the basis for building up your skills and confidence. The tasks you will undertake in the workshops contained in this chapter will cover the main techniques you will encounter in subsequent chapters of this book.

4.2 A Guide to Excel

You should read through this guide with the Excel worksheet on the computer screen. Excel operates from the Windows Program Manager, which was explained in Chapter 1, together with instructions for starting Excel. A summary, however, is provided below:

1. Start the Windows program.
2. You will see on screen the Windows Program Manager. Take the mouse pointer to the Excel IV main icon in the Program Manager window.
3. Double-click the left-hand button on the mouse and the Microsoft Excel icon will appear in the applications window.
4. Double-click the Microsoft Excel icon and the program will start.

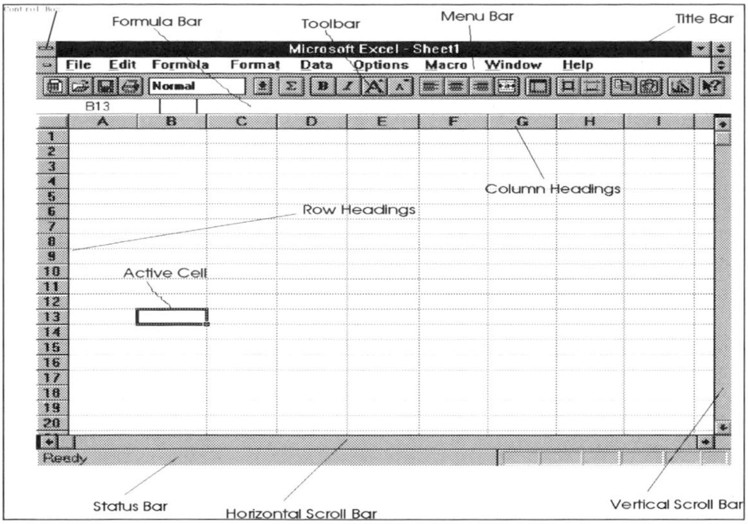

Figure 4.1 The worksheet screen

Learning About the Worksheet Screen

When you first start Excel a blank worksheet appears on your screen like the one shown in Figure 4.1. This is called the 'worksheet screen' and contains two windows: the worksheet document window and the Excel application window.

The Worksheet Window

The worksheet window is called the *active window* and is the area in which you enter your data. A worksheet (which is simply another name for a spreadsheet) is the main document used to store and work with data. We will use the term 'worksheet' for a spreadsheet when we are referring to Excel throughout the rest of this book. The worksheet window is a two-dimensional grid containing a possible 256 columns and 16,384 rows. The column headings are labelled sequentially from A upwards (A to Z, AA to AZ, BA to BZ, and so on), and the row headings are labelled sequentially from 1 through to 16,384. At any one time, of course, you only see a small number of columns and rows displayed in the worksheet screen. The grid structure of the worksheet allows you to enter and organise your data easily. There are three methods of moving around the worksheet window:

- By using the arrow keys located on your computer keyboard
- By using the **Pg Dn** (page down) and **Pg Up** (page up) keys located on your computer keyboard
- By clicking on the horizontal and vertical scroll bars which are shown in Figure 4.1.

Experiment with these three methods. First, use the four arrow keys on the keyboard to move around the worksheet. Second, use the **Pg Dn** key to move down a page and then use the **Pg Up** key to move back up the page. Finally, locate the horizontal and vertical scroll bars on the screen and using the mouse pointer click with the left-hand button first on the horizontal scroll bar and then on the vertical scroll bar.

The Excel Window

The Excel window contains a number of applications which allow you to operate the worksheet. As Figure 4.1 shows, it is divided into four bars at the top: the title bar, the menu bar, the tool bar and the formula bar; and one bar at the bottom: the status bar.

The Title Bar

The top bar of the Excel window is the title bar which contains the name of the worksheet. When you start Excel the worksheet is always titled **Sheet1.** When you save a worksheet to disk under a specific name then the title bar changes to reflect this. You will learn how to name a worksheet in the next workshop.

The Menu Bar

The second bar down is the menu bar and you will use this frequently in the workshop exercises with Excel. The menu is the primary device you use to give instructions to Excel. The menu bar shows the menus which are available to you at any given time. There are eight menu selections plus an Excel Help menu. You select a menu by using the mouse to click on the menu of your choice. You will use some of these menus to design your worksheets. You open the menus by clicking once on the menu title with the mouse pointer. Do this, and, when you have viewed the contents, press the **Esc** (escape key) on the keyboard and the menu will close.

The Tool Bar

The third bar down, under the menu bar, is the tool bar. The tool bar provides numerous buttons (tools) to perform tasks that would take several steps using the menu, and to do tasks that are not included in the menus. You use the mouse pointer to click the buttons and bring the tools to work. Where necessary, you will be shown how to use the tool bar to perform tasks quickly in the workshops. The Excel tool bar is shown in Figure 4.2. Look at the tool bar on your screen and locate the various tools.

The Formula Bar

The fourth bar down, under the tool bar, is the formula bar. This is the area which records

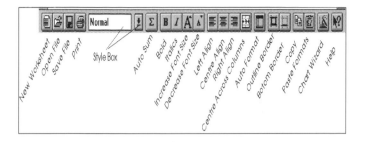

Figure 4.2 The tool bar

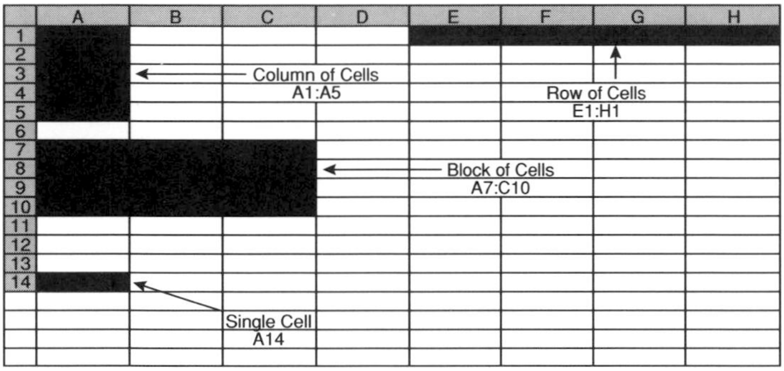

Figure 4.3 Worksheet cell ranges

the information (text, numbers, formulas) you type into the worksheet, and allows you to change (edit) the information you store. You will see how useful the formula bar is when you enter information into the worksheet.

The Status Bar

The status bar, at the bottom of the Excel window, displays messages on the left and keyboard indicators on the right. The most common message you will see is **Ready** which indicates that Excel is waiting for you to type in data or select a menu. This is the Ready mode. Another mode is the Edit mode. When you are editing data, for example in the formula bar, the message will change to **Edit**. The keyboard indicators tell you that a certain key has been pressed, e.g. **Cap** indicates the **Caps** (capitals lock) key.

The Cell Address

A worksheet is made up of a large number of columns and rows. Where a row and a column intersect is called a *cell* and this is where you enter (type) and store information. Each cell is identified by an address. When information is stored in a worksheet it is typed into the individual cells and can be located by reference to the cell address. For example, in Figure 4.3 the single cell is identified by the address A14 and is the intersection of column A and row 14. You build a worksheet by entering text, or numbers and formulas, into the individual cells. It is important you understand the concept of the cell address, because it is used frequently when building a worksheet.

Cell Ranges

A group of adjacent cells in a worksheet is called a *range*. Figure 4.3 shows the four kinds of ranges which can exist on a worksheet: a row of cells (range E1:H1), a column of cells (range A1:A5), a block of cells (range A7:C10), and a single cell (range A14). Each range is identified by the first and last cell address separated by a colon, e.g. range E1:H1 is a row of cells. In this book, when we refer to a range of cells we will use this notation to identify a range of cells. The range specifies a group of cells you want to work on. For example, later in this chapter you will perform calculations and you will need to specify the range of cells you want to calculate. Study Figure 4.4 which gives two sets of figures: a column range, A1:A4, and a row range, B6:D6. If, for example, you wanted to calculate the total for the column of numbers, you would type the formula =Sum (A1:A4). This specifies that the calculation is to be performed on the column range A1:A4. What would you type to produce the total for the row of cells in Figure 4.4?

	A	B	C	D
1	10			
2	20			
3	30			
4	40			
5				
6		20	30	40

Figure 4.4 Specifying range cells for formulas

Selecting Cell Ranges

You will select cell range frequently when working with a worksheet. When you see the term 'select' in this book it instructs you to use the mouse to highlight a range of cells on which you want to operate. For example, you might want to centre the data in a range of cells or format the data by selecting bold. You select a range of cells by pointing on a cell with the mouse in one corner of the range, pressing the left-hand mouse button, and dragging the mouse (pressing and holding the mouse button while moving the mouse) to the opposite corner. For example, the highlighted range in Figure 4.5 shows the result of dragging the mouse from A1 to A10. Try this: take the mouse to A1 and, keeping the mouse button depressed, drag the mouse to A10. To turn the selection off, simply click with the mouse anywhere on the highlighted range. You should now practise selecting the following ranges:

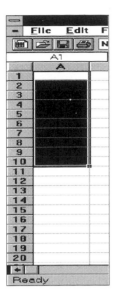

Figure 4.5 Selecting a cell range

A1:A6
C6:E12

Practise selecting until you are confident in this technique.

The Active Cell

The active cell is where you type information, and you make a cell active by clicking on it with the mouse pointer. The shape of the mouse pointer, in the worksheet window, is a white cross. The active cell is recognised by the rectangular border around the cell (see Figure 4.1). In the bottom right-hand corner of the active cell is a small square containing a white cross. This is called the 'fill handle' and is used to position the mouse pointer to copy information in the active cell by dragging the contents of the cell. You will learn how to use the drag facility in the workshops. When you first start Excel, the active cell is always A1. You build a worksheet by moving from one active cell to another and entering information.

When you are satisfied that you have understood the concepts introduced in this section you can move on to the workshops. However, you might wish to break off here and the following instructions show you how to exit the Excel program:

1   Take the mouse pointer to Excel's control menu box located in the upper left-hand corner of the Excel application window (see Figure 4.1)
2   Double-click (click twice in rapid succession) on the Excel control menu box. You return to the Windows Program Manager window.

3   We have assumed that you have not entered any information into the work-sheet. If you have, then the **Save Changes** box opens. Click on **No** as you do not wish to save the worksheet.

(4.3) Workshop Exercises

Workshop 1
Saving and
Opening
Files

During the workshops you may be frequently adding to or amending a worksheet, and it is important that you learn to organise your files. This workshop takes you through a number of tasks designed to teach you:

- How to save worksheet files on a floppy disk and how to save changes to your worksheet
- How to gain access to the saved worksheets by opening the files
- How to open more than one worksheet file and use the Window menu.

Task 1
Naming and saving worksheets to disk

There are a number of ways to save worksheets, but we recommend that when you create a new worksheet to store historical information you should always name and save the worksheet first before you enter information. To name and save a worksheet to disk, follow these instructions:

1   Start the Excel program. (If you require a reminder of the procedures for starting Excel then return to the Excel guide in Section 4.2.)
2   A blank worksheet appears on your screen with the title displayed in the title bar: **Sheet1**. This is the default name given to every worksheet you create.
3   When you use historical information, to build a worksheet, it is important that you name the worksheet so that it can be easily identified with the information it contains. This is especially important as you store more worksheet files on your disk. You now need to change the default name

File	Edit	Formula	F
New...			
Open...	Ctrl+F12		
Close			
Links...			
Save	Shift+F12		
Save As...	F12		
Save Workbook...			
Delete...			
Print Preview			
Page Setup...			
Print... Ctrl+Shift+F12			
Print Report...			
1 CENSUS.XLS			
2 CENSUS1.XLS			
Exit	Alt+F4		

Figure 4.6 File menu box and its contents

(**Sheet1**) in the title bar. Take the mouse pointer to the menu bar in the Excel window. As you pass over the boundary between the worksheet window and the Excel window the mouse pointer changes from a cross to an arrow. Click on the **File** menu. The options available in the **File** menu are shown in Figure 4.6.

4   Click on the **Save As ...** option. You are going to give the file a name and save it on your disk. The **Save As** dialogue box now appears as shown in Figure 4.7. When you open an Excel menu, you will often be required to provide additional instructions, and this is the function of a dialogue box. As you progress through these workshops you will use more menus and their related dialogue boxes. The dialogue box contains these main features:

- **File Name**: This is a text box, i.e. you enter the text for the worksheet name in this area. Directly under the **File Name** text box is a drop-down list box which lists the names of the files you have stored on your disk. You move down the files by clicking on the scroll bars on the right of the list box.
- **Drives Box**: This is a drop-down list box, so called because you click down on the arrow to the right of the box to view the contents of the box. You use it to change the drives for storing your worksheet files.
- **OK, Cancel, Help**: These are command buttons. The **OK** button is used to command Excel to carry out an instruction. The **Cancel** button is used if you want to cancel the dialogue box. The **Help** button provides instruction on how to use the dialogue box.

5   To store worksheets permanently, you need to save them either to the hard drive (drive C:) or to a floppy disk in the A: drive (see Chapter 1). When the **Save As** dialogue box appears, the drive for storing your files is sometimes

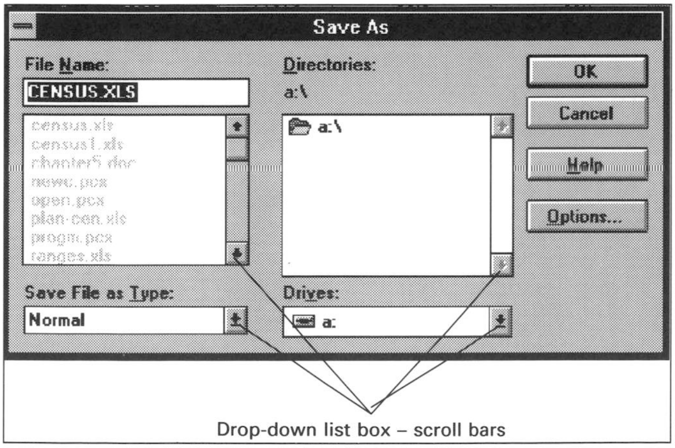

Drop-down list box – scroll bars

Figure 4.7 **Save As** dialogue box

automatically set to the C: drive. To change the drive to the **A**: drive you need to click down on the **Drives** drop-down list box. The **a**: sign will appear in the box. Click on this and you are ready to save to the **A**: drive.

6   You can now name the file in the **File Name** text box. Take the mouse pointer to the **File Name** box and insert the arrow in the left-hand side of the text area. As you do so, the mouse pointer turns to an I-bar shape. This is the insertion point for typing text. When you have the insertion point positioned click once and the insertion point becomes a flashing black line instructing you to enter the file name. A worksheet file name can be up to eight characters long. Type PRACT. This will be a practice worksheet file for you to use in this workshop.

7   When you have finished typing the name take the mouse pointer to the **OK** button and click. A summary information box appears: you can either type information which describes the data in the worksheet, or leave blank and click on **OK**. You will be returned to the blank worksheet. You will notice that the title bar now registers the name of your worksheet file followed by the usual suffix denoting an Excel worksheet file: Microsoft Excel – PRACT.XLS

Task 2 **Closing worksheet files**	You will now close the worksheet file PRACT.XLS. To close the file: 1 Click on the **File** menu box and the list of options appears. 2 Click on **Close**. The file will now close and the worksheet screen will be replaced by a blank window as shown in Figure 4.8. You can now produce a new worksheet, as shown in Task 3.
Task 3 **Creating a new worksheet**	To create a new worksheet follow these instructions: 1 Click on the **File** menu box and click on **New**. 2 The **New File** dialogue box opens showing a list of new files you can create. The type of file you want to create is a worksheet, so click on **Worksheet**. 3 **Worksheet** is highlighted in the list area. Click on **OK** and a blank worksheet will open with the title Worksheet2.XLS.

4   Use the **Save As** option shown in Task 1 to name the file PRACT1.XLS and save to disk.

Now go on to task 4.

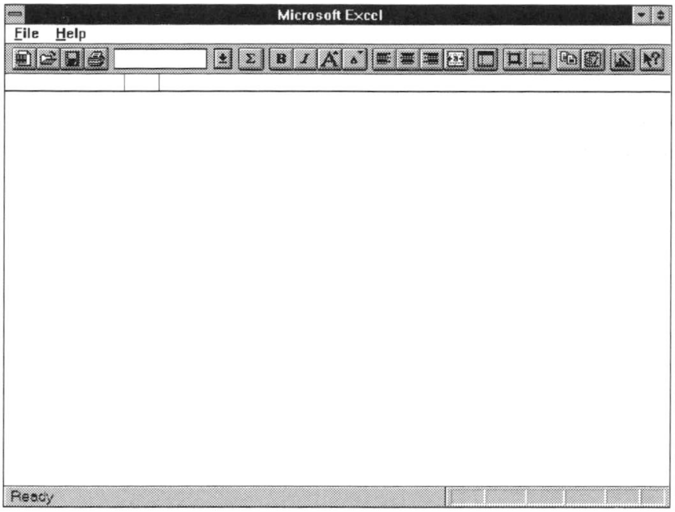

Figure 4.8 A blank window

| Task 4 |
| Opening |
| worksheet |
| files in |
| Excel |

You will frequently need to load files which contain the information on your disk. You can open a number of files simultaneously. To show this, open the original worksheet file you created: PRACT.XLS. To do this:

1. Click on the **File** menu box.
2. From the options click on **Open** and the **Open** dialogue box will appear as shown in Figure 4.9.
3. The files stored on your disk are shown in the **File Name** list on the left of the dialogue box. Click on the file PRACT.XLS. (Note that if you had many files on the disk, some would be hidden in the name box so you would have to use the scroll bars on the right-hand side to locate your file.)
4. When you clicked on the file name it was highlighted. Now click on the **OK** control button and the worksheet PRACT.XLS will be loaded.

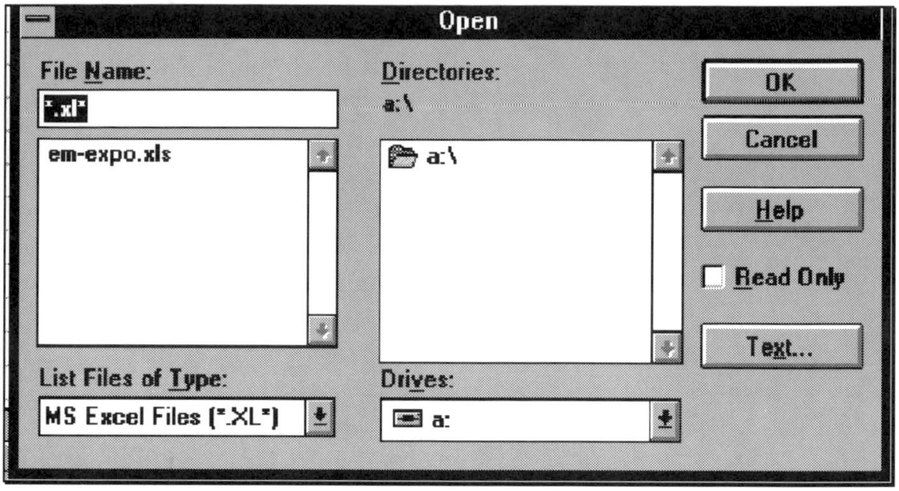

Figure 4.9 The Open dialogue box

Figure 4.10 The Window menu

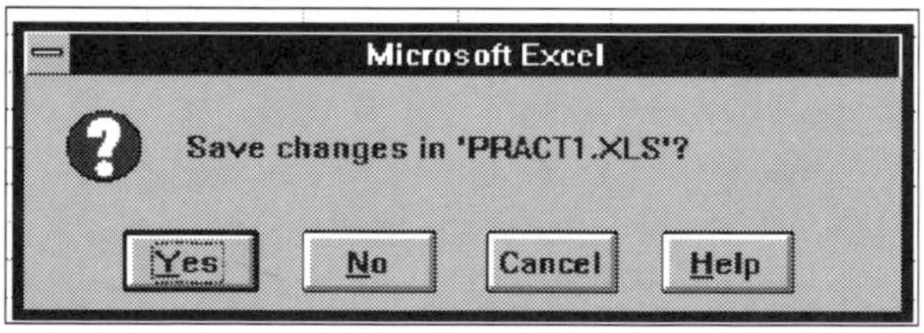

Figure 4.11 Save changes question box

<table>
<tr><td>

Task 5
Using the window menu to move between files

</td><td>

You now have the worksheet PRACT.XLS on the screen and this is the active worksheet. You can move between worksheets quickly by using the **Window** menu box shown in Figure 4.10. To demonstrate this, move between the two files PRACT.XLS and PRACT1.XLS:

1 Click on the **Window** menu box.

2 The two files you have opened are listed in the bottom

</td></tr>
</table>

section of the menu. A tick appears next to the worksheet file PRACT indicating this is the active worksheet. To make PRACT1 the active worksheet click on it and the worksheet PRACT.XLS appears on screen.

3 Click on the **Window** menu again, but this time make PRACT the active worksheet.

So far you have not entered information into the practice worksheets you created. When you open a saved file and make changes to the worksheet then it is necessary to save the changes you made. To demonstrate this complete this exercise:

1 Close the file PRACT.XLS. When you do this the next active file, PRACT1.XLS, appears on screen.
2 Close PRACT1.
3 From the **File** menu select **Open** and then open the file PRACT. In the blank worksheet click on cell A1. Type A1 and press **Enter**. You have now made a change to the worksheet.
4 Open the **File** menu and select **Close** file.
5 A question box appears as shown in Figure 4.11
6 Click on the **Yes** button.

<table>
<tr><td>

Task 6
Saving changes to worksheet files and quitting Excel

</td><td>

In Task 5 you saved the changes in PRACT but remained within the Excel program. Often, however, you may wish to leave the Excel program after making changes to a worksheet. To demonstrate this, open the file PRACT1.XLS. In cell B1 type: B1 and press **Enter**. To close the Excel program, click the control box situated at the left-hand side of the title bar (see Figure 4.1). From the options that

</td></tr>
</table>

appear in the control box click on **Close**. The Question Box appears as in Figure 4.11. Click on the **Yes** button, the worksheet changes will be saved, and you will be returned to the Program Manager window.

There are three categories of information you will want to enter into a worksheet: text, numbers and formulas. You will learn how to enter formulas for calculations in Workshop 4. In this workshop you will create a worksheet, and then enter text and numbers. The historical data we have chosen is information from the 10-year census returns on the numbers of males and females in the British labour force between 1841 and 1931 (see Appendix 1). It was chosen because it is an easily manageable time series and will allow you to get started quickly. It should not take you long to build this small worksheet and then proceed to the next workshop where you will learn to enhance the presentation of the worksheet.

Task 1
Naming the worksheet for the census data and saving to disk

The first task is to create a named workset to store the information from the census returns. The procedure for naming and saving worksheets was discussed in Workshop 1, Task 1, so refer back if necessary. Save the worksheet file as: Census.XLS.

Task 2
Designing a worksheet

You could start to build a worksheet from the information in Appendix 1 by simply entering the necessary information, and as you become more confident you will probably build them this way. However, in this workshop you will plan the worksheet first. Planning involves visualising what the worksheet layout will look like on the screen. You should ask several questions:

Table 4.1 Plan of worksheet for census data

Rows	Columns	Information to be typed
1–3	A	The first three rows will be used to enter the text for the titles of the worksheet and will be typed in column A. Row 1 will contain the main title (The British Labour Force 1841–1931); row 2 will contain the sub-title (Males and Females) and row 3 will be left blank.
4–5	A–E	Row 4 will be used to enter text for the five column headings across the columns A–E: Date, Male Workers, Female Workers, Proportion Male, Proportion Female. Row 5 will be used to enter text describing the statistical information to be entered across columns A–E: (Thousands), (Thousands), (%), (%).
6–15	A–E	Rows 6–15 are the data area and will be used to enter the numerical data for the relevant five column headings across columns A–E. Only the date, male and female workforce is given in Data Set 4A; the two columns for percentages you will calculate later.

- How many rows will you need?
- How many columns will you need?
- What information will be contained in the columns and rows, i.e. where will headings be placed, and where will you type in the statistics?

If you cannot visualise the worksheet in your mind then use a piece of paper to plan out the worksheet layout. You are only planning a rough sketch of the layout and as you will see later, the worksheet is flexible and allows you to alter the design by inserting rows and columns. Table 4.1 shows a worksheet plan for the census data in Data Set A. The worksheet plan signals where you will type text (for titles and headings) and numbers in the data area. This is important because you cannot enter both text and numbers into a worksheet cell. The plan is a data matrix which represents the way you organise data in a worksheet. Once you have understood the plan you can begin to enter the information into the worksheet.

Task 3
Entering text for titles

Before you start entering data it is useful to know about the **Undo** option, a safety device. This option can be selected by opening the **Edit** menu box. If you make a mistake in typing or any other action carried out in these workshops then select **Undo** and this will cancel out your last entry or instruction.

Refer back to the plan in Table 4.1. The first three rows (rows 1–3) will contain the following:

Row 1 – Main Title: **The British Labour Force 1841–1931**
Row 2 – Sub-Title: **Males and Females**
Row 3 of the worksheet you should leave blank to split the title from the main body of the worksheet.

You enter both text and numbers into cells. The left-hand side of the status bar at the bottom of the Excel screen displays the word **Ready**, informing you that Excel is waiting for you to enter information. The text for the title and sub-title is entered in column A, rows 1 and 2. Use the following instructions for entering the two rows of text in the column:

1   Make cell A1 the active cell by clicking on it. The usual rectangular border appears, indicating that A1 is the active cell. The address for the active cell is also recorded in the reference area of the formula bar. Now type the main title: The British Labour Force 1841–1931 in cell A1. As you type you will see the text go into the edit area of the formula bar as well as into cell A1, and this is shown in Figure 4.12.

2   If you make a mistake when you are typing, then use the Backspace key to correct it. When you have finished typing you will notice that the completed title is displayed in the edit area of the formula bar (Figure 4.12) but only the end portion of the text is displayed in the cell. This is because the text is longer than the width of the cell. Do not worry about this. To enter the text

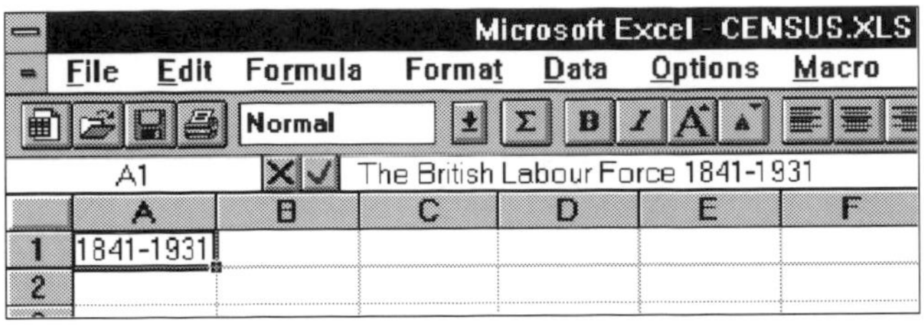

		Microsoft Excel - CENSUS.XLS

File **Edit** **Formula** **Format** **Data** **Options** **Macro**

| Normal | | ± | Σ | B | I | A | A | | | |

| A1 | X ✓ | The British Labour Force 1841-1931 |

	A	B	C	D	E	F
1	1841-1931					
2						

Figure 4.12 Typing text in a worksheet cell

into the cell press the Down Arrow key on the keyboard. When you press the Down Arrow key, the text shown in the edit area of the formula bar disappears because the active cell moves down to cell A2, and the text in A1 adjusts itself so you can see it all, although the active cell remains A1. This may at first sound confusing, but when you enter text you always type in a single cell and if the adjacent cells are blank then the text will always adjust itself across the worksheet row. To demonstrate this, click on cell A2. No text appears in the edit area. Now click on A1 and you will see the contents of the cell appear in the edit area, as in Figure 4.13. You are now ready to enter information into row 2. Note: to enter information you can also use the **Enter** key on the keyboard.

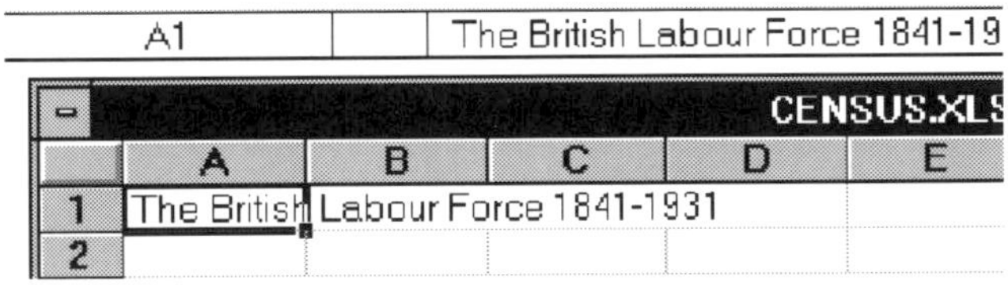

| A1 | | The British Labour Force 1841-19 |

| | | CENSUS.XLS |

	A	B	C	D	E
1	The British Labour Force 1841-1931				
2					

Figure 4.13 Text displayed in a worksheet cell and in edit area

3   You should now check that the text you have typed contains no mistakes. To see the contents of the cell make sure that A1 is the active cell. If there are any mistakes then they can easily be edited. To edit the cell contents take the mouse pointer to the edit bar. The mouse pointer turns to an I-bar shape representing the insertion point. Take the insertion point to where you want to change the text and click the mouse button. The insertion point becomes a flashing black line indicating the point for inserting the changes, as shown in Figure 4.14. Note also that the status bar now records the message **Edit**. When you have finished editing the text then click the edit box, shown in Figure 4.14, and the changed text will be entered into cell A1.

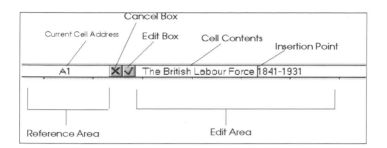

Figure 4.14 Edit bar

4 The text for the sub-title is entered in row 2 of column A. Make cell A2 the active cell and type: Males and Females. When you have finished typing press the Down Arrow key and the active cell becomes A3. Check that you have typed in the text correctly. If there are mistakes then make the necessary edits.

5 Row 3 will be blank so simply use the down arrow key on your keyboard to move to cell A4.

6 The title area on the worksheet is now complete and the first two rows of the worksheet should look like Figure 4.15.

	A	B	C	D	E	F	G	H	I	
1	The British Labour Force 1841-1931									
2	Males and Females									

Figure 4.15 Title area of worksheet

Task 4
Entering text for headings

Refer back to the plan in Table 4.1. You need two rows (rows 4–5) for the column headings. There are five column headings required to capture the information:

Date (cell A4)
Male Workers (ocll B4)
Female Workers (cell C4)
Proportion Males (cell D4)
Proportion Females (cell E4)
(Thousands) (cells B5, C5)
(%) (cells D5, E5)

Use the following instructions for entering the text across the rows:

1 Make cell A4 the active cell and type: Date. Press the Right Arrow key on the keyboard. The text is entered in cell A4 and the active cell moves to B4. The quick way to enter data across a row of cells is to use the Right Arrow key.

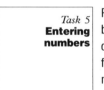

	A	B	C	D	E	F	G	H	I	
1	The British Labour Force 1841-1931									
2	Males and Females									
3										
4	Date	Male Worl	Female W	Proportion	Proportion	Females				
5		(thousand:	(Thousand	(%)	(%)					
6										

Figure 4.16 Truncated text in worksheet cells

2   In cell B4 type: Male Workers and press the Right Arrow key.

3   In cell C4 type: Female Workers and press the Right Arrow key. You will notice that when you type in C4 the text in B4 is truncated. This is because the width of the cell is not great enough to hold all the text (see Figure 4.16). Do not be concerned about this at present as you can easily increase the width of the cell to view all the cell contents.

4   In cell D4 type: Proportion Males and press the Right Arrow key.

5   In cell E4 type: Proportion Females and press the Right Arrow key.

6   In cells B5 and C5 type: (Thousands) and in cells D5 and E5 type: (%) so that your worksheet will look like Figure 4.16.

Task 5
Entering
numbers
Refer to the plan in Table 4.1. The data area for entering numbers begins at row 6. At present you will need to enter the numerical dates and the two columns of numbers in Data Set A. The columns for percentages will be calculated later by entering formulas. The numbers are entered in columns A, B and C, starting at row 6.

Start by entering the numbers for the dates. Click on A6 and type: 1841, the first date. Press the Down Arrow key and the active cell becomes A7. The data you are entering for dates is a time series that increases in a fixed 10-year sequence. When you have to enter any sort of consecutive series of numbers you can use Excel's Data Series option to enter the data quickly. To enter a consecutive series of numbers follow these instructions:

1   Click on cell A6 which contains the entry 1841.

2   Click on the **Data** menu located on the Excel menu bar. From the options that appear select **Series**. The **Series** dialogue box appears as shown in Figure 4.17.

3   The **Series** dialogue box contains a number of options which you can select to instruct Excel to perform a function. You select an option by clicking on the circular option buttons which are highlighted in black when selected. The series of numbers you want to enter for the dates is columns, so click on the **Columns** button in the **Series in** area.

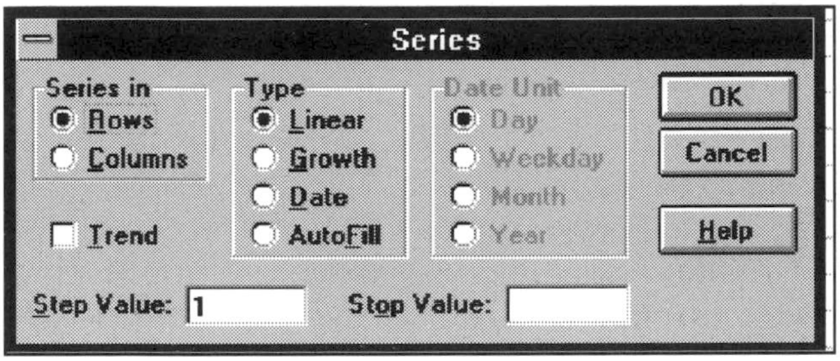

Figure 4.17 Series dialogue box

4 The type of series you want to enter is a linear series, a uniform increase in value of 10. In the series **Type** area, the linear series is pre-set, indicated by the highlighted button.

5 Take the mouse pointer to the area labelled **Step Value**. The mouse turns to an I-bar shape. Click the mouse button and the insertion point appears. Type: 10, the step value for your date series.

6 Press the Tab key to move to the **Stop Value** field and type: 1931, the last date in your series.

7 Click on **OK** and the series will automatically be filled in in the column.

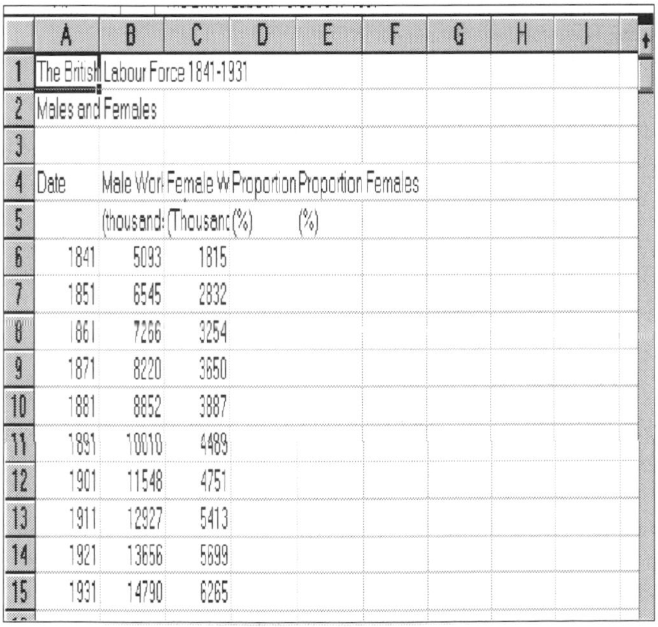

	A	B	C	D	E	F	G	H	I
1	The British Labour Force 1841-1931								
2	Males and Females								
3									
4	Date	Male Work	Female W	Proportion	Proportion Females				
5		(thousands	(Thousand	(%)	(%)				
6	1841	5093	1815						
7	1851	6545	2832						
8	1861	7266	3254						
9	1871	8220	3650						
10	1881	8852	3887						
11	1891	10010	4489						
12	1901	11548	4751						
13	1911	12927	5413						
14	1921	13656	5699						
15	1931	14790	6265						

Figure 4.18 Information entered in a worksheet

Finally you need to enter the numbers for the two columns for male and female workers. Click on B6 and type: 5093. Press the Down Arrow key. The active cell moves to B7. Continue this procedure until all the numbers have been entered for male workers. Click on C6 and enter all the numbers for female workers. Your spreadsheet will look like that shown in Figure 4.18. You can now browse through the worksheet by using the arrow keys on the keyboard, or the vertical and horizontal scroll bars.

Task 6
Quitting Excel and saving the worksheet

If you wish to break off at this point before undertaking Workshop 3 then remember to save the changes in your worksheet as described in Workshop 1, Task 7 and summarised below:

1 Click the control box situated at the left-hand side of the title bar.
2 From the options select **Close**.
3 A question box appears: SAVE CHANGES TO CENSUS.XLS? Click on **Yes**.

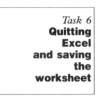

Workshop 3
Enhancing a Worksheet

In this workshop you will learn how to make the worksheet easier to read and more visually presentable. To do this you have to alter the appearance of the worksheet – what is known as 'formatting'. This will entail:

● Changing the widths of columns to show all the text
● Centring titles, headings and numbers
● Creating borders and patterns to highlight the columns and rows
● Changing font styles.

Task 1
Opening the census file

If you broke off at the end of the last workshop, then to begin working on the Census worksheet you must first open it. Follow these instructions:

1 Start the Excel program. A blank worksheet appears (**SHEET1.XLS**). Open the file menu and choose **Open**.
2 The **Open** File dialogue box appears. This was discussed in Workshop 1, Task 4.
3 If necessary, change the active drive to the A: drive.
4 You will see the worksheet file CENSUS.XLS listed in the **File Name** list box. Select the file by clicking on it. The file will be highlighted. Click on **OK**.

Task 2
Changing the width of columns

When you entered the text for headings into the worksheet, the text in columns B, C and D was truncated because the column width was not long enough to display all the text. To increase the width of these columns follow these instructions:

1 To increase the width of column B: place the mouse pointer in the column reference (A,B,C) area of the

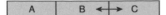

Figure 4.19 Changing column width

worksheet at the intersection of columns B and C. The mouse pointer turns into a two-headed arrow with a line in the middle as shown in Figure 4.19.

2 Keep the mouse button depressed and drag the column intersection to the right. Notice that as you drag the column the size of the column is measured in the right-hand side of the formula bar. Keep the mouse button depressed until you are satisfied with the column width and then release the mouse button.

3 Now you can increase the width of the other columns in your worksheet to meet your requirements. Note: another way you can set the column width is by using the **Format** menu and choosing the **Column Width** option.

Task 3
Centring text for titles across a range

At present, the text for the main title is displayed on the left side of the worksheet. For presentation the main title should be centred across the row of cells A1:E1, i.e. across the length of the worksheet. To do this, follow these instructions:

1 Select the cell range A1:E2. Selecting involves using the mouse to highlight a range in the worksheet you want to work on. In this case you want to select the range A1:E2 and then centre the text across this range. Select the range A1:E2 by clicking on A1 and, keeping the mouse button depressed, drag the mouse over the range A1:E2. As you drag the mouse, the range is highlighted in black. When you have completed the move release the mouse button.

2 To centre the title across the range use the Centre Across Range button on the tool bar. The tool bar was described earlier and is illustrated in Figure 4.2. Locate the Centre Across Range button on the tool bar: the eighth button from the right on the tool bar. When you have located the button click it with the mouse pointer and the text will be centred across the range.

Task 4
Aligning the column headings in cells

When you typed text for the column headings into the worksheet it was automatically aligned on the left-hand side of the cell. However, you will want the text centred in the cell. Follow these instructions for centring the column headings in their cells:

1 Click on cell A4 and select the range A4:E5.

2 There are three buttons on the Excel tool bar for aligning text or numbers in workshop cells (see Figure 4.2): the Right Align button, Centre Align button and Left Align button. To centre the column headings, click on the Centre Align button (the tenth button from the right on the tool bar).

<table>
<tr><td>

Task 5
**Centring
numbers in
columns**

</td><td>

When you typed numbers into the worksheet cell they were automatically aligned on the right-hand side of the cell. To centre the numbers in the columns follow these instructions:

</td></tr>
</table>

1 Click on A6 and select the range A6:E15.
2 Click on the Centre Align button on the tool bar and the numbers will be centred.

<table>
<tr><td>

Task 6
**Borders
and
patterns**

</td><td>

Using Excel you can design a range of different borders to highlight your worksheet. You are going to produce the following borders and patterns for the worksheet:

</td></tr>
</table>

● An outline border for the title area
● A pattern for the title area
● A grid border for the column headings and data area.

To produce an outline border for the title area follow these instructions:

1 Select the title area of your worksheet, i.e. the block of cells A1:E3.
2 Open the **Format menu** and choose **Border**. The **Border** dialogue box opens as shown in Figure 4.20.
3 There are two option boxes to give instructions: **Style** of the border, and **Border**. The latter tells Excel which areas of the worksheet will be bordered. Select your style by clicking on it and then choose **Outline** in the **Border** box.
4 Click on **OK**.

Figure 4.20 Border dialogue box

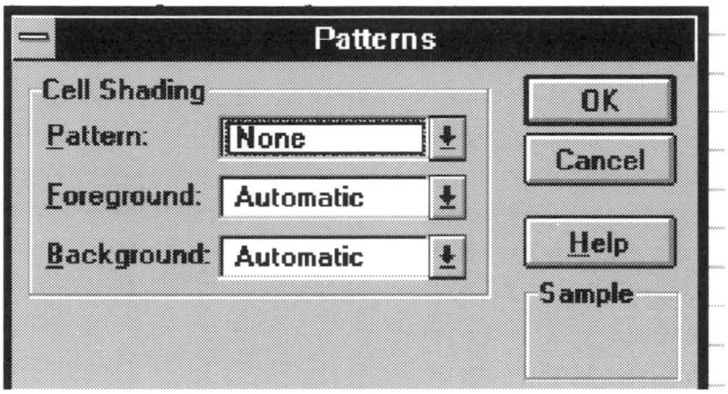

Patterns

Cell Shading

Pattern: None

Foreground: Automatic

Background: Automatic

OK

Cancel

Help

Sample

Figure 4.21 Patterns dialogue box

To produce a pattern for the title area follow these instructions:

1. Select the block of cells A1:E3.
2. Open the **Format** menu and choose **Patterns**. The **Patterns** dialogue box opens as shown in Figure 4.21.
3. Select your pattern from the drop-down menus and then click on **OK**.

To produce a border grid for the headings and data area follow these instructions:

1. Select the block of cells A4:E15.
2. Open the **Format** menu and choose **Border**.
3. Choose your border **Style** and click in all the boxes in the **Border** area.
4. Click on **OK**.

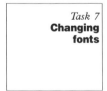

Task 7
Changing fonts

You can choose a range of different fonts and font sizes. Open the **Format** menu and choose **Font**. The **Font** dialogue box opens as shown in Figure 4.22. Experiment with the various fonts and font sizes you see on offer. To provide an example of how this works do the following:

1. Select the whole of the workshop area: cell range A1:E15.
2. In the font **Size** list box choose font size 8 by clicking up on the menu scroll bar.
3. Click on **OK**.
4. Select the cell range A1:A2. Note that, although the text is centred across the range, the text is still contained in cells A1 and A2 for editing purposes. This can sometimes be confusing when you are editing text which has been centred across a range. Open the **Format** menu and choose **Font**. The **Font** dialogue box appears. In the **Font Style** box select **Bold**. A quicker way to

change the font style to bold is to click on the Bold button on the tool bar, labelled **B**.

5   Click on **OK**.

At the end of this workshop your worksheet should look similar to that in Figure 4.23.

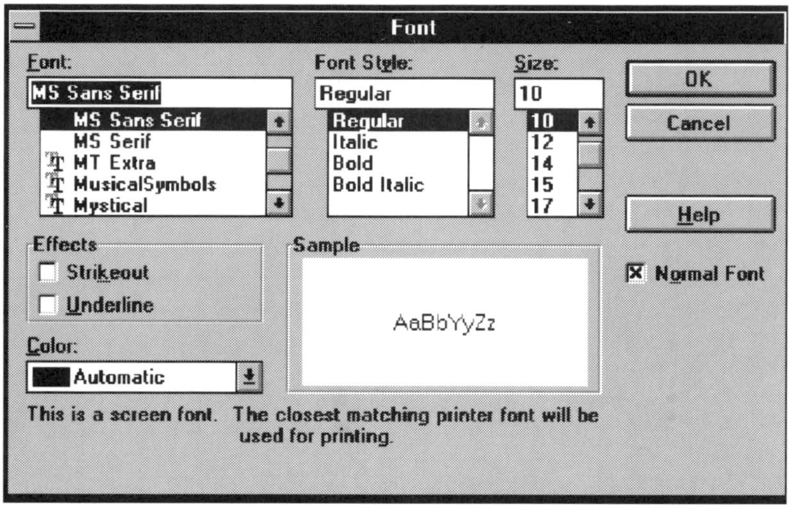

Figure 4.22 Font dialogue box

	A	B	C	D	E
1		The British Labour Force 1841–1931			
2		Males and Females			
3					
4	Date	Male Workers	Female Workers	Proportion Males	Proportion Females
5		(thousands)	(Thousands)	(%)	(%)
6	1841	5093	1815		
7	1851	6545	2832		
8	1861	7266	3254		
9	1871	8220	3650		
10	1881	8852	3887		
11	1891	10010	4489		
12	1901	11548	4751		
13	1911	12927	5413		
14	1921	13656	5699		
15	1931	14790	6265		
16					

Figure 4.23 Completed worksheet

Task 8
**Remember to
save the
changes to the
worksheet when
you quit Excel**

In this workshop you are going to perform calculations by entering formulas into the worksheet. The two obvious calculations to perform are the totals of both male and female workers and the proportion of each category to the total. At present there is no column in your worksheet to contain the information on totals so you will also learn how to insert a new column.

Workshop 4
**Formulas
and
Calculations**

Task 1
**Open your file
containing the
census data**

Task 2
**Inserting
columns**

You are going to insert a column for totals between the column for female workers and the column for the proportion of males. You thus need to create a new empty column D to contain the calculated totals. Follow these instructions:

    1   Click on cell D4, the column headed Proportion Males.
    2   Open the **Edit** menu box and choose **Insert . . .** The **Insert** dialogue box appears. This provides four options: **Shift Cells Right**, **Shift Cells Down**, **Entire Row**, **Entire Column**. The last option is what you want here, i.e. you want to insert an entire column. Choose this option by clicking on it.
3   Click on **OK** and a new blank column D will appear.
4   In the new column D type the new heading. type Total in cell D4 and (Thousands) in cell D5. You are now ready to make your calculations.

Task 3
**Calculating
totals on a
worksheet**

To build in totals you use the sum function. To calculate the totals for male and female workers follow these instructions:

    1   Click on the cell D6. You will want to sum the totals for column B and column C.
    2   First sum the total for B6 and C6. Type this formula: =Sum(B6:C6). The = sign indicates that you are entering a formula and you always type it first when

D6		☒ ✓	=sum(B6:C6)	
	A	B	C	D
1		The British Labour Force 1841–1931		
2		Males and Females		
3				
4	Date	Male Workers	Female Workers	Total
5		(thousands)	(Thousands)	(Thousands)
6	1841	5093	1815	=sum(B6:C6)
7	1851	6545	2832	

Figure 4.24 Typing a formula into a worksheet

using a formula. Sum is a built-in function which allows you to automatically total a column or row. The brackets instruct Excel to carry out a calculation on a range of cells, in this case the range B6 to C6.

3   As you type the formula it is entered in the active cell and in the formula bar of the Excel screen, as shown in Figure 4.24. If you make a mistake when typing then simply click on the edit area of the formula bar and make your changes. When you have finished entering the formula press **Enter** and the calculation will be complete: the total is 6908.

There are 10 totals you have to calculate on the worksheet. This would entail you entering into column D some 10 separate formulas, i.e. =Sum(B7:C7), (B8:C8) and so on. There is, however, a powerful copy function which allows you to copy formulas and automatically fill in calculations. To do this follow these instructions:

1   You first need to copy the original formula =SUM(B6:C6) which you entered into cell D7. When you copy a formula it will automatically fill in the formulas and complete all the calculations, i.e. =SUM(B7:C7), =SUM(B8:C8) and so on. Make sure C6 is the active cell and open the **Edit** menu.

2   Choose **Copy**. The cell D6 is surrounded by a flashing border indicating a copied cell.

3   Click on D7 and select the range D7:D15.

4   Press **Enter** and the calculations for totals will be completed as shown in Figure 4.25.

	A	B	C	D	E	F
1		The British Labour Force 1841–1931				
2		Males and Females				
3						
4	Date	Male Workers	Female Workers	Total	Proportion Males	Proportion Females
5		(thousands)	(Thousands)	(Thousands)	(%)	(%)
6	1841	5093	1815	6908	73.7	26.3
7	1851	6545	2832	9377	69.8	30.2
8	1861	7266	3254	10520	69.1	30.9
9	1871	8220	3650	11870	69.3	30.7
10	1881	8852	3887	12739	69.5	30.5
11	1891	10010	4489	14499	69.0	31.0
12	1901	11548	4751	16299	70.9	29.1
13	1911	12927	5413	18340	70.5	29.5
14	1921	13656	5699	19355	70.6	29.4
15	1931	14790	6265	21055	70.2	29.8

Figure 4.25 Calculation for totals and percentages in worksheet

<table>
<tr><td>

Task 5
**Calculating
percentages for
male workers
and formatting
numbers**

</td><td>

To calculate the percentages for males and females:

1   Click on cell E6, the column for Proportion Males.
2   The percentage for males in 1841 is calculated by
dividing B6 (male workers) by D6 (Total) and
multiplying by 100. Type the following formula:

</td></tr>
</table>

$$=(B6/D6)^*100$$

3   Press **Enter** and the calculation will be inserted in the cell: 73.72611.
4   Make sure E6 is the active cell and open the **Edit** menu. Choose **Copy**. The
cell E6 is surrounded by a flashing border indicating a copied cell.
5   Click on E7 and select the range E7:E15 by dragging the mouse down the
range.
6   Press Enter and the calculations for totals will be completed as shown in
Figure 4.25.

When you first made the calculation the result was displayed with numerous decimal
places. You can, however, choose the number of decimal places to display the data, e.g.
one decimal place as in Figure 4.25. To do this follow these instructions:

1   Select the range E6:E15.
2   Open the **Format** menu and choose **Number**.
3   The **Number Format** dialogue box opens. In the field labelled **Category** click
on **Number**.
4   You can set the number of decimal places by typing in the **Code** field at the
bottom of the box. Take the mouse pointer to the code field and the
I-shaped insertion point will appear. Type 0.0 for one decimal place. If you
want two decimal places type 0.00, and so on.
5   When you have selected the number of decimal places click on **OK**.

<table>
<tr><td>

Task 6
**Calculating
the
percentages
for female
workers**

</td><td>

You can set the number of decimal places before you begin the
calculation. Select the range F6:F15 and follow the procedures in
Task 5 above. To calculate the percentages for female workers use
the formula:

$$=(C6/D6)^*100$$

</td></tr>
</table>

You have now completed the worksheet and you can go on to Workshop 5 which shows
you how to print worksheets.

Task 7
**Remember to
save the
changes to the
worksheet when
you quit Excel**

**Workshop 5
Printing
Worksheets**

In this workshop you will learn how to print the information contained in the worksheet, and develop skills in presentation.

Task 1
**Viewing the
printed
worksheet**

Before you start printing a worksheet you need a vision on screen of how it will appear on the printed page. To do this, open the **File** menu and choose **Print Preview**. An image of how the worksheet will look when printed is shown in Figure 4.26.

There are a number of option buttons located on the second bar of the Print Preview window (i.e., **Zoom**, **Print**, **Setup**, **Margins**, **Close**) which you can use to customise the layout of your printed worksheet. If you want to see an enlarged view of a section of your worksheet, then either move the mouse pointer, which you notice has become a magnifying glass, to the approximate centre of the worksheet and click, or click on the **Zoom** button. This produces an enlarged image of the worksheet. You can now go on to layout the page for the printed worksheet to your own requirements.

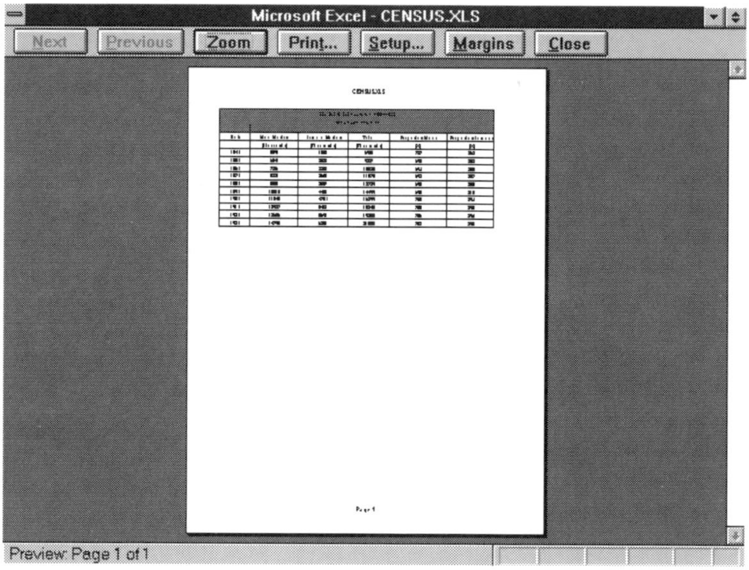

Figure 4.26 Print Preview

Task 2
Page layout

You can view the position of the printed worksheet in relation to the page margins by clicking on the **Margins** option. The right, left, top and bottom margins are now displayed as a skeleton outline as shown in Figure 4.27. You can adjust the width of the margins by using the mouse to drag the handle bars for the top, bottom, left and right margins. For example, if you want to increase the size of the right margin, place the mouse pointer on the handle bar for the right margin. The mouse pointer turns to a double-headed arrow, and you can now drag the margin to the right to expand the width of the margin.

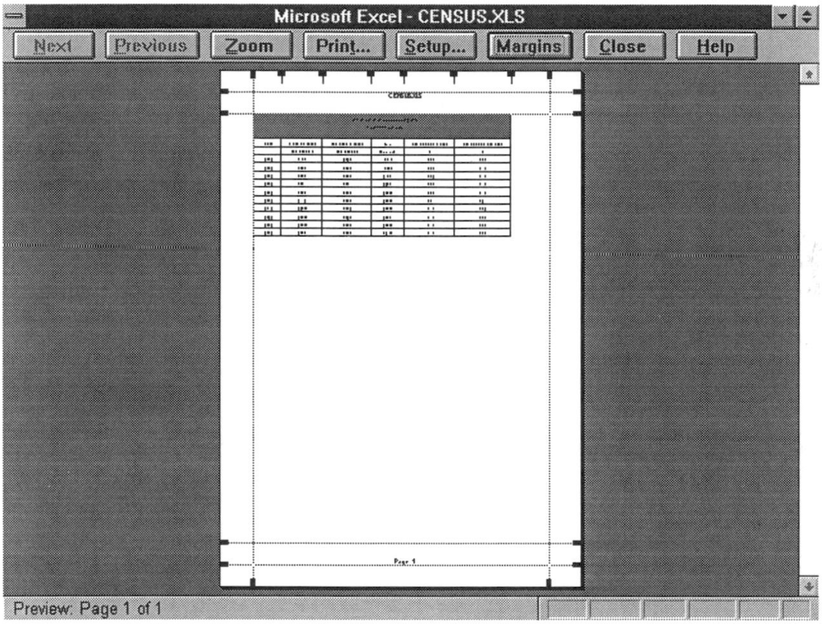

Figure 4.27 Skeleton outline of page layout

There are numerous ways to set up the page for printing, and these can be used by accessing the **Page Setup** dialogue box. Click on the **Setup** button and the **Page Setup** dialogue box, Figure 4.28, appears. This provides a number of options: you can determine the paper size to be used, e.g. A4, or you can print in portrait or landscape. The former prints vertically on the page and the latter prints horizontally. You can also adjust the margins by typing in a measurement and determine whether the gridlines are included in the printed worksheet. Finally, you can insert a title for the printed worksheet page by selecting the **He**a**der** or **F**o**oter** options. You should experiment with these **Page Setup** options before printing the worksheet. When you are satisfied with the layout click on the **OK** button.

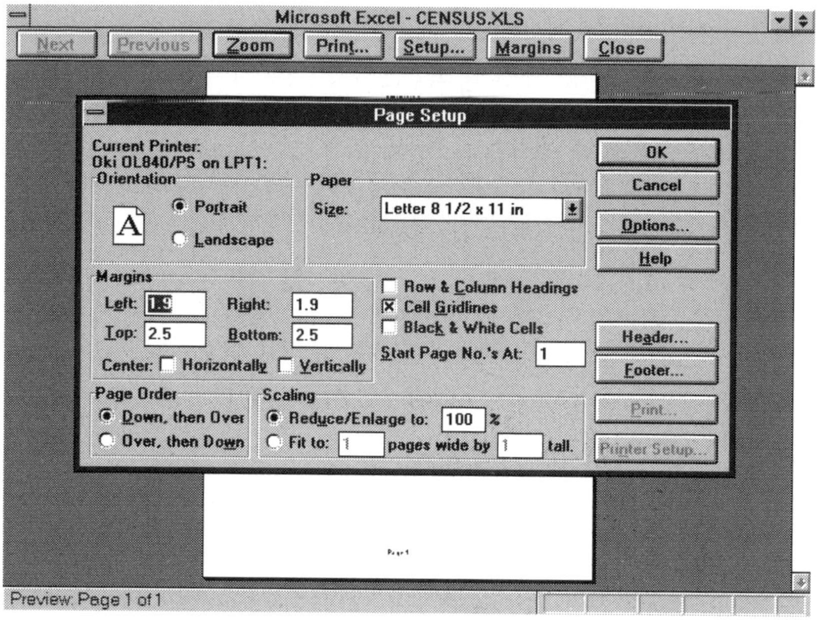

Figure 4.28 Page Setup dialogue box

| Task 3 |
| Printing |

To print the worksheet click on the **Print** button in the Print Preview window. The **Print** dialogue box in Figure 4.29 appears. You use this dialogue box to determine the pages to be printed if the worksheet was more than one page in size, and the number of copies to be printed. To print the worksheet click on **OK**.

Having completed the workshops in this chapter you can now proceed to Chapter 5 and examine the use of charts for presenting historical information.

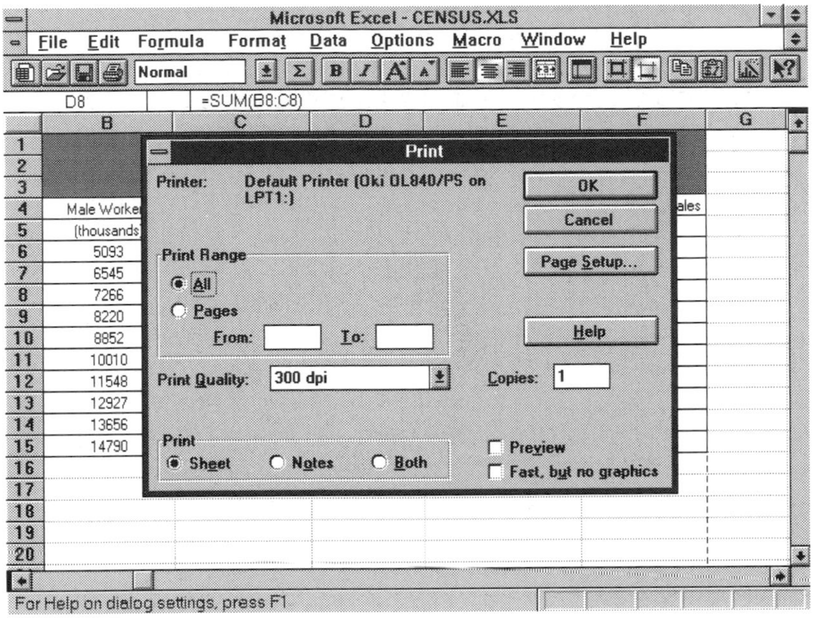

Figure 4.29 Print dialogue box

Chapter 5

Presentation of Historical Information: Graphs

5.1 Introduction

In this chapter you will first learn how to create graphs (charts) from the spreadsheet (worksheet) you produced in Chapter 4. Graphs are a useful and versatile way to present trends in historical data. Using the Excel program you can create numerous types of charts: e.g. column, bar, pie, line, etc. Having constructed charts from the census data you are then encouraged to build additional historical worksheets, and create a variety of chart types. To allow you to do this, Appendix 2 contains two data sets (Data Sets A and B) which you will use to build additional worksheets in the final workshop.

5.2 Workshop Exercises

Workshop 1
Creating and Customising a Column Chart

In this workshop you will first learn how to create a standard column chart, and then customise the chart to a specific design. The historical example is taken from the worksheet you constructed in Chapter 4: the Census Returns on Male and Female Workers (see Figure 4.25 for a representation of the completed worksheet). Load the Excel program from the Program Manager window, and then open the worksheet file: CENSUS.XLS. You can now work through the tasks in this workshop.

> *Task 1*
> **Creating a column chart to display the trends for male workers**

The first chart you are going to produce is a column chart to display the trends in the male workforce between 1841 and 1931. The final chart will look like that shown in Figure 5.1. The data for the male workforce is contained in column B of the worksheet: range B6:B15. This range will be plotted on the vertical (Y) axis of the chart. The time series of dates is contained in column A of the worksheet: range A6:A15. The dates will form the labels for the horizontal (X) axis of the chart. To create the column chart follow these instructions:

1. Select the range A6:A15 by dragging the mouse down the range. This will be the X axis labels for the dates.
2. Press the Shift and **F8** keys on the keyboard simultaneously. The instruction **ADD** appears in the right-hand side of the status bar. This now means that you can add a series of data to be plotted on the chart.
3. Select the range B6:B15 by dragging the mouse down the range.
4. Open the **File** menu and choose **New**. The **New** file dialogue box appears as shown in Figure 5.2. Select **Chart** and click on **OK**. The **New Chart** dialogue

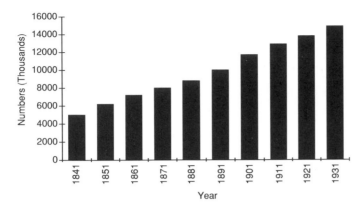

Figure 5.1 Bar chart showing trends in male workforce, 1841–1931

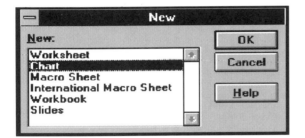

Figure 5.2 New File dialogue box

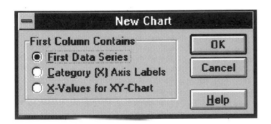

Figure 5.3 New Chart dialogue box

box opens as shown in Figure 5.3. This dialogue box contains a number of option boxes for you to determine the way the chart is to be plotted. The information in the worksheet is organised in columns, and you are instructed to indicate what the **First Column Contains**: **First Data Series**, **Category (X) Axis Labels**, **X-Values for XY-Chart**. The first column you selected contained the dates, the category X axis labels; select this option by clicking in the circular box which will correspondingly be highlighted.

5   Click on **OK** and the Chart screen window will open as shown in Figure 5.4. A column chart is automatically created: this is the standard type produced by Excel and most other programs.

Before moving on to customise the chart in Task 2, familiarise yourself with the Chart screen window shown in Figure 5.4. Finally open the **File** menu and **Save As ...** Call the file CENSUS1.

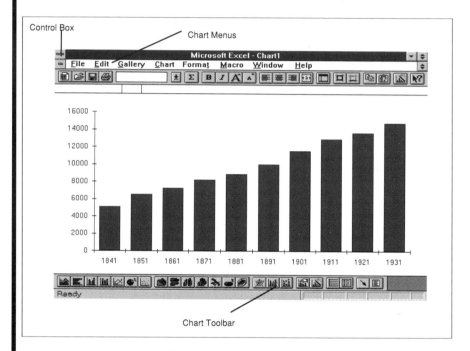

Figure 5.4 Chart screen window with column chart

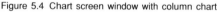

Task 2 Customising the chart by adding annotation	Annotation includes adding titles in several locations, i.e. for headings and axes, and legends to highlight the data plotted in the chart. Producing legends will be shown in Workshop 2, and here you will simply add a main title and titles for the X and Y axes.

To add a main title to the chart follow these instructions:

1   Open the **Chart** menu and choose **Attach Text**. The **Attach Text** dialogue box opens as shown in Figure 5.5.
2   Click on **Chart Title** and then on **OK**. You are now ready to enter the title.
3   Type the title of the chart: Male Workers 1841–1931.
4   Press **Enter** and the title is placed in the chart as shown in Figure 5.6. Note that you can change the font styles by clicking once with the mouse pointer

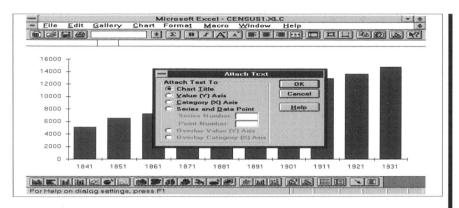

Figure 5.5 Attach Text dialogue box

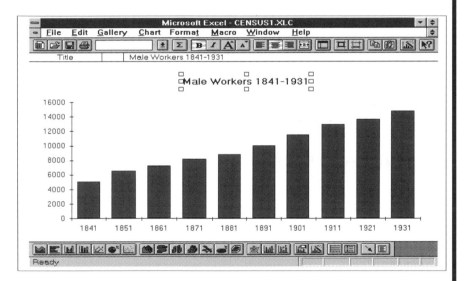

Figure 5.6 Title placed on chart

on the positioned text in the chart. When you do this, the text is surrounded by an outline box. You can now open the **Format** menu and choose **Font . . .** The **Font** dialogue box opens and you can select your options. You can position the text box anywhere in the chart by dragging it with the mouse pointer. Position the mouse pointer on the handles of the outline box (i.e. the black squares) and drag with the mouse to the desired position. To remove the box outline simply press the **Esc** (escape) key on the keyboard.

To place text for the Y and X axes follow these instructions:

1 From the **Chart** menu choose **Attach Text**. The **Attach Text** dialogue box opens. Click on **Value (Y) Axis** and click on **OK**.

2 A **Y** symbol will be placed on the Y axis prompting you to type the title. Type: Numbers (Thousands).

3 Press **Enter** and the title will appear on the Y axis.

4 Choose **Attach Text** from the **File** menu, click on the **Category (X) Axis**, and click on **OK**. An **X** symbol will appear on the X axis. Type: Years, and press **Enter**. When you have finished entering text press the **Esc** key. This clears all machine codes from the screen.

You can now proceed to Task 3, and construct a column chart of your own.

Task 3
Constructing a chart for female workers

Using the skills you have learnt so far, construct a column chart displaying trends in the female workforce from 1841 to 1931. You will first want to close the chart file Census1 and return to your worksheet. To do this click on the control box shown in Figure 5.4. Choose **Close**, and a message box will appear: Save Changes in CENSUS1.XLC? Click on the **Yes** button and you will be returned to the spreadsheet.

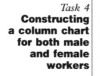
Task 4
Constructing a column chart for both male and female workers

Often, you will want to include in a chart information plotted for two or more variables, such as males and females. You can now construct the column chart in Figure 5.7.

To construct the chart in Figure 5.7:

1 Select the ranges on the worksheet shown in Figure 5.8. First select the range containing the dates (A6:A15): the X axis labels for the dates.

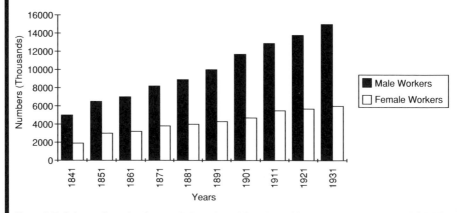

Figure 5.7 Column chart showing trends in male and female workforces

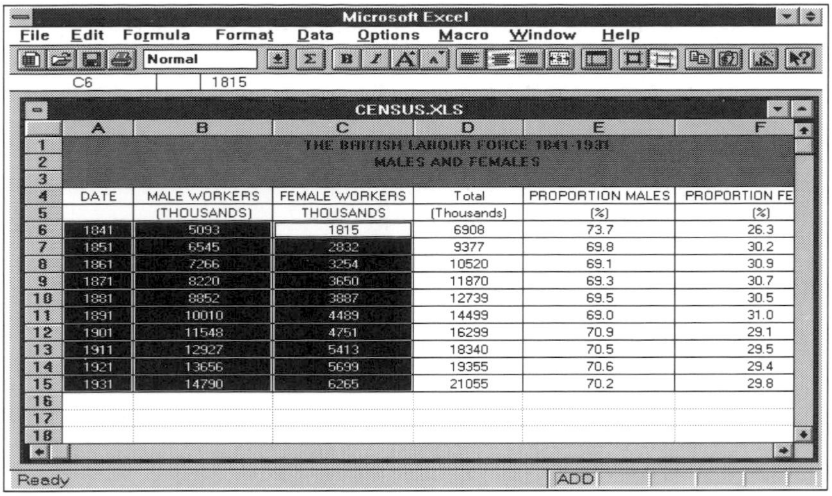

DATE	MALE WORKERS (THOUSANDS)	FEMALE WORKERS THOUSANDS	Total (Thousands)	PROPORTION MALES (%)	PROPORTION FE (%)
1841	5093	1815	6908	73.7	26.3
1851	6545	2832	9377	69.8	30.2
1861	7266	3254	10520	69.1	30.9
1871	8220	3650	11870	69.3	30.7
1881	8852	3887	12739	69.5	30.5
1891	10010	4489	14499	69.0	31.0
1901	11548	4751	16299	70.9	29.1
1911	12927	5413	18340	70.5	29.5
1921	13656	5699	19355	70.6	29.4
1931	14790	6265	21055	70.2	29.8

Figure 5.8 Ranges to be plotted for chart

2 Press the Shift and **F8** keys on the keyboard simultaneously. The instruction **ADD** appears in the right-hand side of the status bar. You can now add the two data series to be plotted.
3 Select the range B6:B15 for male workers, and then select the range C6:C15 for female workers.
4 Open the **File** menu and choose **New**. The **New** File dialogue box appears. Select **Chart** and click on **OK**. From the **New Chart** dialogue box click on **Category (X) Axis labels** and click on **OK**. A column chart showing the two data series will be displayed.
5 Open the **File** menu and **Save As . . . .** Call the file CENSUS2.

You should now place a main title and titles for the Y and X axes on the chart. When you have done this you can then produce a legend to define the two sets of data plotted on the chart. To do this follow these instructions:

1 Either open the **Chart** menu and select **Add Legend** or click on the Legend tool button on the Chart tool bar (the third button from the right-hand side of the tool bar). The legend appears on the right-hand side of the chart as shown in Figure 5.9.
2 The legend indicates the two series plotted on the chart: Series1 (the red column of the chart, and Series2, the green column of the chart. You now want to indicate what these series represent in the chart, i.e. Series1 is the Male Workforce and Series2 the Female Workforce. To rename the series click on the **Chart** menu and choose **Edit Series. . . .** The **Edit Series** dialogue box appears as shown in Figure 5.10. In the **Series** field click on

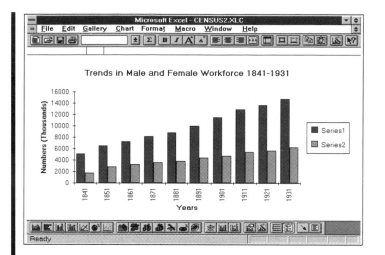

Figure 5.9 Legend placed on chart

Series1. Now take the mouse pointer to the **Name** text box. The mouse
pointer turns into an I-bar shape; click on the mouse button and type: Male
Workers.

3 Click on **Series2**. A Question box appears: Save **Changes to the Current Series?**
Click on **Yes**. Now type in the **Name** text box: Female Workers.

4 Click on **OK** and the legend will be complete.

5 You can position the legend in the chart in two ways. You can click on the
legend box until it is surrounded by a series of black squares. These are the
drag handles, and by clicking on these handles, and keeping the mouse button
depressed, you can drag the legend into a position of your choice. Alter-
natively, click on the legend and open the **Format** menu. Choose **Legend ....**

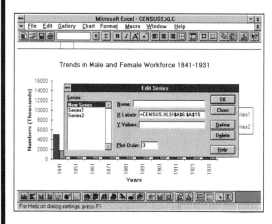

Figure 5.10 The Edit Series dialogue box

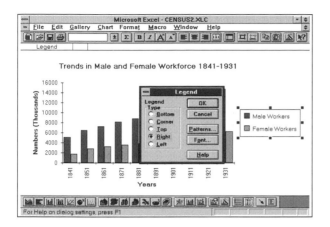

Figure 5.11 Legend dialogue box

The **Legend** dialogue box appears as shown in Figure 5.11. You are given a number of options for positioning the legend in the chart. Choose the position which suits you. Also, you can change the patterns of the legend by clicking on **Patterns ...**, and selecting the choices in the **Patterns** dialogue box.

Remember when you close the file to save the changes. The final task is to construct a series of charts on your own.

Task 5 **Constructing your own charts from the census data**	Construct the following chart. Using the data you calculated in the worksheet, on the proportional distribution of the male and female workforces, construct a bar chart showing these trends over the period 1841–1931. If you have not calculated this data then refer back to Chapter 4. When you have completed this task proceed to the next workshop which examines the use of pie charts.

Pie charts display information as a proportional distribution. In this workshop you will first learn how to construct a pie chart and then go on to produce your own charts.

**Workshop 2
Constructing
Pie Charts**

Task 1 **Constructing a pie chart: proportion of males and females in 1841**	You are going to produce the 3-D pie chart shown in Figure 5.12. To construct the chart follow these instructions: 1 Open the Census worksheet and select the range of data to be plotted on the chart. This is the range B6:C6. 2 From the **File** menu choose **New**.

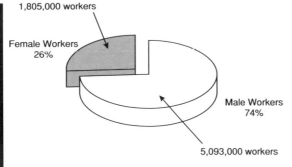

1,805,000 workers

Female Workers
26%

Male Workers
74%

5,093,000 workers

Figure 5.12 Pie chart showing the distribution of male and female workers

3   From the **New** File dialogue box choose **Chart**.
4   A standard column chart is automatically produced with two columns labelled 1 and 2 on the X axis.
5   **Save As**: Census3.

You can now go on to customise this chart by changing the chart type to a pie chart in Task 2.

| *Task 2* **Customising a chart: changing the chart type** | There are numerous chart types you can produce, ranging from column charts to bar charts to line charts to pie charts. These chart types can also be displayed in a variety of different ways, i.e. 3-D or flat charts, or different types of design. To convert the standard column chart to a 3-D pie chart follow these instructions: |

1   Open the **Gallery** menu. This menu contains all the options for creating the range of chart types.

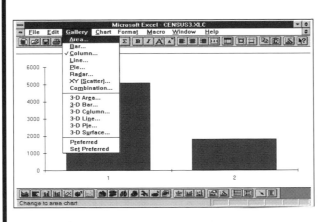

Figure 5.13 Gallery menu

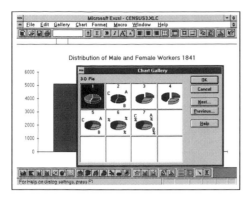

Figure 5.14 Pie chart Gallery menu

The **Gallery** menu is shown in Figure 5.13. Note: you can also choose chart types by using the options on the Chart tool bar, this is a short cut.

2   Choose **3-D Pie ....** The 3-D pie **Chart Gallery** menu opens as shown in Figure 5.14. This offers seven different types of 3-D pie chart.

3   Choose chart type number 6 by clicking on this option. Now click on **OK** and the pie chart appears in the window.

Task 3
Adding text and arrows

The next task is to add text to identify the wedges of the pie chart and to add arrows as shown in Figure 5.12. Before doing this add the title to the chart: Distribution of Male and Female Workers 1841. To add the text and arrows, follow these instructions:

1   Click on the Add Text button on the Chart tool bar, the first button from the right of the tool bar.

2   A box appears in the middle of the chart with the word **TEXT**. Now type: Male Workers, and press **Enter**.

3   The text you have typed appears in the text box as shown in Figure 5.15. Position this text in the chart, as shown in Figure 5.12. Click on the text box and, keeping the mouse button depressed, drag the text to the appropriate area on the chart.

4   When you are satisfied, press the **Esc** key and you are ready to enter the next piece of text.

5   Click on the Add Text button on the Chart tool bar. Type: Female Workers, and press **Enter**. Position this text in the chart, as shown in Figure 5.12. When you are satisfied, press the **Esc** key and you are ready to enter the next piece of text.

6   The next text to enter is the figures for male and female workers, as shown in Figure 5.12. Add this text and position it accordingly. Note: if you want to

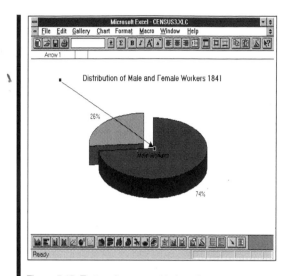

Figure 5.15 Text and arrows added to chart

delete text, click on the text box and press the **Del** (delete) key on the keyboard.

7   Finally, add the arrows as shown in Figure 5.12. Click on the Add Arrow tool button on the Chart tool bar, the second button from the right of the tool bar. The arrow appears, as shown in Figure 5.15. You can position and size the arrow to your requirements. This is largely done by trial and error. Click on the black box at the top or bottom of the arrow. Keep the mouse button depressed and drag the arrow to position it, i.e. pointing from the text for number of male workers, as shown in Figure 5.12. To size the arrow, click on the black box and drag the mouse along the line of the arrow. This may well take a bit of practice, but you will get it right eventually. When you have positioned the arrow to your satisfaction press the **Esc** key and you are ready to insert the second arrow. Do this now, and position the arrow pointing from the text for the number of female workers, as shown in Figure 5.12.

Task 4 **Creating** **your own** **pie chart**	Create a 3-D pie chart showing the distribution of male and female workers for 1931. You have now constructed a pie chart but you should also experiment with the other types of pie chart you can create in the chart gallery before proceeding to the next workshop.

Workshop 3 Further Examples of Historical Data

This workshop explores further the presentation of historical data using different historical examples. The data for the exercises is contained in Appendix 2 as Data Sets A and B. The former provides information on the electoral position of the political parties in the House of Commons for the four elections between 1900 and 1910. This was an important period in twentieth-century political history and witnessed significant political debate over issues such as foreign policy, commercial policy, social reform and the power of the House of Lords. Using this data you can examine the changing electoral performance of the parties in this period. Data Set B contains information on two key areas of state expenditure for the period 1870–1914: education and defence. Using this information you can explore the priorities given to these sectors of public expenditure, and examine change over time.

Task 1
Creating a worksheet from political history data

Create a worksheet from the information in Data Set A. Save your file as Polit.XLS. Figure 5.16 shows an example of a worksheet we have created. Having created the worksheet, proceed to Task 2.

Task 2
Presenting data as a percentage

What was the percentage of the total seats held by each party in 1900? You could, of course, make calculations on the worksheet to present this data. However, to more effectively highlight this data construct the pie chart in Figure 5.17. Follow these instructions:

1 Select the column range containing the information on the names of the parties: range A5:A8 in Figure 5.16. If your worksheet is constructed differently then select the appropriate range.

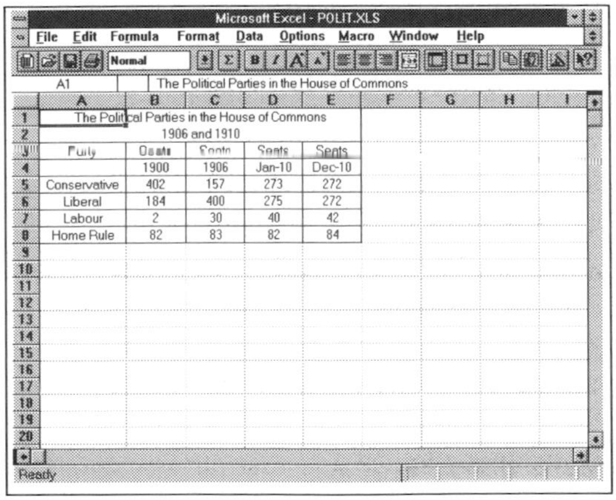

The Political Parties in the House of Commons				
1906 and 1910				
Party	Seats	Seats	Seats	Seats
	1900	1906	Jan-10	Dec-10
Conservative	402	157	273	272
Liberal	184	400	275	272
Labour	2	30	40	42
Home Rule	82	83	82	84

Figure 5.16 Worksheet POLIT.XLS

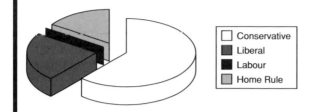

Figure 5.17 Pie chart showing the state of parties in the House of Commons, 1900

2 Press Shift and **F8** simultaneously to add the series of data to be plotted.
3 Select the range containing the information on the seats won by each party: range B5:B8 in Figure 5.16. If your worksheet is constructed differently then select the appropriate range.
4 Open the **File** menu and choose **New**. The **New** File dialogue box opens; choose **Chart**. A column chart appears with the parties labelled accordingly on the X axis. Open the **Gallery** menu and choose **3-D Pie**; the 3-D Pie **Chart Gallery** opens. Click on chart option number **4** and then click on **OK**.
5 Attach an appropriate main title for the chart.
6 Click on the Legend tool button, which is the third from the right on the Chart tool bar. The legend is automatically produced, with the parties listed.
7 Save the file as HC1900, indicating that the chart contains information for the House of Commons for 1900.

| *Task 3*
Examining changes in the position of the parties | The period 1903 to 1906 witnessed considerable political debate over the question of tariff reform and created splits in the Conservative Party. Examine the changing fortunes of the parties between 1900 and 1906 and create a pie chart showing the percentage distribution of the parties in 1906. |

So far you have only examined changes between two time dates, but you can create a chart which examines the percentage change for four dates. Figure 5.18 shows the changing distribution as a bar chart. This was created by:

1 Selecting the dates across the row of cells (range B4:E4 in Figure 5.16) and pressing Shift and **F8** to add the series.
2 Selecting the row of cells containing the information on the number of seats for each party; i.e. selecting the ranges B5:E5; B6:E6; B7:E7; B8:E8 in Figure 5.16 in sequence.
3 Creating a standard column chart and then using the **Gallery** menu to choose the **3-D Bar ...** chart option, and selecting option **3**. You should now construct the chart in Figure 5.18 yourself.

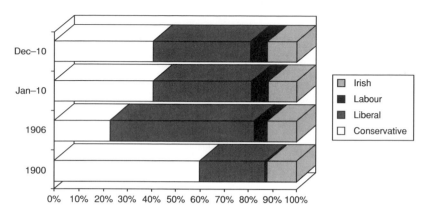

Figure 5.18 3-D bar chart showing distribution of parties in the House of Commons

Another type of chart you can create is shown in Figure 5.19: a 3-D area chart. This shows how the number of seats held by each party changed over the period. You can create this chart by selecting **3-D Area . . .** chart option **3** from the chart **Gallery** menu.

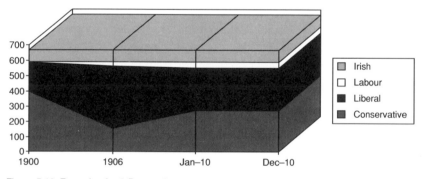

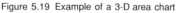

Figure 5.19 Example of a 3-D area chart

Task 4 **Creating a worksheet to examine trends in public expenditure**	Examine the information in Data Set B, open a new worksheet file and **Save As**: EXPEND.XLS. Now construct a worksheet to capture this information. An example of how the worksheet might look is shown in Figure 5.20. The data provides a time series showing the amount spent on two key components of government expenditure.

To highlight the trends in the data construct a line chart:

1 Select the column range containing the information on dates: range A5:A49 in Figure 5.20. If your worksheet is constructed differently then select the appropriate range.

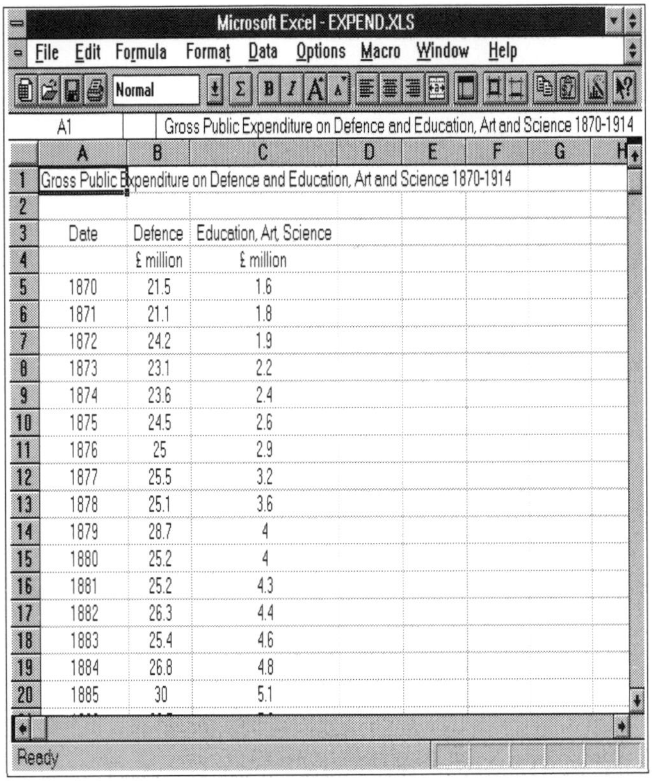

	A	B	C	D	E	F	G
1	Gross Public Expenditure on Defence and Education, Art and Science 1870-1914						
2							
3	Date	Defence	Education, Art, Science				
4		£ million	£ million				
5	1870	21.5	1.6				
6	1871	21.1	1.8				
7	1872	24.2	1.9				
8	1873	23.1	2.2				
9	1874	23.6	2.4				
10	1875	24.5	2.6				
11	1876	25	2.9				
12	1877	25.5	3.2				
13	1878	25.1	3.6				
14	1879	28.7	4				
15	1880	25.2	4				
16	1881	25.2	4.3				
17	1882	26.3	4.4				
18	1883	25.4	4.6				
19	1884	26.8	4.8				
20	1885	30	5.1				

Figure 5.20 Worksheet EXPEND.XLS

2 Press Shift and **F8** simultaneously to add the series of data to be plotted.

3 Use the vertical scroll bar to move up to the top of the worksheet and select the range containing the information on defence expenditure: range B5:B49 in Figure 5.20. Use the scroll bar to move back to the top of the worksheet and select the range containing the information on education expenditure: range C5:C49 in Figure 5.20.

4 Open the **File** menu and choose **New**. From the **New** File dialogue box choose **Chart**. In the **New Chart** dialogue box click on **Category X Axis Labels** and click on **OK**. A column chart showing the two data series will be displayed.

5 Save the file, e.g. as EXPEND1.

6 Choose from the **Chart Gallery** a line chart which you think best displays the data. For example, Figure 5.21 shows a 3-D line chart. You can also produce combination charts from this data. Figure 5.22 display the trends for defence expenditure as a line chart and expenditure on education as a bar chart. This chart was produced by selecting **Combination . . .** chart option **4** from the **Chart Gallery**.

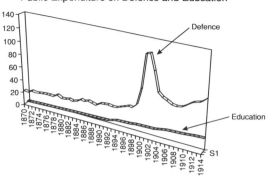

Figure 5.21 Example of a 3-D line chart

In this chapter you have examined a range of historical data using the Excel worksheet and charts. In the next chapter you proceed to examine in more detail information based on a study of the material conditions of the working class, 1850–1914.

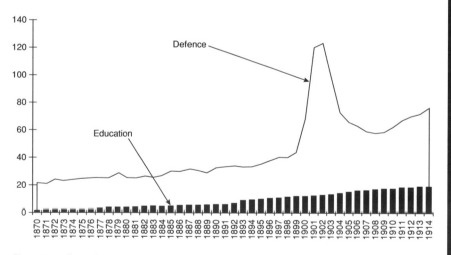

Figure 5.22 Example of a combination chart

Chapter

6

The Historian and Data: The Material Conditions of the Working Class in Britain, 1850–1914

 Introduction

In Chapters 4 and 5 you learnt how to use a worksheet (the term for a spreadsheet used in the Excel program), and you are now going to apply your skills to investigate a historical theme: the debate over the material conditions of the working class in Britain between 1850 and 1914. Using spreadsheets and graphs you will explore the question: did the working class gain from the process of industrialisation and reap the benefits of higher wages and earnings after 1850? Section 6.2 sets the historical context for the investigation and defines the indicators used by historians to measure changes in working-class conditions: wages, earnings, and the cost of living. Historians often organise this data as a series of index numbers, and this technique is also discussed. Section 6.3 outlines the main historical sources which will be used in the workshop exercises in this chapter, and examines some of the historical problems in using this information. The final section, 6.4, is organised as a series of workshops which examine the historical evidence by using spreadsheets and graphs. You start by building a spreadsheet from local data on earnings and the cost of living for workers in the 'steel city' of Sheffield for 1851–1911. As the workshops progress additional data sets are introduced which allow you to expand the analysis and make comparisons between the data sets. By progressing through the workshops you will learn:

- To expand your skills in designing spreadsheets and graphs using a range of historical data
- To organise the data to your requirements
- To perform basic calculations from the data
- To interrogate and critically analyse the trends in the data
- To extend your understanding of working-class earnings and the cost of living.

 Working-Class Wages, Earnings and the Cost of Living, 1850–1914

Even more than the experience of work, it was the level of working class purchasing power that affected the nature of everyday life. It was the interaction of wages, incomes and the cost of living that determined working class purchasing power; and it was working class purchasing power that, together with work, influenced every aspect of working class life.

(Benson 1989: 39)

Clearly it is the purchasing power of people which is the key to understanding the changing standard of living of the population. To explore this process further we need to identify a set of statistical indicators which help determine the degree of change in living standards. The following are the key indicators used:

- *Money wages:* the prevailing wage rate in an industry or firm set by the employer. It is the rate of payment per unit of work done (Benson 1989: 40). For example, the wage rate can be a given rate of payment for work done per unit of time, e.g. £10 per hour; or per unit of volume, e.g. £10 for every ton of a product produced.

- *Money earnings:* the actual payment for work over a period of time. This is the worker's take-home pay, for a nineteenth-century worker usually in the form of cash. Earnings are a more representative indicator of a person's income from work than wages because they do not depend simply upon the prevailing wage rate but are influenced by the hours that workers were able and willing to work as well as the hours that employers were willing to provide (Benson 1989: 40–41). For example, the hours of nineteenth-century piece workers (i.e. workers paid by the volume of work completed) was determined by the intensity at which work was carried out, and also by the efficiency of management in setting the context for work. Such factors were particularly influential in determining earnings in industries such as cotton where piece work was commonplace. Further, in the coal industry, miners' earnings were affected by the introduction of short-time and overtime. In the coal industry of the Black Country, for example, there were wide fluctuations in earnings and the stability of wage rates for many sections of workers over long periods of time (Barnsby 1971: 223). Thus workers' earnings would decrease during periods of short-time work and increase during periods of overtime, even though the prevailing wage rate remained the same.

- *Money income:* a person's final disposable income including various supplements to earnings. This may include earnings from non-wage labour (begging, petty crime, penny capitalism) and welfare payments and fringe benefits not calculated in earnings (Benson 1983, 1989: 41).

- *Real wages, earnings and incomes.* So far we have expressed wages, earnings and incomes in money terms, but what matters is the purchasing power of these indicators, e.g. the purchasing power of earnings. The indicator in this case is termed 'real earnings' and is the actual volume of goods and services that money earnings will be able to purchase. We thus need to consider the effect of the cost of living on purchasing power. The cost of living for a typical nineteenth-century worker would include the prices paid for necessities such as rent, fuel, clothing and food (Gourvish 1979: 16–17; Gazeley 1989: 209). Prices are determined by prevailing market conditions, i.e. demand and supply, and it therefore follows that real earnings are money earnings divided by the cost of living. This distinction between money indicators and real indicators is an important one. For example, in periods of inflation (rising cost of living) a person's money earnings may increase without any increase in their real

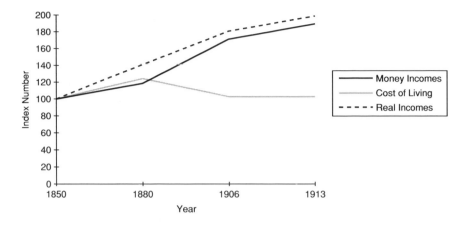

Figure 6.1 Trends in incomes and expenses

Source: Benson 1989: 55, Table 7

earnings. This is because the prices of goods and services that they buy may increase (on average) at the same rate as their money earnings (Craven 1984: 96). Indeed real earnings may actually fall if the rise in the prices of goods and services exceeds the rise in money earnings. Study the trends in Figure 6.1 which demonstrate the interaction between cost of living, money incomes and real incomes (money incomes/cost of living) for British workers between 1850 and 1913. What happens to real incomes when the cost of living rises or falls?

Having defined these indicators, how does the historian represent this information. A technique frequently used for measuring statistical data such as earnings is that of index numbers. Index numbers have the great advantage of being easily organised on a spreadsheet. An index number is a multiple of 100 calculated from a base year. For example, assume that average money earnings in 1900 are £10 per week and that 1900 is the base year. The base year is the fixed standard from which all other index numbers are measured. As historians what we are concerned with is what happens to the index number when there are changes in earnings over time. Assuming that money earnings rose to £11 per week in 1901 then the index number would be 110. The movement of earnings from £10 to £11 per week represents a rise of 10 per cent and thus the index number will correspondingly increase by 10 per cent to 110. If, on the other hand, earnings had fallen to £9 in 1901 the index would have become 90. Try an example yourself by calculating the impact a £2 rise or fall in weekly earnings would have on the index number for 1901.

6.3 Historical Data on Earnings and the Cost of Living

Most middle-class writers who turned their attention to the subject of poverty in the middle decades of the nineteenth century tended to assume – for relatively few explained the

> question statistically – that the bulk of the working class had an income sufficient to both
> guarantee them reasonable standards of housing and feeding and enable them to provide
> cover, through friendly societies and savings banks, for all the ordinary contingencies of life.
>
> (Treble 1979: 8)

The above statement sets the context for the investigation of the standard of living of the working class and you should consider the following proposition: did the standard of living of the working class increase during the period 1850–1914? You will proceed to test this proposition in the following workshop exercises, but at this stage there is a need to outline the issues raised by historians and the sources used to investigate the standard-of-living question.

The period from the early 1890s to 1914, which historians such as Gourvish have loosely defined as the Edwardian years (Gourvish 1979: 13), has fascinated historians. In particular they have examined the views of contemporaries that 'living standards slowed or even stagnated' during the period (Wardley 1994: 63). There was an increasing interest by the Edwardians in the question of poverty and in the collection of statistical indicators on the standard of living (Gourvish 1979: 13). The most influential statistical series compiled in the Edwardian period was undertaken by A. Bowley, and was consequently brought together in his major work published in 1937 (Bowley 1937; Wardley 1994: 63–64; Gourvish 1979: 13). This pioneering work provided 'the origin of most subsequent historical analysis' (Gourvish 1979: 16). There have been numerous revisions by historians of Bowley's original calculations on wages, earnings, and the cost of living (Gazeley 1989: 207), and the most recent by Feinstein has produced a new time series from the data (Feinstein 1990a, 1990b). However, it still remains a key starting point for any investigation of the standard-of-living question and consequently we will use this data.

In Appendix 3 Data Sets C and D provide information taken from the Bowley time series. Data Set C contains information on real earnings for workers in three major sectors of the economy: coal, engineering and shipbuilding, and cotton textiles. Data Set D contains Bowley's national aggregate data on real earnings between 1850 and 1902 (Mitchell and Deane 1962). These data sets will be used in the workshops that follow, but it is worth recognising some of the problems associated with this data. Bowley, himself, recognised that his data was open to question and could only provide an estimate of trends. For example, the indexes for earnings in Data Sets C and D were adjusted to account for unemployment, but this was based on returns from a limited number of trade unions which also largely represented skilled workers. Thus, this may distort the impact of unemployment on earnings. There was also a problem with the information on food prices which formed the cost of living index for Bowley to produce his real earnings index. Food prices were taken from London price lists, and do not represent variations in prices across the country. In particular, aggregate data in Data Set D must be used with caution because it does not capture cross-industry and cross-regional variations in real earnings (Gourvish 1979: 16–19; Gazeley 1989: 201–208).

To overcome the bias of using aggregate data historians have focused on local, industrial and regional studies, although again the fragmentary nature of this information must be kept in mind (see Hunt 1973, 1986). Thus, in the workshops we begin by examining local evidence on steel workers in Sheffield (Pollard 1954, 1959). The data for this study is provided in Data Sets A and B. Data Set A contains information on money earnings and the cost of living for the light and heavy steel trades in Sheffield for 10-year periods between 1851 and 1911, and Data Set B contains the same information on a year-to-year basis. The data is extracted from Sidney Pollard's excellent study of labour in Sheffield and constitutes a long-run time series. The series is based on index numbers with the base being 100 for 1900. Sheffield was a large industrial town with a heavy concentration of workers in the steel and allied trades, and in 1870 some 70 per cent of UK steel output was produced in the town (Lloyd-Jones and Lewis 1994a: 267). For simplification and analysis of the data on workers' earnings Sheffield's steel and metal-making trades have been divided between the heavy and light trades. The former include workers in armaments, engineering and steel production, and the latter constitute the traditional employment sector of cutlery and tool production. In the heavy trades, there were giant firms employing thousands of workers, such as John Brown's, Charles Cammell's and the Vickers enterprise. By the late nineteenth century these firms were major employers in Sheffield and dominated the industrial landscape in the East End of the city. But even in the heavy trades the typical firm was small-scale, as was certainly the case in the light sectors of the industry. In the light trades, small firms were commonplace, and employed inworkers and also large numbers of outworkers. Small workshop production persisted and the use of skilled artisans was crucial to the handicraft technology of the cutlery and tool trades. Similarly, in the specialist steel trades craft traditions predominated even in 1914. Thus traditional craft workers persisted alongside those employed in modern large-scale plant. The work process in Sheffield underwent significant organisational and structural change in the second half of the nineteenth century and we would expect this to be shown in the pattern of workers' earnings and their material conditions (Lloyd-Jones and Lewis 1993b; Pollard 1959: 54, 59; Tweedale 1993; Taylor 1993).

The evidence from Sheffield provides an excellent local source which you can use to test out the following propositions:

- What were the trends in real earnings in Sheffield over 1851–1911?
- Was the pattern of change similar in both sectors of the industry: the light and heavy trades?
- What factors may account for changing real wages in Sheffield?
- Did the trend in real wages in Sheffield over 1851–1911 suggest an improvement in living standards?

You can now proceed to the analysis of the data in the workshops, but given the problems we have raised concerning this data you should think of the study as an exercise in interpretation. As Pollard reminds us: 'Any attempt to trace the course of earnings of labour before 1914 must, in view of evidence available, remain an essay in interpretation rather than an exercise in statistics' (Pollard 1954: 49). The data can only provide statistical estimates but is sufficient for you to use your historical skills to identify and interpret trends and thus build a picture of changes in the standard of living of workers over time.

6.4 Workshop Exercises

In this workshop you are going to plan and build a spreadsheet to examine the conditions of the Sheffield working class. The first spreadsheet you should build is from the information in Data Set A on money wages and the cost of living for 10-year periods. Data Set A only contains information on the cost of living and money earnings, but you should also leave space to enter formulas for calculating the real earnings for both the light and heavy trades. We will again use the Excel program as the exemplar in this chapter; thus we will refer to a spreadsheet as a 'worksheet' and a graph as a 'chart'.

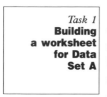

Workshop 1
Planning a Worksheet for Earnings and the Cost of Living in Sheffield

Task 1
Building a worksheet for Data Set A

From the information in Data Set A construct a worksheet to capture this information. Figure 6.2 shows a worksheet we have constructed under the file name Sheff-10, i.e. a name which indicates that it is data for Sheffield for 10-year periods. Chapter 4 examined the techniques for building worksheets but for this first exercise we will repeat the procedures.

The first task is to enter the text for the main title, sub-titles and column headings. Follow these instructions:

1. Make cell A1 the active cell by clicking on it.
2. In cell A1 type the main title: Index of Cost of Living and Money Earnings. Press the Down Arrow key, and the active cell becomes A2.
3. Check that the text you have typed contains no mistakes. If there are mistakes then edit the cell contents.
4. In cell A2 type: Sheffield Light and Heavy Trades 1851–1911, the first sub-title. Press the Down Arrow key, and the active cell becomes A3.
5. In cell A3 type the second sub-title: (1900=100), and press the Down Arrow key. Cell 4 becomes active.
6. Leave row 4 blank.

	A	B	C	D	E	F
1	Index of Cost of Living and Money Earnings by Decade					
2	Sheffield Light and Heavy Trades 1851–1911					
3	(1900=100)					
4						
5	Year	Cost of Living	Money Earnings	Money Earnings	Real Earnings	Real Earnings
6			Light Trades	Heavy Trades	Light Trades	Heavy Trades
7	1851	100.5	78	71.0		
8	1861	115.9	75	73.0		
9	1871	116.4	100	89.0		
10	1881	110.8	86	87.0		
11	1891	101.5	96	83.0		
12	1901	101.0	95	94.0		
13	1911	105.9	98	109.0		

Figure 6.2 Worksheet for Data Set A

7 Make A5 the active cell and type: Year. Press the Right Arrow key to enter the text. The active cell moves to B5.

8 In cell B5 type: Cost of Living. Press the Right Arrow key.

9 In cell C5 type: Money Earnings. Press the Right Arrow key.

10 In cell D5 type: Money Earnings. Press the Right Arrow key.

11 In Cell E5 type: Real Earnings. Press the Right Arrow key. Finally in cell F5 type: Real Earnings.

12 Underneath both of the money earnings and real earnings columns you want a heading for the light and heavy trades. Make C6 the active cell and type: Light Trades; press the Right Arrow key and type: Heavy Trades, in cell D6. Do the same for both the real earnings columns.

Having entered the text you can now proceed to enter the numbers: year and cost of living and money earnings. The data for real earnings in columns E and F will be calculated later by entering formulas. The numbers are entered in columns A, B and C starting at row 6. Start by entering the numbers for the dates. Click on A7 and type: 1851, the first date. Press the Down Arrow key and the active cell becomes A7. Dates must be ordered chronologically and you must enter the 10-year time series from 1851 to 1911. As shown in Chapter 4, Workshop 2, there is a quick way of entering a consecutive series of numbers:

1 Click on cell A7 which contains the entry 1851.

2 Click on the **Data** menu in the Excel menu bar and from the options that appear select **Series**. The **Series** dialogue box appears.

3 Click on the **Columns** button in the **Series in** area.

4 The type of series you want to enter is a linear series, a uniform increase in value of 10. In the series **Type** area, the linear series is pre-set.

5 Take the mouse pointer to the field labelled **Step Value** and type: 10, the step value for your date series.

6 Press the Tab key to move to the **Stop Value** field and type: 1911, the last date in your series.

7 Click on **OK** and the series will automatically be filled in the column.

You should now complete the data entry by typing the numbers for cost of living and money earnings in columns B and C, starting at row 6. When you have finished entering you should enhance the presentation of the worksheet. This was explained in Chapter 4, Workshop 3, and you should refer back to that if necessary. To enhance the worksheet:

1 Increase the width of the columns so that the full text is shown.

2 Centre the text for the title and sub-titles across the worksheet range, i.e. across the block of cells A1:F3.

3 Centre the column headings and the numbers in their cells.

4 Use the **Format** menu to design borders and patterns.

When you have designed the worksheet to your satisfaction you can proceed to Task 2 and construct a chart to display your data.

<table>
<tr><td>

Task 2

Constructing a chart showing the cost of living and money earnings for the light and heavy trades

</td><td>

The techniques for constructing charts were introduced in Chapter 5. To display the trends on money earnings and the cost of living, construct the line chart shown in Figure 6.3. On the X axis, you want the labels for the dates, and on the Y axis you want three data series: Cost of Living, Money Wages Light Trades, Money Wages Heavy Trades. To construct this chart follow these instructions:

</td></tr>
</table>

1　On the X axis of the chart you want the labels for the dates. The dates are contained in column A. Select the range A7:A13.

2　Press Shift and **F8** and the Add series function will be activated.

3　To add the first data series for the Y axis, the cost of living in column B, select the range B7:B13.

4　To add the second series for the Y axis, the money earnings for the light trades, select the range C7:C13.

5　To add the third series for the Y axis, money earnings for the heavy trades, select the range D7:D13.

6　Open the **File** menu and choose **New . . .**. The **New** dialogue box opens. Choose **Chart**, and click on **OK**.

7　You must now give instructions as to how the data is to be plotted in the chart. You are asked what the **First Column Contains**. The first column selected contained the date labels for the X axis. Click in the selection box titled **Category (X) Axis Labels**. Finally click on **OK**. A column chart appears on the screen.

8　Name the chart file and save it to your disk by opening the **File** menu and choosing **Save As . . .**. Call the file Sheff-10, reflecting the information for 10-year periods.

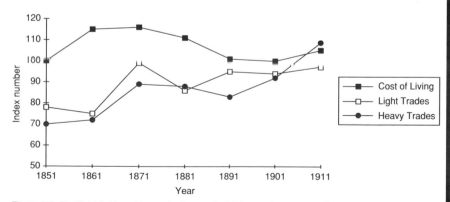

Figure 6.3 Sheffield light and heavy trades: cost of living and money earnings

You can now design the chart to your own requirements:

1   Change the chart type from a column chart to a line chart. Click on the Line Chart button on the Chart tool bar (see Figure 5.4). This is the fifth button from the left of the tool bar. You can also select different types of line charts by opening the **Gallery** menu and choosing **Line . . .** chart.

2   Insert a main title for the chart. Open the **Chart** menu and choose **Attach Text**. The **Attach Text** dialogue box opens. Choose **Chart Title**. You can now type the main title into the edit area of the chart screen. When you have finished, press **Enter**.

3   To label the X axis (year) and Y axis (index number) follow the same procedures as in 2 above for **Value Y axis** and then for **Category (X) axis** in turn.

4   Place a legend on the chart to indicate the three series of data. Click on the Legend tool button on the Chart tool bar at the bottom of the **Chart** screen (see Figure 5.4). This is the third button from the left of the tool bar. The legend appears on the right-hand side of the chart. Open the **Chart** menu and choose **Edit Series . . .**. In the **Edit Series** dialogue box there is a field labelled **Series**. In this field click on **Series1**. Take the mouse pointer to the field labelled **Name** and type: Cost of Living. Now click on **Series2** in the **Series** field. A question box appears: **Save Changes in Series1?** Click on **Yes**. Now type: Money Earnings Light in the **Name** field. Click on Series3, save the changes to Series2, and type: Money Earnings Heavy in the series **Name** field. When you have finished, click on the **OK** button. To change the position of the legend in the chart window (i.e. top, bottom, centre), click on the legend box in the chart window and then open the **Format** menu and choose **Legend**. You can now choose an option to position the legend. In Figure 6.3 we have chosen the **Right** of the chart.

5   Finally you will want to change the scale of the Y axis to highlight the trends in the data. At present, the Y axis series starts at 0. Depending upon the sequence of numbers in a given series you might want to start the Y axis series at a higher value than 0. In our example in Figure 6.3, 50 is a more appropriate starting value (think about this?). To change the starting point to 50, click on the top point of the Y axis and a box will appear at the top and bottom of the Y axis. Open the **Format** menu box and choose **Scale . . .**. In the field labelled **Minimum** type: 50, the minimum point on the Y axis.

6   When you have finished designing the chart make sure you save it. Click on the **File** menu and choose **Close**. A question box appears: **Save Chart Sheff-10.XCL?** Click on **Yes**.

You can now proceed to the next task which deals with calculating data for real earnings.

> **Task 3**
> **Calculating data for real earnings**

In Section 6.2, a crucial distinction was made between money earnings and real earnings. Real earnings are determined by the amount of goods and services that money earnings will purchase in the market place. In statistical terms real earnings are money earnings divided by the average price of goods and services that the worker buys. To calculate the real earnings for the Sheffield trades you would therefore use the equation:

$$Y = \frac{W}{P}$$

where:

   Y = real earnings

   W = money earnings

   P = the average cost of living.

Start by calculating the real earnings for the light trades. To do this follow these instructions:

1   Click on cell E7 and type the following formula:

   =(C7/B7)*100

   This formula divides the money earnings in C7 by the cost of living in B7, and then multiplies by 100. You need to multiply by 100 to convert to an index number which is a multiple of 100.

2   Press **Enter** and the calculation is displayed in cell E7 (77.6119403).

3   So far you have only calculated the real earnings for one year, 1851, but you require the data for all years. You should now copy the original formula =(C7/B7)*100 and automatically fill in the calculations for all years. Click on cell E7 and open the **Edit** menu. Choose **Copy**. Click on E8 and select the range E8:E13. Press **Enter** and the calculations will be filled in. Note: another way of copying formulas is to use the copy and drag method. Click on cell E7. The drag box is located on the bottom right of the active cell: a small square. Position the mouse pointer on the drag box: it turns into a black cross. Keep the mouse button depressed and drag to E13 and the calculations will be filled in.

4   At present the calculations are displayed with numerous decimal places. For display purposes you would only want one decimal place. To change the number format open the **Format** menu and choose **Number . . .**. The **Number Format** dialogue box opens. In the field labelled **Category** choose **Number**, and in the **Code** field type 0.0 (i.e. one decimal place). Click on **OK**.

5   Finally, in column F calculate the real earnings for the heavy trades. Use the formula:

   =(D7/B7)*100

Copy this formula for all the years. Your final calculations should match those shown in Figure 6.4.

Real Earnings Light Trades	Real Earnings Heavy Trades
77.6	70.6
64.7	63.0
85.9	76.5
77.6	78.5
94.6	81.8
94.1	93.1
92.5	102.9

Figure 6.4 Calculated data for real earnings in Sheffield

Task 4
Constructing a chart showing real earnings

Construct the line chart in Figure 6.5 showing the real earnings for both the light and heavy trades on one chart. Remember, the X axis will include the date labels, and the Y axis the two data series: Real Earnings Light and Real Earnings Heavy. Figure 6.5 is only an illustration and you should design the chart to your own specifications.

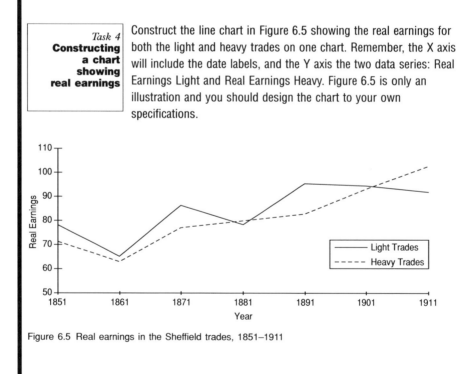

Figure 6.5 Real earnings in the Sheffield trades, 1851–1911

Task 5
Remember to save all your work when you leave the program

Study the chart you have created for real earnings (Figure 6.5). In Chapter 3 we pointed out the problems of long-run versus short-run time series. Often, the long-run series irons out short-run fluctuations. If you look at the trends in Figure 6.5 they suggest the following:

Workshop 2
Long-run and
Short-run
Time Series:
Building a
Worksheet
for Annual
Time Series

- For the light trades there were sharp long-run fluctuations in real wages from the 1850s to the 1880s and, following a sharp upward movement in the 1880s, workers experienced fairly constant real wages from the 1890s to 1911.
- Workers in the heavy trades experienced real wages falling in the 1850s, rising sharply in the 1860s, rising gradually in the 1870s and 1880s, and displaying a marked upward shift from the 1890s to 1911, i.e. during the Edwardian period.

You must, however, be cautious of such a reading of this data. Consider the following statement from Sidney Pollard concerning the 10-year period 1893 to 1903: 'The years 1893–6 formed a period of grave distress, particularly in the winter months, and after some years of prosperity . . . unemployment again became widespread in most trades in 1903' (Pollard 1959: 182). This suggests that workers were highly vulnerable to short-term unemployment due to the downturn of the trade cycle. Short-term unemployment was a reality of everyday working life and in 1891 its consequences were remarked upon by A. J. Mundella, the Liberal MP for Sheffield Brightside: 'I am afraid that my poor constituents are passing through a period of great suffering. Are any subscriptions coming in response to the Mayors appeal? I should like to give something' (Lloyd-Jones and Lewis 1993b: 220). Further, employers reacted to the downturn of the trade cycle by introducing short-term work and pushing wages downwards. Thus, for example, in the depressed climate of 1894, one Sheffield cutlery firm informed their workers of the introduction of a three-day week and claimed that they should 'be permitted to run short-time by giving a weeks notice' (M. J. Lewis, 1990: 100). In the depression of 1886 wages were severely reduced for unskilled workers and short-time introduced for skilled workers (Parliamentary Papers 1886: 21, 84, 103, 106). Unemployment, short-time working and wage reductions coloured the life of the working class in Sheffield, and these factors very likely led to a decrease in earnings in the short run. Your task in this workshop is therefore to build a worksheet to explore the annual time series data contained in Data Set B.

Task 1
Build a
worksheet from
the data on cost
of living and
money earnings
per annum (Data
Set B)
Data Set B contains information on an annual basis for cost of living and money earnings for both the light and heavy trades for 1851–1911. Figure 6.6 shows part of the worksheet we have created to capture this information, and also includes the calculations we have made for real earnings. The column headings for the data are the same as those you created in Workshop 1, for the 10-yearly series, but of course there is now a great deal more

Cost of Living, Money Earnings and Real Earnings					
Sheffield Light and Heavy Trades 1851–1911					
1900=100					
Date	Cost of Living	Money Earnings Light Trades	Real Earnings Light Trades	Money Earnings Heavy Trades	Real Earnings Heavy Trades
1851	100.5	78	78	71	71
1852	100.5	79	79	73	73
1853	107.6	82	76	77	72
1854	121.5	82	67	72	59
1855	125.1	80	64	72	58
1856	124.6	89	71	68	55
1857	119.0	88	74	75	63
1858	110.8	82	74	65	59
1859	109.7	82	75	65	59
1860	113.3	83	73	68	60

Figure 6.6 Worksheet for Data Set B

data to enter. You should now construct your worksheet from Data Set B. Remember that the dates can be filled in automatically, and that you should create the columns for real earnings to perform the calculations discussed in the next task.

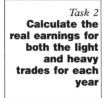

Task 2
Calculate the real earnings for both the light and heavy trades for each year

The calculations are the same as those carried out in Workshop 1, although you will be working on different cell ranges. Remember that you need only enter one formula and then copy the original formula, or use the copy and drag method, to fill in the rest of the calculations. The finished calculations for real earnings, for the first ten years, are shown in Figure 6.6.

Task 3
Remember to save the changes to the worksheet

Workshop 3 Constructing Charts to Display Annual Time Series Data

You now need to construct a number of charts to display the trends in the annual series for Sheffield. Construct charts for the following:

- A line chart containing three data series: the cost of living and money earnings for both the light and heavy trades for each year
- A line chart containing two data series: the real earnings of the light and heavy trades for each year.

The two charts are shown in Figures 6.7 and 6.8. An important tip when selecting your columns for the X axis and Y axis is to use the scroll bar to move around the worksheet. For example, when you select the date column and press Shift and **F8** (add) use the scroll bar to move up the document and then select the column for money earnings for

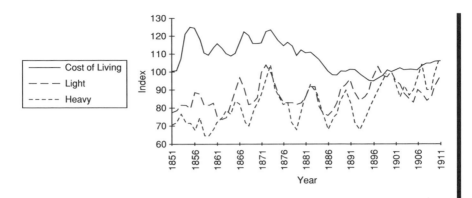

Figure 6.7 Cost of living and money earnings in Sheffield

the light trades. As you will find out, this is a much easier way of selecting data in larger worksheets.

Note that we have designed the Y axis at a minimum point of 60 in Figure 6.7 and 50 in Figure 6.8 to highlight the trends (see Workshop 2, Task 3). You can also change the dates on the X axis (e.g. labels for 5-year intervals as shown in Figures 6.7 and 6.8). To do this click on the intersection of the Y and X axes, open the **Format** menu and choose **Scale . . .**. In the field labelled **Number of Categories Between Ticks** (the ticks are the small vertical lines on the X axis), type a number, i.e. 5. In the field labelled **Number of Categories Between Tick Labels** (the tick labels are the dates themselves), type a number, i.e. 5. Click on **OK**. You should design the axis the way you think best highlights the trends in the data.

When you have finished producing the graphs print them so that you can use them in the final workshop to analyse the trends.

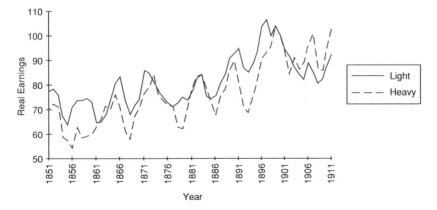

Figure 6.8 Real earnings in Sheffield

Having built the charts you can now interpret the trends, and we suggest that you produce a report on your findings based on a consideration of the following questions:

● What interpretations can be placed on the trends displayed in the charts you have created? For example, assuming that a worker entered the labour market aged 10 in 1851, what generalisations can you make concerning his standard of living in Sheffield over the next 60 years? (Note: national pension became available following the 1909 'People's Budget' for males aged 70+, and consequently our worker would have become eligible in 1911.) Remember also to consider the different trends in the light and heavy trades.

● Consider the following statement from Charles Belk, a Sheffield cutlery manufacturer, talking about the depression in Sheffield's light trades between 1883 and 1886:

> The depression is probably more intense and general than any within my experience – suffering, however, is not so great . . . attributable mainly to the extraordinary low prices at which nearly all commodities required by the operatives are obtainable.
>
> (Parliamentary Papers 1886: 75)

Is this observation borne out by the trends you have produced for Sheffield? Did a falling cost of living cushion the working class in Sheffield?

● We can use different types of charts to display trends. For example, if we wished to chart real wages we might use:

(a) A linear chart (year by year or decade by decade)
(b) A moving average (e.g. 5-year/10-year average).

You may find that these two different approaches provide different historical interpretations of the trends displayed. Consider the proposition that for the Sheffield working class conditions steadily improved over 1851–1911. Look at the chart we have created in Figure 6.9 which plots real earnings as 10-year moving averages; what conclusions would you draw? Now look at the chart you produced earlier for real wages per annum (Figure 6.8); you might well now draw a different conclusion. Which of the charts do you think most accurately reflects changes in real wages experienced by the working class in this period?

● Many contemporaries, including government advisers, argued that 'the rate of increase of living standards slowed or even stagnated during the Edwardian period (1890–1914) and this was a cause of widespread industrial conflict in the period 1908–1914' (Wardley 1994: 63). Is this view substantiated by the Sheffield data, i.e. do real earnings show significant changes over 1890–1914?

● Sheffield represents only one location for a study of the standard of living in the second half of the nineteenth century. You might want to ask how typical

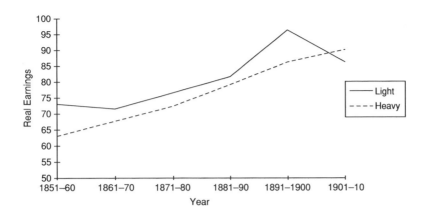

Figure 6.9 Real earnings in Sheffield (10-year averages)

was Sheffield, and how representative are the trends for real earnings in a local industry? We pointed out in Chapter 3 the importance of using comparative data (see Function 7). To test the representative nature of your data you would want to ask the following questions:

(a) How does Sheffield fit in with the national trends for real wages in the British metal and metal-making industry?
(b) How do the metal trades fit in with the trends in other key staple industries – the export-oriented industries of coal, cotton, shipbuilding and engineering?
(c) How does the Sheffield data fit in with national trends for the whole economy?

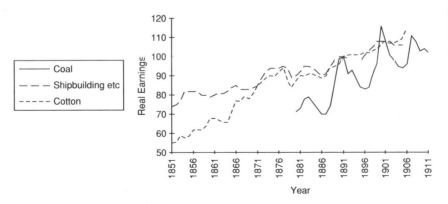

Figure 6.10 Real earnings for three UK staples (1891 = 100)

Note: The data are adjusted to take account of unemployment

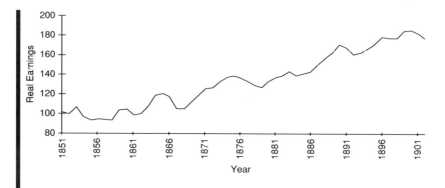

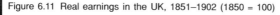

Figure 6.11 Real earnings in the UK, 1851–1902 (1850 = 100)

Note: This data is adjusted to take account of unemployment

(d) Long-run data series on real wages for the iron and steel industry nationally are not available and this highlights one of the points we made in Chapter 3 concerning the fragmentary nature of historical evidence. However, a reasonably good long-run time series exists for the three staples mentioned above and also for the national trends. You can build worksheets and construct charts from the information in Data Sets C and D. However, to allow you to make some preliminary comparisons Figure 6.10 shows the trends in real earnings for the three staples and Figure 6.11 shows the national trends. What interpretation can you place on this evidence and was the experience of Sheffield's workers typical in this period?

There are obviously further issues you might want to explore on the question of the standard of living. You can find more information in the excellent statistical compilation by Mitchell and Deane (1962: Chapter 7) and we recommend that you use this source. Further, if you want to compare the national figures compiled by Bowley in Data Set D with recent revisions then see the work by Feinstein and Wardley (Feinstein 1990a, 1990b; Wardley 1994). Finally, you should also consider other sources of evidence on the standard of living for this period. For example, diet and nutrition (Oddy 1970), family and community, housing (Benson 1989: Chapters 3–5; Rodgers 1989: Chapter 7; Englander 1983), and also the amount of leisure available to the working class with the reduction of working hours from 10 to 8. As Gourvish reminds us: in the early twentieth century there was still 'the existence of widespread poverty in the midst of plenty' as exemplified by the social investigations of the time by Booth and Rowntree (Gourvish 1979: 13). The statistical indicators relating to real earnings are obviously important indicators, but you should also consider qualitative indicators to get a fuller picture of the standard of living of the working population.

Having explored in detail the specific theme of the standard of living, the next chapter will introduce you to a range of historical information relating to a number of different themes.

Spreadsheets and Graphs: The Historian and Data

7.1 Introduction

This chapter provides three exercises which use different types of historical data sets: disaggregate data, comparative data, relational data. The exercises will use spreadsheets and graphs to examine specific historical themes using Excel as an exemplar. The themes are drawn from a range of historical disciplines: political history, economic and social history and demographic history. Each exercise starts with an introduction outlining the historical theme and setting the historical context. The data sets used to examine the theme are then explained, and you are prompted to build worksheets and charts from the material provided. You are finally asked to examine a number of historical questions in relation to each data set you examine. The data sets for the exercises are located in Appendix 4.

7.2 Historical Themes

This exercise uses worksheets and charts to capture the trends from a number of disaggregated data sets, and examines the composition of the House of Commons in a volatile period of Britain's political history, 1906–1910. Before using worksheets to examine the evidence on composition the next section provides a brief discussion on the major political issues of the period and sets the historical context.

Historical Theme 1 **The Composition of the House of Commons, 1906–1910**

Historical Context **British party politics, 1900–1910** In January 1906, a Liberal Government, supported by Labour and Irish Nationalist MPs, came into office after 10 years of Conservative Party rule (the General Election was actually held in December 1905, but convention dates the election/office of this government from 1906). The British electorate gave this government an enormous vote of confidence and it swept to power in a landslide victory. The magnitude of this victory is shown in Figure 7.1 which compares the state of the parties in the Commons in 1900 and 1906. In 1900, the Conservatives, with their political allies the Liberal Unionists (the Liberal Unionists split from the Liberals in 1886 after Gladstone's Home Rule Bill and by 1906 had effectively merged with the Conservative Party), had a comfortable majority but by 1906 there had been a dramatic turn-around in the fortunes of the parties.

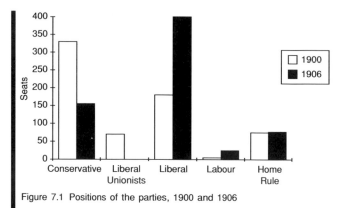

Figure 7.1 Positions of the parties, 1900 and 1906

Source: A.R. Ball 1987: 16

The Liberal Governments after 1906 have received considerable attention from historians, not least for their programme of social reform: 'In the history of social policy in Britain, the years between 1906 and 1914 stand out as one of the periods of major reform' (Hay 1986: 11). Given the sweeping victory of 1906 the Liberal Party had a clear mandate to carry out its policies, and the origins of the Liberal reforms have been extensively debated by historians (see Hay 1986: Chapter 3). The Liberal Government was not, however, elected on a social reform ticket, and it should be borne in mind that issues of foreign affairs played an important role in all the elections of this period (the Khaki Election of 1900, and questions of the arms race in 1906–1910), as did the question of Britain's international trading policy. Certainly, during the election campaign, a major political issue centred on whether Britain should retain free trade, a central plank of the Liberal's political agenda, or should adopt tariffs and develop closer economic ties with the Empire. In 1903 the Colonial Secretary, Joseph Chamberlain, had resigned from the Cabinet, and launched a national campaign to support tariff reform and greater Imperial unity. This split the Conservatives and they entered the election as a divided party in sharp contrast to the Liberals who had united around the banner of free trade (see Blewett 1968; Cain 1979; Marrison 1977; Wardley 1994). Thus, social reform was by no means the main campaign issue of the election and whilst a number of backbench MPs sought to raise it up the political agenda the leadership remained reticent. Indeed:

> The Liberal Party achieved its overwhelming victory . . . mainly because of mistakes and lack of electoral appeal of the Conservative Party. The election manifesto and the themes echoed by Liberal leaders outlined no new policy departures.
>
> (A.R. Ball 1987: 79)

Nevertheless, the administration, especially after 1908 (when Asquith became PM on the death of Campbell-Bannerman), has been correctly viewed as a 'strong reforming government' with an emphasis on social welfare and intervention in the social and economic arenas. This 'New Liberalism' emphasised a changed role for the state: intervention to tackle the social and economic inequalities of the nation by collectivist action (A.R. Ball 1987: 79–81). Social reforms were carried out, especially in relation to education, employment and the old-aged. Table 7.1 lists these reforms and you can find more information in Hay (1986: Chapters 3–4) and Thane (1982: Chapter 3):

Table 7.1 Major Acts of Parliament relating to social reform, 1906–1914

1906 Trades Disputes Act	1908 Children's Act
1906 Education (Provision of Meals) Act	1908 Old Age Pensioners Act
1906 Workers Compensation (Extension) Act	1908 Smallholdings and Allotments Act
1907 Notification of Births Act	1909 Trade Boards Act
1907 Education (Administrative Provisions) Act	1909 Housing and Town Planning Act
1907 Probation Act	1911 National Insurance Act
1908 Matrimonial Causes Act	1914 Education (Provision of Meals) Act

Source: Thaine 1982: 359–360

These reforms were challenged by Conservative forces, leading to two General Elections in one year in 1910. The period after 1906 saw a heightening political tension amongst the parties especially focused on constitutional issues, notably the power of the House of Lords (Fair 1986: 80). Between 1906 and 1909, the Unionist majority in the House of Lords did everything possible to wreck the legislative programme of the Liberal Government (Fair 1986: 80; Ridley 1992: 235, 251). Underlying the constitutional crisis was the major issue of taxation and the vexed political question of how social reforms were to be financed. Fiscal policy cannot be divorced from social policy and 'ought to be considered as part of the process of social reform' (Hay 1986: 57). Chamberlain, for example, had argued that the revenue raised from tariffs could be used to finance old-age pensions while the Liberals argued that progressive taxation should be used to help fund social reform. Lloyd-George's 'People's Budget' of 1909 proposed a radical solution to the raising of revenue for social expenditure: an increase in the basic rate of tax to 1s 6d in the pound, a super tax on incomes over £3,000, death duties increased on estates valued at over £5,000, and a tax of 20 per cent on the sales valuation of land; lower-income groups were compensated by a £10 abatement of tax for each child under the age of 16 (Thane 1982: 87–88). The rejection of this budget by the House of Lords led to the General Election of January 1910 and created a tense political environment (Hay 1986: 57–59; S. Ball 1991: 243; Ridley 1992: 251).

In the exercises that follow, you are first going to explore the electoral support for the various parties between 1900 and 1910, and then examine the economic interests in the House of Commons during 1906–1910. What does this tell you about the balance of economic interest in the House of Commons during this period of heightened political tension? This question is important because, although historians have written a great deal on the major political issues of this period, less has been said about the politicians who made and opposed policy: 'Parliament has been viewed as the place where events occur, rather than as a factor shaping the events themselves' (S. Ball 1991: 243). Having considered the historical theme you can now go on and do the exercises.

<table>
<tr><td>

Exercises
The composition of the House of Commons

</td><td>

You are provided with three small but very informative data sets to examine this theme (see Appendix 4: Data Sets for Historical Theme 1).

</td></tr>
</table>

Analysis of Data Set 1A

Before exploring the economic structure of the Commons it is worth considering the electoral support for the parties. In Chapter 5 you performed an exercise using information on the number of seats for each party between 1900 and 1910 (see Figure 5.18). This provides an indication of the electoral support for each party. However, given the first-past-the-post system in British politics a more representative indicator of electoral support is provided in Data Set 1A which gives the total votes cast for each party in the elections of 1900, 1906, and January and December 1910. Now perform the following tasks:

1. From the data set build a worksheet to capture the information.
2. Calculate the total votes for all parties and then calculate the percentage share for each party. To do the latter you simply enter a formula which divides the votes for each party by the total votes for all the parties. For calculating percentages refer back to Chapter 5, Workshop 4, Task 5.
3. Using the calculated data in your worksheet for the percentage votes of the parties construct a chart showing the proportion of the vote for each party in 1906–1910. Figure 7.2 shows an example that we have produced. We have selected a column chart from the chart **Gallery** menu and selected column chart option 10. This is only one example of a way you can display data in chart form and you should experiment with different chart styles by using the options in the chart **Gallery** menu. For example, you could produce four separate pie charts to display the data, or build 3-D charts.

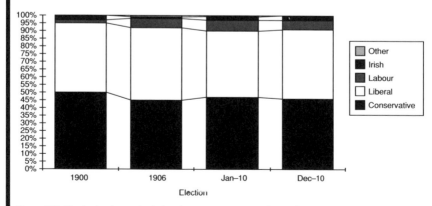

Figure 7.2 Stacked column chart showing percentage vote for each party

Now consider the following questions:

- What does your chart tell you about the electoral fortunes of the parties in 1900–1910?
- Turn back to Chapter 5 and examine Figure 5.18. This shows the distribution of seats in the House of Commons for each party. Compare the trends with the trends in Figure 7.2. What does this tell you about the representative nature of the British electoral system in this period?

Analysis of Data Set 1B

This data set is compiled from a study of the economic and social character of the House of Commons undertaken by J. A. Thomas (1958: 14–16). The data set provides information on the economic interests of all MPs returned at the General Elections of 1906 and January and December 1910. Individual MPs might have two or more economic interests; thus, 'the number of interests returned to Parliament was never equal to the numbers of members elected'. Keeping this information in mind, perform the following tasks:

1   From this data set build a worksheet to capture the information.
2   Express the data for each interest group as a percentage of the total number of MPs in the Commons for the three elections. Remember, there are more economic interests than members, and to perform this calculation you will have to divide the number of MPs in each interest group by 670, the total number of MPs in the Commons. For example, the number of interests recorded in the Landowner category in 1906 is 129. The formula would be, for example, =(Cell Address/670)*100.
3   Use this calculated data to construct charts to highlight the pattern of economic interests in the Commons for the three elections. You should experiment with displaying the data in a variety of chart forms, e.g. column

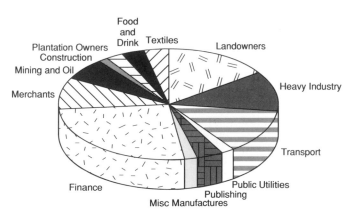

Figure 7.3 Economic composition of the House of Commons, 1906

charts for each election, stacked column charts, or pie charts. We decided to display the data in three pie charts, and one of these, for 1906, is shown in Figure 7.3.

Now consider the following question:

- What interpretation can be placed on the pattern of economic interests displayed in your charts?

Analysis of Data Set 1C

Data Set 1C contains information which breaks down the economic interests for the two main parties in the Commons: the Liberals and the Conservatives. Perform the following tasks:

1   From this data set build a worksheet to capture the information.
2   Express the data for each interest group as a percentage of the total number of MPs in each party for the three elections. To perform this calculation you will have to divide the number of MPs in each interest group by the total number of MPs for each party, which is provided for you in Table 7.2.
3   Construct charts to display the trends.

Table 7.2 Total numbers of seats held by main parties

Party	Seats 1906	Seats Jan 1910	Seats Dec 1910
Conservative	157	273	272
Liberal	400	275	272

Source: A. R. Ball 1987: 15–16

Now consider the following question:

- What interpretation can be placed on the pattern highlighted in your charts concerning the economic interests represented in the two parties?

After you have completed the exercises we recommend that you write a report outlining the main findings of your investigation. Further information on class and social indicators of the House of Commons, for example occupations and educational background can be found in the study by Thomas as well as those by Stuart Ball and David Butler (J. A. Thomas 1958; S. Ball 1991; Butler 1972). There is also an excellent discussion of the influence of businessmen in the Liberal Party by G. R. Searle (Searle 1993). You should also consider the problems raised by the limitations of numerical data when dealing with political issues.

This exercise will use worksheets and charts to explore the trend of economic recovery in these two major economies in the decade before the outbreak of the Second World War. Both these economies suffered huge economic contractions between 1929 and 1933; they abandoned traditional economic methods and sought to implement novel economic policies to tackle, in particular, the problem of mass unemployment. The American and German governments both acknowledged the role of the state in economic management but of course this process was taken much further by the Nazis. You will be using comparative data sets providing indicators of economic performance. For those of you unfamiliar with economic terms the basic indicators used are defined for you as follows:

> **Historical Theme 2**
> **Economic Recovery in the USA and Nazi Germany in the 1930s**

Aggregate Demand	The total demand in the economy, made up of consumer demand + investment demand + export demand + government demand. The two main indicators used are private consumption demand for durable and non-durable goods, and services, and private investment, i.e. the demands by businessmen for capital goods.
GNP	Gross National Product: the total value of output of the economy excluding international trade.
GNP per capita	GNP per head of the population, i.e. total GNP divided by the population. This is a more accurate measurement of economic performance over time because it accounts for population change.

Before you undertake the worksheet exercises, you should read the following section which discusses the main economic trends and policy implications in the two economies between 1929 and 1939.

Historical context
The US and German economies in the interwar period

In the 1920s the performance of these two major industrial economies diverged markedly: the US experienced boom conditions and unprecedented prosperity, while Germany adjusted only slowly to the post-war economic environment (Potter 1985: Chapter 3; Fearon 1987: Chapter 3; Overy 1982: Chapter 2; Temin 1971; Eichengreen 1992). Certainly, in the case of the US in the 1920s there seemed to be little need for government intervention: Americans enjoyed a period of post-war prosperity. During the election campaign of 1928, Herbert Hoover, the Republican candidate and soon to be elected President, stated:

> We in America are nearer to the final triumph over poverty than ever before in the history of any land . . . We shall soon, with the help of God, be in sight of the day when poverty shall be banished from the nation.
>
> (Quoted in Potter 1985: 91)

By the end of his term of office American GNP had been approximately halved, unemployment had risen from 1.6 million to 12.8 million, manufacturing employment had fallen by 40 per cent, and farm wage rates by 52 per cent (Potter 1985: 95). The prosperity of the 1920s and the impact of the collapse is illustrated by the data for per

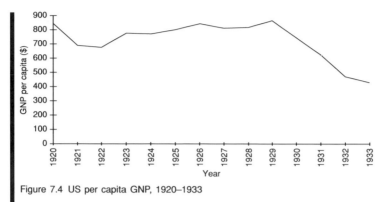

Figure 7.4 US per capita GNP, 1920–1933

Source: calculated from Potter 1985: 57, 95

capita GNP shown in Figure 7.4. Apart from a sharp recession in the early 1920s, trends are upward until the devastating slump of 1929. The impact of this collapse is put superbly by Jim Potter:

> We must not allow . . . cold statistics to conceal the human faces behind them. The resultant physical hardship was intense and affected millions of Americans. But more serious still was the demoralisation that affected people in all walks of life . . . The Jazz-man had sung in the twenties: The more I get, the more I want it seems. His words now became: if you can't give me a dollar give me a lousy dime.
>
> (Potter 1985: 94–95)

The inauguration of Franklin D. Roosevelt as President on 4 March 1933 brought into existence the first period of the New Deal and witnessed feverish activity on the part of the government to combat the enormous social and economic problems of the depression. This period was known as 'The 100 Days' and brought into existence a number of new state-directed policies to alleviate the problems of mass unemployment. The major policies of the New Deal era, March to June 1933, were as follows:

- Agricultural Adjustment Act
- Banking Reform Act
- Civil Works Administration
- Civilian Conservation Corps
- Federal Emergency Relief Administration
- National Industrial Recovery Act created the National Recovery Administration and the Public Works Administration
- Tennessee Valley Authority.

The New Deal has received a great deal of attention from historians and there is a wealth of literature on the subject (Potter 1985: Chapters 5–6; Fearon 1987: Chapter 12; Badger 1989: Chapters 1–2).

In contrast to the US, the German economy under the Weimar republic (1919–1933) did not experience boom conditions in the 1920s, but was plagued by hyper-inflation in the early 1920s, financially weakened by reparation payments (war debts to the allies), and faced problems in world export markets. It was not until 1928 that industrial output and trade reached the pre-1914 levels. From 1925 to 1929 German industry did rapidly modernise its technology and rationalise the heavy capital goods sector, and consequently there was a 17 per cent increase in productivity in major industrial sectors. However, the German economy of the 1920s was fragile and from a long-run perspective the performance of the economy over the interwar years as a whole was disappointing compared with the pre-1914 or post-1945 achievements (Overy 1982: 13–14). There is little doubt that the depression which hit the economy in 1929 made the situation very much worse, and it was in the context of economic crisis that the Nazis led by Adolf Hitler came to power in January 1933. German governments before the 1930s had intervened in the affairs of the economy but, as Overy points out, the advent of Hitler meant a major 'shift away from the mixed liberal economy of the Weimar period' (Overy 1982: 29). A main objective for the regime was to tackle the problem of unemployment, and the work creation schemes introduced in the 1930s in road building and agriculture have been well documented in the literature. At a broader level, however, the Nazis increasingly regulated economic activity and sought to direct the economy towards rearmament in preparation for war. It is important to note that private enterprise was not extinguished. Nazi Germany was not a command economy, nor were the Nazis the mere puppets of big business (Turner 1969; Schweitzer 1964), but by the end of the 1930s the Nazis had acquired an extensive network of controls over the economy.

In the exercises that follow you will examine a number of economic indicators to gauge the extent of the recovery in the two economies. You can then consider recovery in the context of the policies of the New Deal in America and the Nazis in Germany. Finally, you can compare the pace of recovery across the two economies. There are five data sets (Data Sets 2A–2E) for the exercises and they are located in Appendix 4: Data Sets for Historical Theme 2.

Exercises
Indicators of economic recovery in Germany and the US

Analysis of Data Set 2A

Data Set 2A provides a time series for GNP between 1929 and 1940. This is a key indicator of economic growth and frequently used by economic historians to measure the performance of an economy. You are also provided with information on the civilian population during the same period, and you can use this data to calculate the per capita GNP. Perform the following tasks:

1 Build a worksheet to capture the information in Data Set 2A.
2 Perform the following calculation:

- Calculate the per capita GNP for 1929–1940. This calculation is performed by dividing the total GNP by the total civilian population and multiplying by 1000. For example, the first formula would be:

(104.4/121.8)*1000

You will need to include in the formula the multiplication by 1000 because the two data series use different values: the data for GNP is in billions and the data for population in millions. A billion is a thousand million, and thus you need to multiply the first part of the formula by 1000.

3   Construct two charts: one to display the trends in total GNP and one to display the trends in per capita GNP.

4   A technique often used by historians is that of counterfactual analysis. For example, if the American economy had continued to grow at the same average annual rate that it achieved before 1929 and after the depression, what would have been the potential GNP of the economy for each year between 1929 and 1940? This is a counterfactual measurement of the potential performance of an economy compared to its actual performance. Consider the following statement:

> It is reasonable to assume that the productive potential of the economy should have increased at a . . . rate of at least 3% per annum after 1929. An average growth rate at least this high had been achieved during most earlier decades and was achieved again after the end of the depression.

> (Chandler 1970: 4)

Assuming, then, that the potential growth of GNP should have been 3 per cent per annum, calculate the potential GNP for each year from 1929 to 1940. The GNP for 1929 is 104.4 and to calculate the potential GNP for 1930 you should enter the following formula:

$$=(104.4/100)*3+(104.4)$$

The result is a potential GNP of 107.5. To calculate the potential GNP for 1931 enter this formula:

$$=(107.5/100)*3+(107.5)$$

The answer is 110.7. Continue to perform these calculations for all the years 1929–1940.

5   Construct a chart to display the calculated data series for the potential GNP plotted against the actual total GNP achieved.

Having completed these tasks consider the following question:

●   From the trends in GNP, what conclusions do you reach concerning the growth performance of the American economy after Roosevelt came to office in 1933?

Analysis of Data Set 2B

Data Set 2B provides information on the total civilian labour force and the numbers unemployed in 1929–1940. Perform these tasks:

1 Build a worksheet to capture the information in Data Set 2B.
2 Calculate the following: the proportion of the total civilian workforce unemployed for each year.
3 Construct separate charts to display the changes in the total civilian labour force, the total unemployed, and the percentage unemployed.

Now consider the following question:

● Did the New Deal put American workers back to work after 1933?

Analysis of Data Set 2C

Data Set 2C contains information on the value of two indicators of aggregate demand:

● personal (private) consumption for durable, non-durable and service goods, and
● private investment.

Perform the following tasks:

1 Build a worksheet to capture the information in Data Set 2C.
2 Express total private consumption and total private investment as a proportion of total GNP. Consumption and investment are often expressed by historians in this way to distinguish between consumer demand for consumption goods and producer demand for capital goods (investment).
3 Build charts to display the data trends.

Having completed these tasks consider the following questions:

● From the trends in the data:

(a) Which component of aggregate demand is the most important?
(b) Which component is the most volatile?

● What does the data tell you about the level of confidence of

(a) Consumers
(b) Businessmen?

Analysis of Data Set 2D

Data Set 2D contains information on manufacturing performance, a key indicator of economic activity. You are provided with an index of total manufacturing output, and the production of passenger cars, the latter being an important consumer durable goods industry. Perform these tasks:

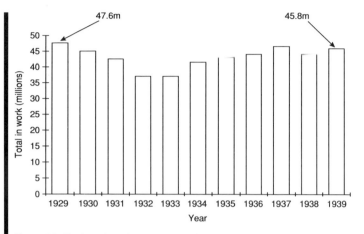

Figure 7.5 Total numbers in work in the USA, 1929–1939

1   Build a spreadsheet from the data in Data Set 2D to capture the information.
2   Construct charts to display the trends.

Consider the following questions:

● From the trends in total manufacturing output what can you tell about the
recovery of American manufacturing industry after 1933?
● From the trends in passenger car output what can you tell about:

(a) the performance of this key sector, and
(b) the level of consumer demand?

● Figure 7.5 shows the total of people in work in millions between 1929 and
1939. Compare the trends in this chart with the trends in total manufacturing
output for the same period. What does this tell us about the performance of
American manufacturing in productivity terms? Compare the number in work
in 1929 with that for 1939 and then compare the manufacturing output
figures for the same years.

Analysis of Data Set 2E

Data Set 2E provides a number of similar indicators for the German economy over the
years 1928–1938. Detailed information on the German economy is more difficult to
accumulate (see Overy 1982: Chapter 3; Schweitzer 1964: 334–336) and, as you will
find, there are some inconsistencies compared to the data sets for the USA.
Nevertheless, the data provides a sufficient number of indicators to compare the recovery
of the Nazi economy with that of the USA. Perform these tasks:

1   Build a worksheet to capture the information in Data Set 2E.
2   Construct relevant charts to display the trends.

Now consider the following questions:

- From the trends in the data, what conclusions do you reach concerning the effectiveness of Nazi economic policy after 1933?
- Was German economic policy more successful than that of the US in creating recovery after 1933?

After you have completed the exercises we recommend that you write a report outlining the main findings of your comparative investigation.

This exercise studies emigration patterns from Britain in the nineteenth century. The first data set used contains disaggregated data showing the geographical pattern of emigration. Having studied the trends from this data set you can then go on to examine relational data which tests out possible factors which led to the out-flow of population in this period. The next section provides a brief discussion on the causal explanations of migration and sets the historical context.

Historical
Theme 3
**Emigration
from the
British Isles
in the
Nineteenth
Century**

Historical context
**Nineteenth-
century
emigration**

The emigration question became a major issue of social concern following the end of the Napoleonic Wars in 1815. Influential political economists, such as the Reverend Thomas Malthus, drew attention to the rapidly rising population and the inadequacy of domestic food supplies. Emigration was seen as a possible remedy to address the demographic and social problems of the nation. By directly encouraging emigration the assumed crisis of over-population would be avoided by removing redundant labourers to the new colonies in North America and Australia and New Zealand. In the 1820s an emigration policy was specifically expounded by Robert Wilmot Horton, who became Under-Secretary for the Colonies in 1822. Influenced by Malthus, he argued that assisted emigration schemes should be implemented to remove paupers from Britain. Although these proposals created heated debate at the time, Parliament only voted a limited amount of money for assisted emigration schemes. The question of emigration was later taken up by the reformer Edward Gibbon Wakefield. In the early 1830s Wakefield proposed the creation of a fund, supported by the sales of land in the colonies, to assist the emigration of labourers, especially to Australia and New Zealand. Although limited-assistance schemes were introduced they were short-lived and the mass exodus of British people in this period cannot be simply explained by government intervention. In fact the bulk of British emigrants did not go to the colonies in the nineteenth century, but rather to an ex-colony, the US. Between 1820 and 1899 an estimated 15 million people emigrated from the British Isles, which was roughly equal to the total population in 1801 (see Shaw 1969; Glass and Taylor 1976; H. J. M. Johnson 1972; Carrothers 1929). The pattern of emigration is well documented in the Parliamentary Inquiries of the period and there is a good long-run series of annual data on emigration. These data sets show quite distinctive trends and the total emigration from Britain is shown in Figure 7.6.

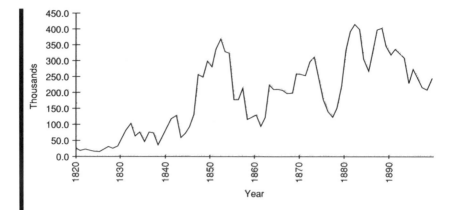

Figure 7.6 Total numbers of emigrants, 1820–1899

There is clearly no unilinear pattern to emigration flows and the data demonstrates marked fluctuations; emigration was cyclical. During the nineteenth century large numbers of people emigrated not just from Britain but also from Scandinavia, Germany, and later from Southern and Eastern Europe, notably Italy and Russia. This movement of population has given rise to controversy amongst historians over the causes of emigration.

Explanations fall into two broad categories: push and pull factors. Were people pushed out due to the prevailing social and economic conditions in their country of origin? Or were migrants pulled by the socio-economic conditions prevailing in the destination countries? To test these propositions you need to look at a number of indicators relating to the socio-economic conditions of the country of origin (push factors) and of the country of destination (pull factors). For example, we might hypothesise that there would be a rapid movement of population from Britain to the US if the former's economy was in depression and the latter's in boom (see B. Thomas 1954). Indeed, studies show that emigrants themselves are part of the prevailing pull factors operating, with earlier migrants creating the financial means and communal environment which attract future emigrants. In the exercises that follow, you are going to first examine the geographical pattern of emigration from Britain and then explore the relationships between the flows of emigration and indicators of economic prosperity in both the US and Britain. Is there a strong correlation between emigration and push and pull factors for 1820–1899? There are two data sets in Appendix 4: Data Sets for Historical Theme 3 (3A and 3B).

| *Exercises* **Emigration from the British Isles** | **Analysis of Data Set 3A** |

Analysis of Data Set 3A

This data set contains information on the numbers of emigrants from the British Isles for 1820–1899, and their geographical destinations. The data was extracted from an investigation on emigration patterns in 1929 (Carrothers 1929). The information was compiled from the official returns of the British customs, and the data provides a useful long-run series on emigration patterns. There were, of course, numerous problems in counting emigrants in the nineteenth century. For example, the customs returns take no account of emigrants who did not pass through customs and in all probability 'the number of emigrants would be larger than the returns' (Carrothers 1929: 357). Nevertheless, this is a valuable data source and provides an excellent compilation of data to investigate the theme of emigration.

With these caveats in mind, perform the following tasks:

1 Build a worksheet to capture the information in Data Set 3A.
2 Calculate the following:

● The total number of people emigrating to each geographical region
● The percentage distribution of migrants to each region annually.

3 Construct charts to illustrate the trends in the data. For example, you could build a line chart displaying the numbers of emigrants to each location and another showing the proportional distribution by region. Figure 7.7 shows a line chart we have constructed for emigrants to North America and the US. This is only one way to display the data, and Figure 7.8 shows a combination chart (combination chart option 4) showing the percentages for the US and Australia and New Zealand. There are numerous ways of displaying this data and you should take advantage of the options open to you.

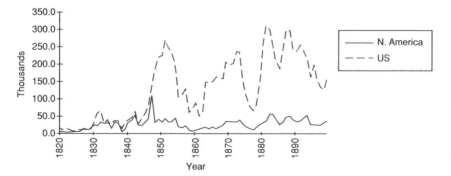

Figure 7.7 Line chart of numbers emigrating

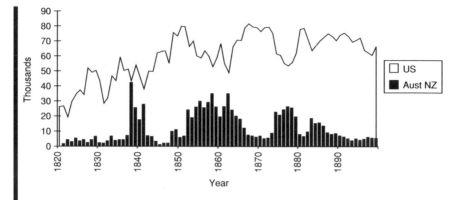

Figure 7.8 Combination chart of numbers emigrating

Having completed the tasks consider the following questions:

- What interpretation can you place on the trends in your charts concerning the geographical pattern of emigration in this period?
- Identify what you consider to be the major peaks and troughs in the trends for each destination area.

Analysis of Data Set 3B

This data set contains information on the number of emigrants to the USA and also four indicators of economic conditions. Economic factors are usually considered paramount in considering the forces of emigration. The economic indicators used are as follows:

- The first indicator, exports by value to the USA for 1820–1899, is important because it provides evidence on the economic conditions in the US. If exports rise, this suggests an upturn in prosperity in the USA as boom conditions sucked in British exports. In the nineteenth century, the two economies were mutually interlinked:

  the links connecting Western Europe, and particularly Britain, with America were so strong, the ties of mutual self-interest so binding and persuasive, as to constitute an identifiable entity known as the Atlantic Economy.

  (Bagwell and Mingay 1987: 18)

  Given this interdependence, we would expect emigration to be closely related to the trading patterns between the two economies. Here we have an indicator relating to both push and pull factors and you can test out the proposition that emigration was causally linked to the cyclical pattern of exports between Britain and the US. Other pull factors that you might want to look at are the levels of consumer expenditure, capital investment, house building, manufacturing employment and railway construction in the US.

● The other three indicators relate to push factors in Britain: real earnings 1851–1899; numbers of outdoor paupers 1840–1899; the percentage of unemployment of trade union members, 1851–1899. Using these indicators you can test out the relationship between emigration and prevailing push factors. Real earnings and unemployment are obvious indicators of the economic conditions of the population. The information on outdoor paupers is also interesting because it relates to the debates discussed earlier concerning the notion of shovelling out paupers. The numbers for outdoor, not indoor, paupers are used because outdoor paupers would contain the able-bodied unemployed, the most likely section of the pauper population to emigrate. Note, however, that the time series are incomplete and you do not have a full run of information to match that of the emigration data. This highlights a problem discussed in Chapter 4, namely the fragmentary nature of historical information.

You can now perform the following tasks:

Build a worksheet which captures the information for the number of emigrants from the US and the value of British exports to the US for 1820–1899. In this first exercise you should enter the data as shown in Figure 7.9.

	A	B	C
1	Relationship Between Exports to the USA and Emigration		
2	Exports in £ million and Emigrants in thousands		
3			
4	Year	Exports	Emigrants to the USA
5	1820	3.9	6.7
6	1821	6.2	5.0

Figure 7.9 Worksheet showing exports and emigrants

Enter the column headings in the range A4:C4. Enter the dates in column A starting at row 5, the information on exports in column B starting at row 5, and finally the information on emigrants in column C starting at row 5. This will allow you to follow the instructions provided below in calculating the statistical relationship between these two variables. You have already entered the information on emigrants to the US in the worksheet you constructed from Data Set 3A, so you can copy this information and paste it into the new worksheet starting at cell C5.

From the worksheet you can test the following propositions:

● If exports from Britain to the US rise we would expect the number of emigrants to increase.
● If exports from Britain to the US fall we would expect the number of emigrants to decrease.

Thus, you need to test whether emigration is dependent on variations in the levels of exports, which in turn provide a measure of the economic climate in the US. We should therefore think of the export data as the independent variable and the emigration data as the dependent variable, i.e. dependent on changes in the value of exports.

To test the strength of this relationship you can produce an X-Y chart, known as a 'scatter chart', to plot the relationship between the two variables. The scatter chart plotting the relationship between the two variables is shown in Figure 7.10. The export data is plotted on the X axis (the X variable) and the emigration data on the Y axis (the Y variable). The closer the various dots lie to a straight line drawn through them, then the greater is the statistical relationship between the two variables. This might sound complicated, but the relationship is important to understand so we advise you to read what follows carefully.

To produce the chart in Figure 7.10 follow these instructions:

1   Select the range B5:B84 which contains the data on exports and will be plotted on the X axis of the chart.
2   Press Shift and **F8** to add a series and then select the range C5:C84 which will be the data plotted on the Y axis.
3   From the **File** menu choose **New** and then choose **Chart**. The **New Chart** menu dialogue box opens. Click on the selection box labelled **X-Values for XY-Chart**. The first column of data contains the values for the X values. Click on **OK** and the scatter chart will be produced.
4   Give the chart a heading and title the X and Y axes.

Looking at the points on the scatter chart, there would seem to be a close relationship between the two variables: the points on the chart clearly cluster. Can we give this relationship a statistical expression? You could draw a straight line through the dots and determine the degree of closeness to which dots approximate to the line. The measurement devised by statisticians to determine the deviation of dots from a line is called the 'correlation coefficient'. The nearer the correlation coefficient is to one, the greater is the strength of the relationship between the two variables. You can quickly calculate the correlation coefficient by following these instructions:

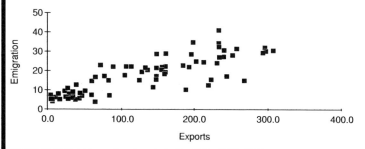

Figure 7.10 Exports and emigrants to the USA, 1820–1899

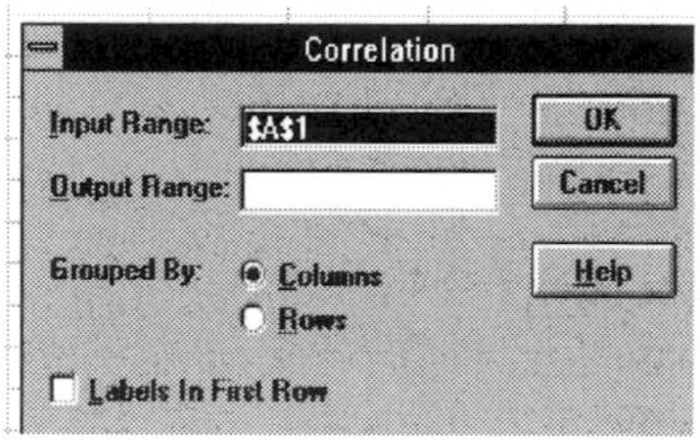

Figure 7.11 Correlation dialogue box

1   Open the **Options** menu and choose **Analysis Tools . . .**.
2   A list of statistical tools appears in a drop-down menu box. Choose
    Correlation and then click on **OK**.
3   The **Correlation** dialogue box shown in Figure 7.11 appears. In the field
    labelled **Input Range** you type the range of worksheet data you want to
    correlate. This should be the block of cells containing the two variables.
    Type: B4:C84.
4   Select the **Columns** option button in the **Grouped By** check box to indicate that
    the data in the input range is arranged in columns.
5   The input range includes column headings which are not calculated. Click on
    the **Labels In First Row** check box.
6   Finally you must specify the output range. This is the range on the
    worksheet in which you want the calculation of the correlation coefficient to
    appear. In the **Output Range** field type: D5. Now click on **OK** and the
    correlation coefficient will be calculated.

The correlation coefficient is 0.83 and such a high number suggests a strong correlation
between the two variables. You should now test out the relationship between emigration
and the other three variables contained in Data Set 3B; these are variables related to
push factors. Build separate worksheets for each of the variables, plot scatter charts and
measure the correlation coefficients.

Having completed these tasks consider this question:

●   From your calculations of the correlation coefficients on the four economic
    indicators, what conclusions do you draw concerning the relationship
    between pull and push factors and emigration in the nineteenth century?

After you have completed the exercises we recommend that you write a report outlining
the main findings of your investigation.

Part 3

Databases

Databases and the Historian

8.1 Introduction

Richard Trainor has claimed that historians on both sides of the Atlantic are increasingly realising that 'information technology will enable students to learn about the past in deeper and more complex ways' (Trainor 1990: 146). In particular a database management system (DBMS), the program which allows you to build and operate a database, is an ideal tool for organising, managing and interrogating historical information. For most history students databases may be a relatively new experience, and indeed their application to the history curriculum is still in its infancy. However, as historical information is increasingly becoming available in machine-readable form, historians will want to acquire the means of effectively using it, and therefore they need an understanding of a DBMS (Lloyd-Jones and Lewis 1994b: 42).

With relatively little set-up time you can learn how to use a DBMS, and apply your acquired skills to independent study, i.e. project and/or dissertation work in your own particular area of historical studies. There are two ways in which you might be introduced to working with a database:

- Using a database which has been prepared for you
- Using historical information to design and build your own database.

While we recognise the merits of using an existing database, for example, in bringing research information closer to the student audience, we nevertheless believe that constructing your own will provide you with a deeper appreciation of the structure and complexity of historical data. You will be brought into closer proximity with actual historical data, in particular primary sources. Constructing your own database is a 'highly educative process' (Ayrton 1989: 67). Before proceeding, there is a matter of technical clarification: we need to distinguish between a database and a DBMS. The former is the collection of records (in our case historical records) related to a specific class or subject, while the latter is the computer program which allows you to organise and manage the information stored in the database.

Section 8.2 will define the properties of a database and then proceed to examine the functions of a DBMS. Section 8.3 will then briefly examine some of the developments in using databases in historical research, before setting out a set of guidelines you may wish to adopt in using a database for your own independent study. However, before proceeding to the next section take some time to study Table 8.1 which provides a guide to the terminology used in this and subsequent chapters on databases.

Table 8.1 Database terms

Term	Definition
Database	A collection of data compiled in machine-readable form (i.e. can be read by a computer) related to a particular topic or purpose.
Database record	Information on a specific subject contained in the database (i.e. information on a particular person such as age, gender, income).
Database table	The way data is organised in a database. Each row in the table contains information for each record, and each column contains fields of information for each record (e.g. fields for age, gender and income).
Database field	The area where you enter information into the database table. Each column in a database table is a field of information. A field is a category of discrete information relating to a particular record.
Field name	A unique name which identifies the information contained in a database field (e.g. Age, Gender, Income).
Field width	The width of an individual field contained in a database table. In other words, the maximum number of characters, either letters or numbers, which can be entered into a database field.
Data (field) type	The data type specifies the type of data contained in the field. The most common data types are Text field which contains textual data (words and letters), Number field which contains numerical data, and Logical field which contains information based on the premise Yes or No.
Database management system	A computer application which allows you to organise and manage data to meet your requirements.
Relational database	A database compiled from a number of database tables. A relational database allows you to link the information contained in the various fields in the database tables, and thus make relationships between the data.

Historical Databases and Database Management Systems

A database is a collection of records which contain categories of information. These categories are known as 'fields' and each field contains discrete information relating to a particular record. Therefore, historical databases contain records of historical information organised in fields. Databases may be manual or electronic. The former have long been part of the tool kit used by historians to build a bank of empirical information. For example, a standard procedure is to use note cards for each record and then document the information into categories. The historian thus builds up a catalogue of record cards each containing fields of information. Figure 8.1 shows a specimen note card for a study of the death toll of miners in the major coal mining area of South Wales, the Rhondda Valley. Each record contains discrete categories or fields of information relating to colliery explosions between 1817 and 1916 (E. D. Lewis 1959: 279–280). There is a field each for the date of the accident, the name of the colliery, the number of fatal casualties, and the source of the

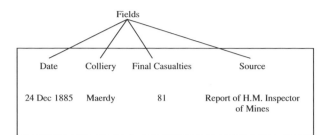

Figure 8.1 Manual database: note card on colliery explosions in the Rhondda

Date	Colliery	Casualties	Source
1817	Abergorchy	1	National Library of Wales
6 Oct 1836	Dinas Lower	4	Mining Journal No. 5 p.50
1839	Dinas Lower	3	Children's Employment Commission p.521
1842	Newbridge	1	Galloway, Annals p.11
1 Jan 1844	Dinas Middle	12	Mining Journal 1844 p.447

Figure 8.2 Electronic database table on colliery explosions

information. In all there are 38 note cards each containing records which record information in discrete fields, i.e. the field names are the same on each of the 38 note cards. By using an electronic system, a DBMS, this information can be organised into a table whose columns also contain discrete fields of information. A view of the first five records of the database table is shown in Figure 8.2. The advantages of an electronic database over a manual system will be explored later, and we now turn to a description of the properties of a database.

Greenstein (1994: 61–65) identifies five common properties of a database which are outlined as follows:

- A database is 'built up from individual records about some pre-defined class or object'.
- The records in the database comprise fields of information.
- The fields associated with each record in the database will determine how the records can be retrieved and classified.
- Each record in the database is unique. No two records are the same.
- When new records are added to a database they must retain their consistency, i.e. they must be unique and be consistent with the existing fields in the database.

These properties are common to all databases whether they are manual or electronic systems. The first property associates a database with a specific purpose, i.e. it is constructed of records relating to a class or object for the purposes of study. A business firm will have a collection of records on customer orders, and a university will have a collection of records

Firm	Location	Process	TEMPLOY
▶ BIRLEY & KIRK	MANCHESTER	I	1692
ORMROD & HARDCASTLE	BOLTON	I	1576
MCONNELL & CO	MANCHESTER	S	1545
BOLLING E & W	BOLTON	S	1356
HOULDSWORTH T	MANCHESTER	S	1201
HORSEFIELD JOSEPH	DHS	I	1183
ASHTON THOMAS	DHS	I	1149
MARSLAND T	STOCKPORT	I	947
TAYLOR HINDLE & CO	BOLTON	I	924
COLLINGE & LANCASHIRE	OLDHAM	I	853
MURRAY A & G	MANCHESTER	S	841
STIRLING & BECKTON	MANCHESTER	I	873
LEES J & SONS	STOCKPORT	I	796
OXFORD ROAD TWIST CO	MANCHESTER	I	774
SMITH WILLIAM	STOCKPORT	I	761
LAMBERT HOOLE & CO	MANCHESTER	S	752
OGDEN T R & T	MANCHESTER	S	712
GUEST JAMES	MANCHESTER	I	712
HOWARD C & T	DHS	I	648
SAMPSON LLOYD & CO	STOCKPORT	I	632

Figure 8.3 Example of business history database table (Microsoft Access database management system)

on a student's profile. For the historian, a database is built up from individual records which relate to the object of their historical study. Thus, both the manual and electronic databases, used as examples earlier, explore the theme of safety in the mining industry by examining records on colliery explosions. Similarly, a business historian might be interested in a database that studied firms in particular industries or towns (Lloyd-Jones and Lewis 1994b: 46–49). Figure 8.3 shows a partial view of an electronic database table constructed to study the business structure of the nineteenth-century cotton industry. In total the database table contains 118 records on cotton firms in 1833. The information was extracted from returns to the factory inspectors by S. Stanway, and later reproduced in a book by Dr Andrew Ure (Ure 1836).

Table 8.2 Names and description of fields in business history database

Field name	Field description	Field data type
Firm	The name of the individual cotton firm.	Text
Location	The town in Lancashire in which the firm is located.	Text
Process	Information on the business activity of the firm. This information has been coded: S = a firm engaged only in the process of cotton spinning; W = a firm engaged only in the process of cotton weaving; I = an integrated firm which combined both the processes of cotton spinning and weaving.	Text
TEMPLOY	The total number of workers employed by each firm.	Number

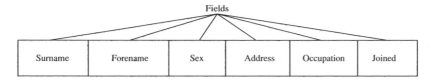

Figure 8.4 Database fields: Blueshirt database

Figure 8.3 also illustrates the second property of a database: the records comprise fields of information. There are four discrete fields of information, each given a specific name, and described in Table 8.2. The fields of information also contain information of a specific type: Text or Number. Thus fields are characterised as containing either textual or numerical data. You will learn more about specifying data types in the next chapter.

A further example of a database table is provided in Figure 8.4. This example was provided by Michael Cronin's study of the Blueshirt Movement in Ireland. The Blueshirts are commonly referred to as Ireland's fascist movement and gained a short period of political influence in the early 1930s (Cronin 1994a, 1994b). To examine the socio-economic background of the participants in this movement there are detailed lists of registered members. Figure 8.4 shows the six fields in the database table. Similar to the earlier examples, the database contains fields of information on a specific class or object, i.e. biographical details on members of a fascist organisation.

The fields of information 'associated with each record in a database determine how records can be retrieved and classified', constituting the third common property of a database (Greenstein 1994: 62). For example, in the business history database we might want to retrieve and classify all records of integrated (code I) firms. Thus the existence of a field (Process) which captures this information determines the way we can retrieve and classify records in the database. Similarly, in the example of the Blueshirts, we might want to examine the gender balance (male and female) of registered members of this organisation. The existence of a field (Sex) which contains this information allows the user of the database to engage with the analysis of the data contained in the various fields. Consequently, the fields of a database 'impinge on analysis as well as retrieval' (Greenstein 1994: 62). For example, the business history records are organised into fields which relate to the analysis of the structure of the cotton industry in 1833. By examining the various fields we can retrieve specific records but also address important analytical questions. For example, by examining the TEMPLOY field and the Location field we can determine the different size categories of firms by employment and also look for patterns across the various cotton towns. Did small firms dominate the industry and were they more common in one town than another? Similarly, in the Blueshirts database, was the movement dominated by males (Sex field), and did members come from a particular occupational background (Occupation field)? The range of fields in a database determines how the records can be analysed, and in turn must relate to the aims and objectives of the study. A database allows the systematic analysis of historical records because 'the same range of pre-defined fields is supplied for every record in a particular database' (Greenstein 1994: 63).

The fourth and fifth properties of a database define a database's reliability and consistency. No two records in the database are identical, and new records added must contain information relating to each of the pre-defined fields. For example, if the business history database contained two identical records then the database would produce inaccurate results as the records would be counted twice. These rules of consistency should also govern the addition of new records to a database. Having explored the common properties of a database we now turn to a discussion of the uses of a DBMS, the program which allows you to operate a database.

A DBMS is a computer application which allows the user to build electronic database tables, selectively retrieve, order, group and count records. These are the basic functions or uses of a DBMS. As discussed in Chapter 1, a key task of the historian is to manage information, and a DBMS is a valuable addition to the historian's tool kit. A DBMS allows you to design a database by creating fields to store the information for historical records which you can then type into the individual fields. This, as we saw earlier, was a key property relating to the way information is organised in a database. You can store a vast volume of records which constitute a permanent store of machine-readable information, a computer archive. The database can, however, be easily updated if new records come to light. A DBMS thus allows the historian the flexibility of adding new records to the database. To examine the uses of a DBMS to the historian, let us take some specific examples.

As a starting point consider the example of the business history database on cotton firms used earlier and examine the information on business activity located in the field named 'Process' (see Table 8.2). What firms were engaged in spinning only, what firms were engaged in weaving only, and what firms combined both activities? You want to select all records matching the code S, all records matching the code W, and all records matching the code I in the field Process. In effect you would need to compile three groups of records. If these records were filed manually, i.e. on 118 separate note cards, then the process of selecting and grouping would be a highly time-consuming procedure. You would have to thumb through all the note cards, systematically selecting the records which matched the appropriate codes in the Process field. You would of course end up with three sets of note cards which grouped the appropriate records. Having done this exercise you might well stop at this, but there are clearly other questions you may need to ask of your manual database which entail further selection. For example, how many of the firms in the database by type of business activity were small (employing less than 151 workers), medium (employing 151–500 workers), or large (employing over 501 workers)? These size categories have been defined by historians of the cotton industry to classify firms (Lloyd-Jones and Le Roux 1980). The difficulties of the manual system should now be obvious, you would have to thumb through the three piles of records and again systematically select all firms which matched the above size criteria in the TEMPLOY field. At the end of the exercise you would have nine separate sets of note cards.

The manual procedures tend to be time-consuming, and because of the complexity of handling the data they tend to foreclose on the range of questions you can ask of a database. It is here that a DBMS comes into its own. Unlike the note card system the structure of the computerised database does not impinge upon the retrieval of the records, and quite

Table 8.3 Selected records – spinning only firms (code S in Process field)

Firm	Location	Process	TEMPLOY
ADSHEAD & BROTHERS	DHS	S	209
ASHWORTH H & E	BOLTON	S	517
BELLHOUSE J & W	MANCHESTER	S	211
BOLLING E & W	BOLTON	S	1,356
BRADBURY C	OLDHAM	S	95
BROADBENT & SONS	OLDHAM	S	106
BUCKLEY & HOWARD	DHS	S	82
CARRUTHERS WILLIAM	MANCHESTER	S	143
CHEETHAM & HILL	DHS	S	45
CHEETHAM GEORGE & SONS	DHS	S	560
CLEGG ABRAHAM	OLDHAM	S	88
DUNCUFF JOHN	OLDHAM	S	60
EWART PETER	MANCHESTER	S	251
GLEADHILL JAMES ASSIGNEES OF	OLDHAM	S	146
GOUGH NATHAN	MANCHESTER	S	144
GRAEVES J	STOCKPORT	S	26
GRAY BENJAMIN	MANCHESTER	S	391
HAIGH ABRAHAM	BOLTON	S	210
HALL JAMES & SON	DHS	S	187
HAYWOOD & SONS	MANCHESTER	S	112
HIGGINS WILLIAM	MANCHESTER	S	196
HOULDSWORTH T	MANCHESTER	S	1,201
HOWARD J & R	DHS	S	115
ISLINGTON TWIST CO	MANCHESTER	S	77
KENNEDY JAMES	MANCHESTER	S	599
LAMBERT HOOLE & CO	MANCHESTER	S	752
MCONNELL & CO	MANCHESTER	S	1,545
MCOOL ALEXANDER	BOLTON	S	186
MOORE S M	MANCHESTER	S	189
MOSS & HOWARD	OLDHAM	S	28
MURRAY A & G	MANCHESTER	S	841
NEW BRIDGE MILLS TWIST CO	MANCHESTER	S	450
NIELD JAMES JNR	OLDHAM	S	53
OGDEN & WALMSLEY	OLDHAM	S	186
OGDEN T R & T	MANCHESTER	S	712
OGDEN THOS & SONS	MANCHESTER	S	346
PARROTT & WESTON	STOCKPORT	S	47
PLANT THOMAS	MANCHESTER	S	343
POOLEY & SON	MANCHESTER	S	514
RIGG SIBSON	MANCHESTER	S	66
ROTHWELL J	BOLTON	S	151
SANDFORD BENJAMIN	MANCHESTER	S	382
SCHOFIELD ROBERT	MANCHESTER	S	87
SHAW HUGH & CO	MANCHESTER	S	182
SMITH & RAWSON	MANCHESTER	S	133
WAGSTAFF & SIDEBOTTOM	DHS	S	202
WARING & SONS	OLDHAM	S	49
WILDE EDMUND	OLDHAM	S	90
WILKINSON JAMES	DHS	S	104
WIMPENNY & SWINDELLS	DHS	S	113

Table 8.4 Database selection for spinning firms showing only Firm and TEMPLOY fields

Firm	TEMPLOY
GRAEVES J	26
MOSS & HOWARD	28
CHEETHAM & HILL	45
PARROTT & WESTON	47
WARING & SONS	49
NIELD JAMES JNR	53
DUNCUFF JOHN	60
RIGG SIBSON	66
ISLINGTON TWIST CO	77

complex groupings of records can be achieved in seconds (Greenstein 1994: 68). Table 8.3 shows a view of the retrieved group of records relating to spinning-only firms (code S) in the database. When you select information in a database you use a function called a 'query'. This allows you to ask questions of the information contained in the fields of a database, e.g. how many firms were spinning-only firms? A query automatically filters information, displaying on screen only the records which match your selection criteria.

You should also note that the selected records in Table 8.3 have been ordered alphabetically in the Firm field. The records have therefore not only been grouped by process but also automatically arranged in ascending alphabetical (A–Z) order by name of firm. This function is called 'sorting' and a DBMS can automatically sort records. You could, for example, have sorted the records in the TEMPLOY field and displayed the records in ascending (1 upwards) order of employment. Finally, a DBMS allows you to select records and choose which fields of information you want to display. For example, Table 8.4 shows a partial view of the selection for spinning firms with only the Firm and TEMPLOY fields displayed. In other words you can, for presentation purposes, hide the fields in the selection view. Note also that in this selection we have sorted the records in a different way: ascending order by employment.

The example above shows the outcome of a simple process of retrieval using a DBMS, and you will learn how to retrieve information from a DBMS using queries in the next chapter. However, the importance of a DBMS is its speed compared to a manual system in handling the complex retrieval of information. Think of the following question you might ask of the business history database: from the database how many spinning-only firms were there in the town of Manchester employing less than 151 workers? Just think of the difficulties of performing this task using the manual system of note cards discussed earlier.

A final important use of a DBMS is in its ability to provide summary statistical information. Not only will it display selected information on the computer screen but it will count and perform basic calculations. A DBMS thus allows you to quantify the data you select. Table 8.5 shows the summary information for all Manchester cotton firms in the database.

Table 8.5 Summary statistical data from cotton database: Manchester firms, 1833

Total employment	17286
Average employment	411.5
Minimum employment	66
Maximum employment	1692
Count of all firms	42
Count of all firms employing less than 151	12
Count of all firms employing greater than 150 and less than 501	18
Count of all firms employing greater than 500	12

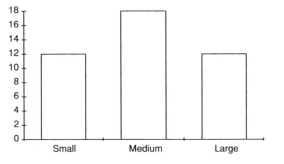

Figure 8.5 Number of firms by size classification: Manchester, 1833

Automatic calculations are performed for employment and counts made for firms by employment size category. From this summary information you can present the information in a tabular form, as in Table 8.5, or use a spreadsheet to construct charts as shown in Figure 8.5.

So far we have explored the use of a DBMS for databases containing only one table, but the nature of the data and the aims of the investigation might require the creation of more than one database table. Most modern DBMSs are relational, that is they allow you to organise data into different tables and then cross-reference the tables to bring the data together. You can therefore create multi-table databases, containing numerous tables of related information. The advantages of relational databases are defined by Harvey and Press (1991: 4) as follows: 'records within one table may be joined with records in another table because the two tables share one or more common fields . . . the database forms an integrated whole, and it is possible to retrieve data from many tables . . . with a single query'. This may sound complicated, but the relational properties of a database are of key importance to historical investigation. To demonstrate the relational properties of a database, consider the example of the medical history database (PATIENTS) shown in Figure 8.6. This contains fields of biographical information recorded by the medical administrators on patients when first admitted to the Wakefield Asylum between 1861 and 1890 (Wakefield

ID	Surname	Forename	Place of Birth	Age	Sex	Occupation
163	Roehan	Isabella	Shipton	30	F	House Servant
164	Samuel	Andrew	Hunslet	20	M	Labourer

Figure 8.6 PATIENTS database table

Admission Records). The biographical information is easily captured and retrieved in the single PATIENTS table. Each record in the table is unique: the asylum administrators gave each patient a unique identification number (the ID field in Figure 8.6).

However, a medical historian would require more than biographical details. For example, they would be interested in the medical diagnosis of the patient's illness when they were admitted and when they were discharged. This is more difficult to manage within the confines of one database table. Does the historian record only the first time that a patient was admitted and the first time they were discharged? If so, what happens to those patients who were admitted and discharged on more than one occasion? For example, Isabella Roehan was admitted on 25 April 1861, again on 10 July 1865, and finally on 10 January 1867, and was consequently discharged on three separate occasions. On each admission her medical diagnosis was different. The problem here is that the database would have to capture multiple-values (entry, discharge) and some records will have more information associated with them than others. To overcome this problem you can use a multi-table database and link them by means of a common field, i.e. a field identical in all tables. This is where a relational database system comes into its own.

Figure 8.7 shows the three independent tables created to capture the multiple values on entries and discharges. The PATIENTS table contains the basic biographical data for patients when first admitted, the ENTRY table contains information on the date of entry and the medical diagnosis on entry, and the DISCHARGE table holds information on the date of discharge and the medical comments of the administrators. The uniqueness of the records in the ENTRY and DISCHARGE tables is maintained by the creator of the database attributing a unique entry number (EntryNo) and discharge number (DisNo) to the records when they are entered. The importance of this method is that it allows you to add the additional records on the diagnosis on entry and discharge to the tables as you discover them in the records. The records are linked (related) to each other by the common field in all three tables, the ID field. This is indicated by the joining line in Figure 8.7, and the double-headed arrow illustrates that for any one record in the PATIENTS table there may be more than one record associated with it in the ENTRY and DISCHARGE tables.

Using a DBMS you can retrieve groups of records on one table or on two or more tables. The latter is clearly an important function of a DBMS for the historian when dealing with complex relationships between fields of information. For example, in the medical history database tables the historian can trace the case history of patients through their records of entry and discharge. This provides valuable information on the changing diagnosis of the insane over the second half of the nineteenth century.

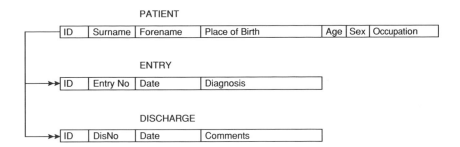

PATIENT

ID	Surname	Forename	Place of Birth		Age	Sex	Occupation

ENTRY

ID	Entry No	Date	Diagnosis

DISCHARGE

ID	DisNo	Date	Comments

Figure 8.7 Multi-table relational database

PATIENT

ID	Surname	Forename	Place of Birth		Age	Sex	Occupation
163	Roehan	Isabella	Shipton		30	F	House Servant

ENTRY

ID	Entry No	Date	Diagnosis
163	A163	25 April 1861	Melancholy
163	A456	10 July 1865	Manic Depression
163	A603	10 Jan 1868	Suicidal Tendencies

DISCHARGE

ID	DisNo	Date	Comments
163	B401	25 Jan 1864	Medical Condition Relieved
163	B708	11 Nov 1867	Medical Condition Same
163	B806	21 Feb 1868	Recovered

Figure 8.8 Retrieved records from medical database

Figure 8.8 shows an example of data retrieved from the three database tables in Figure 8.7. This was achieved by using a query which grouped the records by the common ID field. As one can see, patient 163 was admitted on three separate occasions, first diagnosed as suffering from melancholy, second from manic depression and third from suicidal tendencies. Similarly, the comments on the patient's condition at discharge illustrates the extent to which treatment was effective.

The example above is important to understanding the complexities of data in a database. The relationship between the tables in Figure 8.8 is a one-to-many relationship: 'In a one-to-many relationship, one occurrence of an entity A can be associated with many occurrences of an entity B' (Harvey and Press 1991: 5). In the PATIENT table there can be only one occurrence of a record relating to the biography of the patient, but in the ENTRY and DISCHARGE tables there may be many relationships. There could, of course, in the above example be a one-to-one relationship where 'one occurrence of an entity A can be

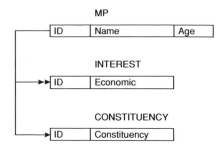

Figure 8.9 One-to-many and one-to-one relationships

related to only one occurrence of an entity B' (Harvey and Press 1991: 5). Thus a patient may have entered the asylum only once and consequently been discharged only once. To further clarify these issues consider the example given earlier in Chapter 7 of the economic interests of MPs in the House of Commons between 1906 and 1910. An MP can have more than one economic interest and thus if we were compiling a database table we might need to create two database tables. The MP table would contain fields of information on name and age while the INTEREST table would contain a field of information relating to their business background. The common field which links the two tables is ID, a unique number given to MPs in both tables. If, however, we were to relate the MP table to a third table on the constituency that they represented then the relationship would be a one-to-one relationship, as an MP can represent only one constituency. Figure 8.9 illustrates the relationships between the tables. The double-headed arrow signifies the one-to-many relationship between the MP and INTEREST tables, and the single-headed arrow the one-to-one relationship between the MP and CONSTITUENCY tables.

Having examined the properties of a database and explored some of the potential uses of a DBMS to the historian we turn now to an examination of the use of databases in historical research and teaching and how they might be applied by you in independent study.

8.3 Databases: Research, Teaching and Independent Study

Databases can be used by historians to interrelate research and teaching. For example, we have produced a large-scale database on Manchester 1815–1825, which reconstructs the city's business system. This allows a series of smaller projects to be undertaken which can focus on certain aspects of Manchester's urban history. In computer workshops students have been able to examine Manchester's factory system, the pattern of ownership of property assets, the role of large cotton masters in Manchester's political elite, etc. In other words, you can take tranches of information from a large-scale database and use it for small project work. We have also produced a large-scale database for the Sheffield metal and metal-making trades, 1880–1920, and R. J. Morris has produced a database on the economic interests of the Leeds middle class in the first half of the nineteenth century.

The latter uses relational database techniques, discussed earlier, to link different sources of records based on the town of Leeds (Lloyd-Jones and Lewis 1988, 1990a, 1993b; Morris 1991). In some areas of history, notably demographic history and psephology (study of poll book data) databases have radically transformed the subject by opening up new interpretations of the past and directing new lines of enquiry (Speck 1994: 29–30). Historians are increasingly realising the potential of databases as a tool in their research and there is an increasing amount of database-related research being published (see Mawdsley *et al.* 1990: 156–203). Large-scale databases will be increasingly available in the future, providing a store of machine-readable historical information for students to access in a workshop context. We believe that research databases are a valuable teaching tool and there 'can be a fruitful relationship between teaching and research' (Lloyd-Jones and Lewis 1994b: 38).

But large-scale research and teaching databases are not produced without costs to the historian; they require a considerable investment in terms of the time involved in data collection, entry and processing, e.g. our Manchester database contained some 17,000 records. We do not expect that after reading this book you will go off and construct a large database. We do believe, however, that it is feasible that you can build small databases. These databases can produce fruitful results (see Munck 1990: 133–138) and will also help you learn the techniques associated with using a DBMS. A small database can be an extremely useful tool in producing information for project work, dissertations and independent study. Let us consider first what we mean by a small database; you might well ask, how small is small? Asking this question is important, for you must remember that time management is of the essence, and it is the time available to you that is largely going to determine the size of the database. The following parameters are offered which help you determine the size of your database:

- A small database, compiled from a single historical source, should not include more than 500 individual records. This estimate is based on a 12-week period (normal teaching contact period for a semester) for the collection, entry and processing of the data.
- The size of the database may well be smaller than 500 records if

  (a) the data is extracted from two or more sources.
  (b) the data contains a large number of variables.
  (c) the original data source is extremely large.

  In the first two cases we suggest that you should reduce the size of the database, thereby accommodating the increased cost of collection and entry of data, and in the third case you should sample the data, a technique which is commonly used by historians.

The size of the database is determined by a feasibility exercise, and you must, at the outset, produce a reasonable estimate of the time required to complete the database given the time constraints you may face. These factors are discussed further in Chapter 9 where an example of a small database is provided. Having defined a small database, we can now offer a set of guidelines, or rules, which can be used by you when applying small databases to project and dissertation work.

Table 8.6 Guidelines for the use of small databases

Stage	Task
1	Selecting the historical topic and outlining the aims of the study
2	Search for and evaluation of data sources
3	Collection of data
4	Conceptualisation of data
5	Design of database tables
6	Entry of data
7	Checking data
8	Data processing
9	Producing summary information
10	Data analysis

The guidelines provide a step-by-step process which represents a model for your use. In other words, they provide a methodology, a way of doing things. By following these guidelines you will quickly be able to develop and gain confidence in using small databases in your work. Table 8.6 shows the guidelines we recommend. They are set out as a sequence of stages, and in each stage you accomplish a set of basic tasks. The guidelines are explained below and are used in Chapter 9 to take you through a number of examples of using small databases for project work.

Stage 1: Selecting the Historical Topic and Outlining the Aims of the Study

The first task is to select the historical topic you are going to investigate and work out the basic aims of the study. You may select a topic for a number of reasons. For example, you may have an interest in that specific topic, it may relate to a key area of your course, or it may be a source of information which is available that lends itself to the construction of a database. Having selected the topic, you should familiarise yourself with any secondary reading in this area of study, and then develop the basic aims of the investigation. The latter is important, because it helps you focus on the relevant questions to be asked in the study, and will help you target in Stages 2 and 3 the data sources and the type of information to be collected. In other words, you need to be clear why you are doing the study and how a database may enhance the investigation.

Stage 2: Search for and Evaluation of Data Sources

Searching for historical sources is, of course, a common task of the historian. The historian must evaluate the information, and this is particularly important when using a database. Is there information which lends itself to the construction of a database, and if so can it be collected, entered and processed in the time available to you? Does the information in the source meet the aims of the proposed study? These are crucial questions: it is obviously easier to design a database from a source of information which comes in a structured form (discussed in Chapter 2), such as lists and tables, than if the data is fragmentary and unstructured. Information on local topics is a useful source of information, and trawling through local history libraries and archives will often produce a profitable outcome. In Chapter 9 we use examples taken from local history sources. Having evaluated the feasibility of the data source you can go on to collect the information.

Stage 3: Collection of Data

The following rules are a useful guide to the collection of information for a database:

- Decide at the outset what information you are going to collect, i.e. do you need to collect all the information contained in the data source? For example, are all the variables contained in the data source relevant to your study, and if you have an extensive source of information, is it possible to sample the data?
- Decide how you are going to collect the data. The data should be collected in a systematic way which helps facilitate the design of the database and makes it easier to enter the information.
- If you can get access to a lap-top computer containing a database program then you can enter the data directly into the database at the place of origin, e.g. library, archive. If you are using a lap-top then you should undertake Stages 4 and 5 before entering the data.

Stage 4: Conceptualisation of Data

Before entering data into the database the data needs to be conceptualised. By this we mean that you have to define the information to be entered and how it is to be entered. You might want to create new variables from the raw data which contains information generated from the original source. For example, you might have a list of names, let us say from a nineteenth-century census. From this you might want to create a variable which indicates the gender of the person entered in the census, male or female. Further, information may need to be coded for ease of entry and later processing of the completed database, e.g. M for male and F for female.

Stage 5: Design of Database Tables

The design of the database tables involves your first formulating a plan which outlines the construction of the database. You have to decide on the number of tables to be included in the database, and the number, names and widths of the fields needed to capture the information contained in the historical source. Further, in a multi-table relational database you will have to decide which is the common field in your various database tables. A simple example of a plan for a database containing information from the census records in one table is shown in Figure 8.10.

Census Database Table

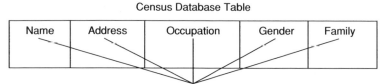

Field Name

Field Name	Data Type	Field Width	Description
Name	Text	40	Information on the names of the head of household recorded in the census returns
Address	Text	40	Information on the address of the head of household recorded in the census returns
Occupation	Text	15	Information on the occupations of the head of household recorded in the census returns
Gender	Text	1	Information on the sex of the head of household recorded in the census returns
Family	Number	3	Information on the number of family members recorded for each head of household in the census returns

Figure 8.10 Plan for a database

Having designed the database layout on paper you can then proceed to construct the database on the computer. In Chapter 9 we demonstrate how to construct a database using the Microsoft Access database management program as our exemplar. This allows you to automatically design tables containing specific fields of information.

Stage 6: Entry of Data

After the database has been designed, you can enter the data for each record into the database fields. This is a basic functional task of building a database and requires you to type the information into your table or tables.

Stage 7: Checking Data

After you have completed the entry of the data you should check the entries for mistakes, and ensure that the database design meets your requirements. If necessary, you can change the design of the database at this stage, i.e. you can delete or add fields. A DBMS allows you flexibility in design.

Stage 8: Data Processing

This is a key stage. Data processing uses the functions of a DBMS discussed earlier: selectively retrieving, grouping, ordering and quantifying information by building queries. In Chapter 9, you will be shown how to select and sort, relate different tables, and provide summary statistical information. You will learn how to create queries which require that you first set out a logical series of questions which you want to ask of the data. This, of course, is a basic task of the historian: before the database can produce an answer by querying the data, it must be provided with a question. This will be explored further in the example given in Chapter 9.

Stage 9: Producing Summary Information

In this stage, you need to work out the summary information which you wish to produce from the processed data. In Chapter 9, you will be shown how to create summary reports and produce quantitative summaries from the processed data.

Stage 10: Data Analysis

The final stage is the analysis of the trends produced by the database. The database provides the raw material for you to analyse trends, but you must use your analytical skills as historians to produce a historical account of your main findings. The findings from the database may well highlight new questions to pose, and open up new routes for you to develop in your project.

This chapter has provided a basic grounding in the potential use of a DBMS, and discussed some of the procedures for using a database in your own independent study. If you want to explore some of the methodological issues involved in using historical databases further then consult the works by Munck and Mawdsley and Greenstein (Mawdsley and Munck 1993; Greenstein 1994). In the next chapter we move to a more practical approach and provide an exercise using a small historical database. The best way to acquire new skills is to learn by doing, and this is the objective of the next chapter.

Chapter 9

Getting Started with a Database

9.1 Introduction

This chapter will adopt the guidelines outlined in the previous chapter to provide a framework for directing you through the various stages of building a historical database for use in your own studies. The example used is an investigation of Sheffield cinemas in the interwar years. The data for the exercise is located in Appendix 5: Data Sets A and B. We examine how the combination of a socio-cultural approach with a local study can provide an ideal type for project or dissertation work. The example used is merely illustrative but the guidelines are generic to any database work you might undertake. By working through this example you will learn to apply a systematic set of rules in using databases in historical studies, acquire a basic understanding of how to use a database management system, and gain confidence in applying databases to your own independent work.

To demonstrate the techniques we will provide basic instruction in the use of the Microsoft Access database program which can be run from Windows. You will be shown how to design database tables, enter the data, process information by doing a series of query exercises and produce reports. Access is used here as the exemplar, but you can easily apply the techniques you learn to other database programs to develop your own work. Before working through the example in this chapter, refer back to Table 8.6 in Chapter 8 and familiarise yourself with the guidelines for using small databases in independent study.

9.2 The Historical Exercise: A Survey of Sheffield Cinemas in 1931

**Stage 1
Selecting
the
Historical
Topic and
Outlining the
Aims of the
Study**

This topic was selected as an area of British cultural history which has received little treatment from historians although the cinema industry represented a new cultural form of mass entertainment for the working class in the interwar years. Much is known about the development of the cinema industry at the institutional level. For example, there are numerous studies of the American and British cinema industries, the entrepreneurs who produced films, and the stars who became household names to millions of people (see Ryall 1986: Chapter 2; Balio 1985). Nevertheless, little is known about the cinema industry at the local level in Britain or its impact on the lives of ordinary people. This project will therefore examine the local structure of the cinema industry in the important Northern industrial city of Sheffield and in particular explore the views of contemporaries on its cultural influence. The cinema was a mass entertainment medium, and by 1930 Sheffield's cinemas could accommodate 1 in 17 of the city's population, and it was estimated that 10 million people visited the cinema in that year. This represented 20 attendances per annum for every man, woman and child of all ages in the population, and about £330,000 was spent on admissions in 1930 (Sheffield Social Survey 1931: 1). It is also worth noting that this was a period of rapidly rising unemployment in Sheffield.

The aims of the study are as follows:

- To explore the structure of the cinema industry at the local level by employing a case study of Sheffield
- To quantify information on the cinema by constructing a small database on relevant information relating to Sheffield cinemas
- To examine the cultural impact of the cinema in a Northern industrial city in the interwar years.

Academic work on the cinema in Sheffield has been limited. There are a few local history studies which examine the cinema largely from a pictorial standpoint, notably R. Ward's *In Memory of Sheffield Cinemas* (Ward 1988). There have also been recent studies on the cultural and recreational features of the city since the nineteenth century which provide general background reading (see Mackerness 1993: 429-462; Renshaw 1993: 463–481). Apart from pictorial images of the cinema in the city there has been no systematic investigation of its structure and cultural influence. An important source for examining local industries and structures is trade and commercial directories. There are annual runs of directories for the interwar period located in the Sheffield local history library. Indeed, you will find such directories in the local history libraries of most major cities and large towns. These provide information on the name of the cinema and its address, and are a useful starting point to quantifying the number of cinemas in the city. However, this source tells us nothing about structural factors such as the size of cinemas, who owned them, or the prices they charged. An examination of the records of the Sheffield Archives, however, produced a valuable official source of information contained in a large survey of cinemas in 1931. In that year Sheffield City Council formed a Social Survey Committee whose remit was to investigate housing conditions, welfare and health provision; it also commissioned volunteers, drawn from the middle classes, to examine the cultural and moral influence of cinemas on the public (Sheffield Social Survey 1931). The need for this investigation was clearly outlined in the opening paragraph of the report:

> The social importance of the cinema has not met the recognition it deserves. It has probably penetrated into the lives of the people more widely than any other cultural institution.
>
> (Sheffield Social Survey 1931: 1)

In compiling the report, volunteers visited the cinema and recorded their observations on:

- The reaction of the audience to the film being shown
- The programme of films over a period of time
- The impact of the cinema on the moral attitudes of the public, especially children.

**Stage 2
Search for and Evaluation of Data Sources**

This is a detailed and valuable source of historical information, and provides a wealth of qualitative evidence on the cultural impact of the cinema. The report also produced an appendix which provides a table of information on the structural features of the cinema industry and allows an examination of cultural factors. Detailed information on 50 cinemas was provided, and the data was compiled under the following eight headings:

- Cinema
- Address
- Financial control
- Date of opening
- Price of entry
- Seating
- Additions
- Remarks.

This provides an ideal source for the construction of a small database. Although there are eight separate headings of information, the number of records is easily manageable, and the presentation of the information in a tabular form allows the efficient collection of data. The estimated time for the extraction of this information was two hours. Having evaluated the source, you can move on to the collection stage.

Stage 3 Collection of Data

For the purposes of this study, it was decided that all the information (except Additions) contained under the eight headings listed was relevant. The data was collected by hand, and the information was systematically recorded in the format shown in Table 9.1 which

Table 9.1 Example of information on cinemas

Record number	Cinema	Address	Financial control	Date of opening	Price of entry	Seating	Remarks
2	Theatre Royal	Attercliffe	W. Bryan	1904	12d/24d	950	No children's matinee provided. No sound equipment installed.
34	Darnall Cinema	Darnall Rd	W. C. Brindley	1912	4d/9d	531	Children's matinee provided on Saturday afternoon. No special programme for children. No sound equipment installed.

shows two examples of the records collected. Note that at the time of collection each record extracted was identified by a unique record number as shown in the table. The next stage is to define the information collected and prepare it for entry into the database. We shall refer to this stage as the conceptualisation of the data.

The conceptualisation of the data takes two forms. First, how do we define the information to be entered into the database and what relationship does it have to the aims of the study? Second, in what form is the data to be entered into the database?

Stage 4 **Conceptual- isation of Data**

The source contained seven headings of information which we can refer to as variables. The seven variables are listed in the left-hand column of Table 9.2. This table also provides a definition of each variable to be entered into the database and its relationship to the main aims of the study. The latter is an important part of working with a database because it relates subsequently to the questions you are going to ask of each variable in Stage 8, data processing.

Having defined the data to be included in the database, you now need to determine in what form the data is to be entered into the database. Apart from the seven variables above, there is also the unique Record Number. This can be entered sequentially (1, 2, etc.,) into the database as recorded in Appendix 5: Data Set A. The information for variables 1–4 and 6 can be entered into the database as recorded in the original source. Variables 5 and 7, however, require further consideration before entry. Remarks (variable 7) consists of three separate pieces of information and these will be entered using the logical codes shown in Table 9.3. A logical code is a Yes or No code which allows you to enter the data easily and to process the information later. The conceptualised information for variables 1–4 and 6–7 are provided for you in Appendix 5: Data Set A.

Variable 5, on price, is more complicated. All the other variables in the database have a one-to-one relationship, i.e. the attributes of the Cinema, Address, Financial Control, Date of Opening, Seating Capacity are common (unique) to each individual cinema. For example, each cinema has only one address. The information on price, however, is in a one-to-many relationship, i.e. each individual cinema may charge one or more prices (see Chapter 8). The conceptualised data for prices is provided for you in Appendix 5: Data Set B. This data set contains the Record Number, the common category of information to both data sets, and the prices each cinema charged. Having conceptualised the data you can now turn to the design of the database tables.

Table 9.2 Definition of data variables and relationship to the study

Variable	Name of variable	Definition of variable	Relationship to study
1	Cinema	Information on the name of the cinema.	Key information for sorting and organising data, and information for cross referencing with other variables
2	Address	Location of the cinema.	Provides information on the spatial distribution of cinemas in the city, i.e. were the majority in working-class or middle-class districts, or neutral districts such as the city centre?
3	Financial control	Information relating to the owner of the cinema. This may be either a single proprietor or a limited company.	Provides information on the business aspects of the cinema in terms of the pattern of ownership of cinemas. This information could be cross-referenced with data sources such as trade directories to ascertain whether the same owners owned other types of leisure property.
4	Date of opening	This records the year in which the building was officially opened, but not necessarily the data it was opened as a cinema. For example, a cinema may be converted from other entertainment activities, e.g. a theatre or music hall.	Provides information for a chronological analysis of the opening of property related to leisure activity.
5	Price of entry	Information on different prices charged to the public for entry, recorded in pre-decimal currency.	Provides information for gauging the cost of leisure to the population, and indicates whether there was a discriminatory pricing policy operating, i.e. more than one price band for entry.
6	Seating	Information on the number of seats in the cinema.	Provides an indication of the size of the cinema in terms of audience capacity.
7	Remarks	This consisted of miscellaneous information which was broken down into three new variables: (a) whether children's matinees were provided on Saturdays, (b) if children's matinees were provided, did they provide a special programme for children, (c) whether sound equipment was installed.	This is a more complex set of information. Variables (a) and (b) provide information on the cultural impact of the cinema in terms of provision of programmes for children. A children's matinee was a screening on a Saturday for children only; adults were excluded. In these matinees some cinemas provided a special programme designed for children which would include material of an educational nature (e.g. newsreels) or new forms of cinematography such as cartoons. Some cinemas which provided these matinees provided no special programme and simply repeated what was screened to the adult audience. Variable (c) provides information on technological developments by way of the advent of sound technology.

Table 9.3 Logical codes for entry of information on Remarks

Code	Description
Yes/No	Yes, the cinema provided children's matinees, or No, it did not provide children's matinees
Yes/No	Yes, the cinema provided a special children's programme, or No, it did not provide a special children's programme
Yes/No	Yes, the cinema had sound equipment installed, or No, it did not have sound equipment installed

In this stage, you are going to design how the data is to be structured in the database. Before using a database management system to construct the database on the computer you should plan the database on a sheet of paper. When designing a database you should ask three basic sets of questions:

**Stage 5
Design of
Database
Tables**

- How many tables are to be included in the database and what information is going to be recorded in each database table?
- How is the table going to be organised, i.e. how many fields are needed to capture the information and what are the names of the fields?
- What is the data type of each field in the database, e.g. is it a Text field, Number field, Logical field?

At this stage, if you are uncertain of the concepts of database table or field, then we suggest that you return to the discussion on databases and database management systems in Chapter 8.

Figure 9.1 shows a plan for the Sheffield cinema database.

The database will consist of three tables:

- The CINEMA table will contain information directly about the cinema itself (variables 1–4 and 6 in Table 9.2). Thus, each record will contain information relating to a set of known attributes of an individual cinema.
- The REMARKS table will contain information on the cultural and technical factors identified in variable 7 of Table 9.2, i.e. provision for children and installation of sound equipment.
- The PRICE table will contain the information on the different prices charged for each cinema.

A common property of a database, discussed in Chapter 8, is that it comprises fields of information. The three database tables all contain specific fields of information. The CINEMA table consists of six fields and the names of these fields are shown in

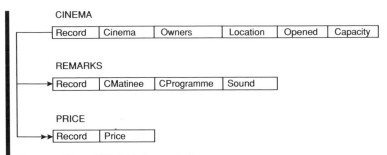

Figure 9.1 Plan of Sheffield cinema database

Figure 9.1. The field name Record is included so as to give each record a unique identification number, and is common to all tables in the database. This is the common field which links the three database tables. The link between the CINEMA and REMARKS tables is a one-to-one relationship because for one occurrence of a value in the CINEMA table there can be only one occurrence of a value in the REMARKS table. For example, a cinema either had sound equipment installed or it did not. The one-to-one relationship is shown by the single-headed arrow in Figure 9.1 which also illustrates the link to the common field: Record. On the other hand, the relationship between the CINEMA and REMARKS tables and the PRICE table is a one-to-many relationship. For every occurrence of a value in the CINEMA or REMARKS tables there may be more than one occurrence in the PRICE table. An individual cinema can charge more than one price to its customers. The one-to-many relationship is shown by the double-headed arrow in Figure 9.1.

The names of the fields in the CINEMA table reflect the variables described earlier in Table 9.2. The field name should identify the information which the field will contain. Figure 9.2 shows the relationship between the names of the CINEMA table fields and the variables in Table 9.2. The REMARKS table consists of four fields. The Record field is again the common field to the tables, and the remaining three fields reflect the information from variable 7 in Table 9.2. This is shown in Figure 9.3. Finally, the PRICE table consists of two fields: the common Record and the Price field from variable 5 in Table 9.2, shown in Figure 9.4.

Variable		Field Name
1 Cinema		Cinema
2 Address		Location
3 Financial Control		Owners
4 Date of Opening		Opened
6 Seating		Capacity

Figure 9.2 Names of fields in CINEMA database table

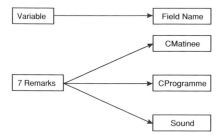

Figure 9.3 Names of fields in REMARKS database table

Figure 9.4 Names of fields in PRICE database table

Table 9.4 Specifications of field data types

Database table	Field name	Data type
CINEMA	Record	Counter
	Cinema	Text
	Location	Text
	Owners	Text
	Opened	Number
	Capacity	Number
REMARKS	Record	Counter
	Cmatinee	Logical
	Cprogramme	Logical
	Sound	Logical
PRICE	Record	Number
	Price	Number

The final step in the planning stage is to specify the data type of each field. Table 9.4 shows the data type of each field in the three database tables. These specifications were determined by an examination of the full range of data to be entered which is contained in Data Sets A and B in Appendix 5. Having thought through the design of the database, you can now go on to use a database management system and construct the database.

The database management system we have chosen as the exemplar is Microsoft Access. Access has many powerful functions, but here we will only deal with getting you started by introducing the basics.

Constructing a Database Using Access

Start Windows on your computer and from the Program Manager double-click on the Microsoft Access icon. Access will start and display the **Welcome to Microsoft Access** box shown in Figure 9.5. This box offers you choices on how to get started with Access by

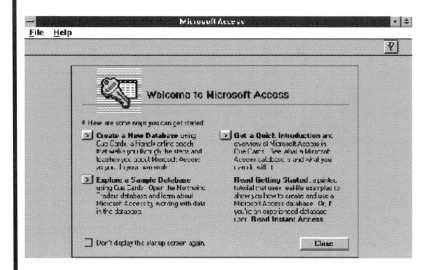

Figure 9.5 Welcome to Microsoft Access box

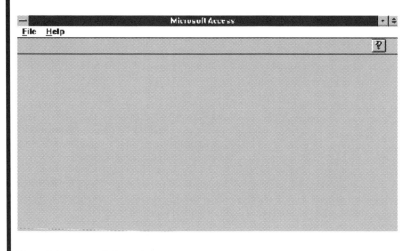

Figure 9.6 Access start-up window

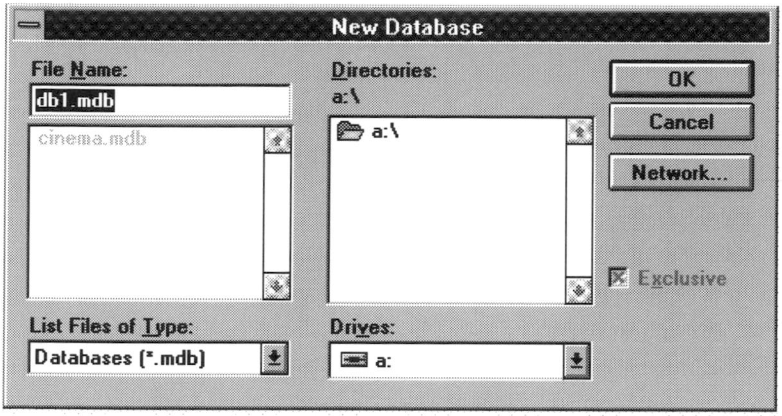

Figure 9.7 New Database dialogue box

using Cue Cards, an automatic learning tool. If you want to use these choices then simply click on the button to the left of the option. At this point, however, you should close the **Welcome** box. Click on the **Close** button and the Access start-up window will be displayed. The Access start-up window, shown in Figure 9.6, allows you to create a new database, open an existing database, or do basic administrative tasks.

To create a new database file follow these instructions:

1   Click on the **File** menu.
2   The **File** menu box opens, providing a number of options. Select **New Database** by clicking on this option. The **New Database** dialogue box appears as shown in Figure 9.7.
3   In the **File Name** text box type the name of the new database file; type: CINEMA.
4   Now click on the **OK** box and the database window will open. You are now ready to design and construct the three databases.

The database window is shown in Figure 9.8, and contains the option buttons you will use to construct database tables, perform queries and produce reports to display your data. You can now construct the three database tables which were designed earlier and illustrated in the plan shown in Figure 9.1: CINEMA table, REMARKS table and PRICE table.

To construct the CINEMA database table follow these instructions:

1   Click on the **Table** button in the database window and then click on the **New** button. The Tables design view appears as shown in Figure 9.9.
2   The Table design view allows you to create fields and structure the information in the table. Refer back to Table 9.4 which lists the field names

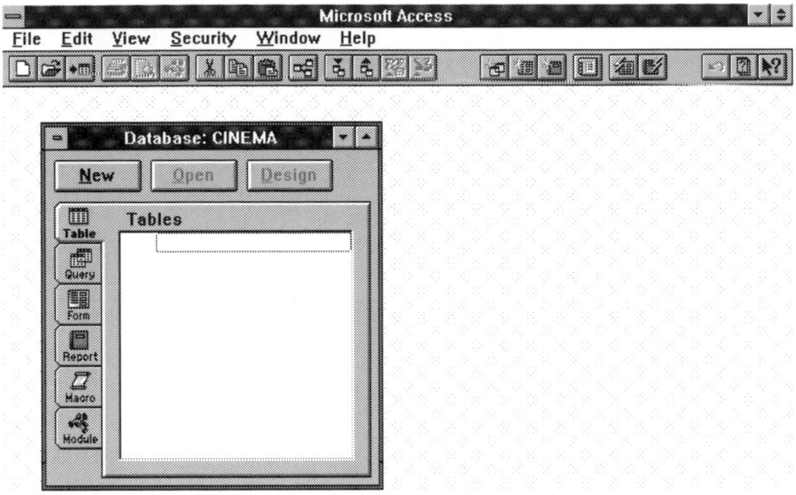

Figure 9.8 Database window

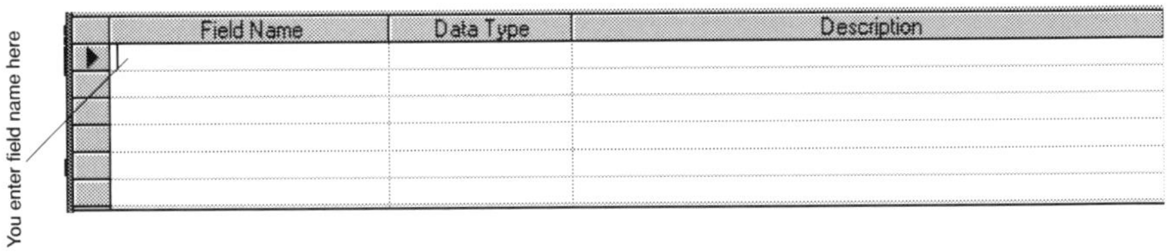

Figure 9.9 Table design view

and the data type of each field. In the **Field Name** column of the design view there is a flashing black line; this is the insertion point which prompts you to type in a field name. Type: Record, the first field in your database. Remember, this is the common field in all three tables. Now press the Tab key on your keyboard and you will move to the **Data Type** column in the design view.

3   You will note that the word **Text** appears. This is the default setting, i.e. the data type is automatically set for Text. To change the data type to Counter click on the drop-down menu box to the left of the column. A selection menu appears, as shown in Figure 9.10. Click on **Counter** and this option will

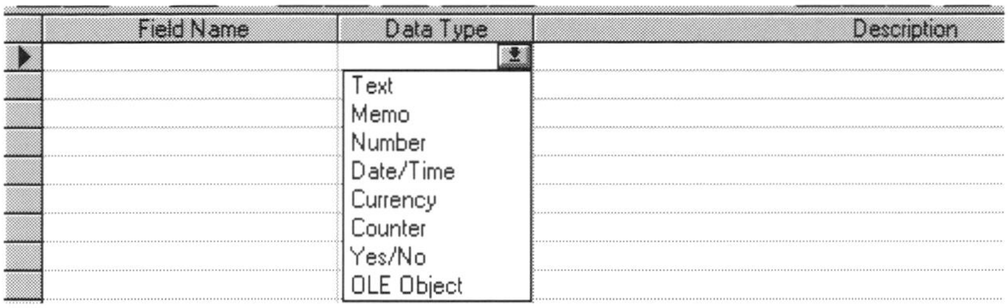

Field Name	Data Type	Description
	⬥	
	Text	
	Memo	
	Number	
	Date/Time	
	Currency	
	Counter	
	Yes/No	
	OLE Object	

Figure 9.10 Selection menu for data type

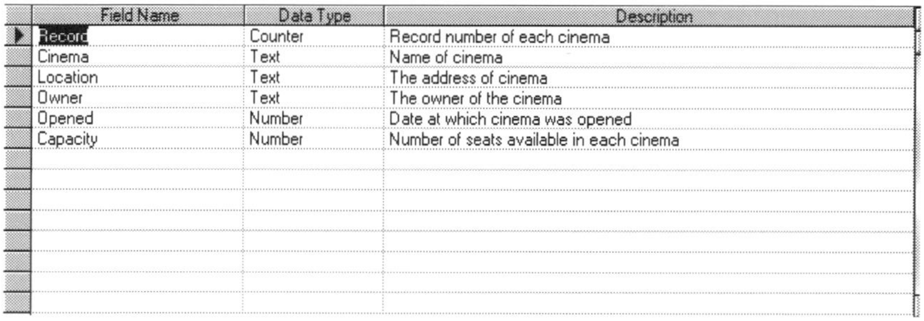

Field Name	Data Type	Description
Record	Counter	Record number of each cinema
Cinema	Text	Name of cinema
Location	Text	The address of cinema
Owner	Text	The owner of the cinema
Opened	Number	Date at which cinema was opened
Capacity	Number	Number of seats available in each cinema

Figure 9.11 Completed table design view for CINEMA table

appear in the **Data Type** column. Press Tab and you will move to the **Description** column in the design view.

4 In the **Description** column type a summary describing the information contained in the field. Type the record number of each cinema. Press Tab and the insertion pointer will move to the next row and you will be ready to create the second field. The second field is called Cinema. Type this name and press Tab. The field type is automatically set to Text so simply press Tab again. Type in a description of the information contained in this field and then press Tab, and you will be ready to create the remaining fields.

5 You should now create the remaining fields, as shown earlier in Figure 9.2. The completed design view is shown in Figure 9.11. Note that two of the

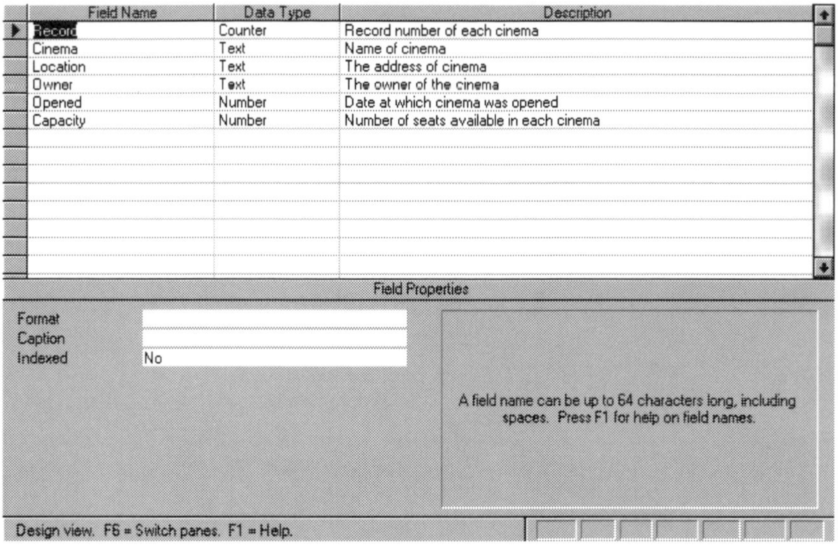

Field Name	Data Type	Description
Record	Counter	Record number of each cinema
Cinema	Text	Name of cinema
Location	Text	The address of cinema
Owner	Text	The owner of the cinema
Opened	Number	Date at which cinema was opened
Capacity	Number	Number of seats available in each cinema

Field Properties

Format	
Caption	
Indexed	No

A field name can be up to 64 characters long, including spaces. Press F1 for help on field names.

Design view. F6 = Switch panes. F1 = Help.

Figure 9.12 Field properties options

fields contain Number data types. To change the data type to Number simply click on the drop-down selection box and select **Number**.

When you are in the design view you can also set the properties for each field in the table. For example, you can set the width of Text fields to your requirements. Do not concern yourself about the Counter and Number fields, they are automatically set for you. To change the width of the Text fields follow these instructions:

1   Click on the field name Cinema.
2   The **Field Properties** options appear at the bottom of the screen as shown in Figure 9.12. In the Field Size box the width of the field is automatically set to 50. To change this to 40, the maximum width you will require to enter information, click in the box and use the delete key to erase the number.
3   Type: 40. Finally, to switch the **Field Properties** options off, click on any field in the tables design view.
4   Now change all the field text widths to meet your requirements. When you have completed this you can then set the primary key and save the database table.

The primary key identifies one or more fields in the database table whose values uniquely identify each record in the table. A field with a Counter data type, e.g. the field named Record, makes a perfect primary key because as you enter the records into the table they are automatically allocated a sequential number. You will see how important the primary key is later when you use the field to link database tables. To set the primary key follow these instructions:

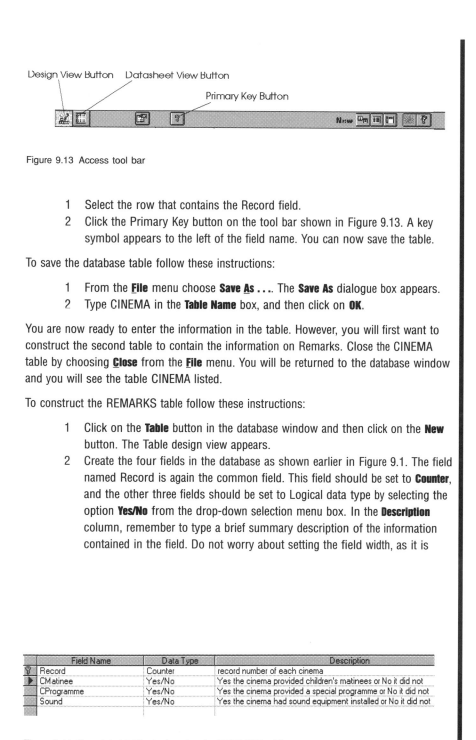

Figure 9.13 Access tool bar

1 Select the row that contains the Record field.
2 Click the Primary Key button on the tool bar shown in Figure 9.13. A key symbol appears to the left of the field name. You can now save the table.

To save the database table follow these instructions:

1 From the **File** menu choose **Save As . . .**. The **Save As** dialogue box appears.
2 Type CINEMA in the **Table Name** box, and then click on **OK**.

You are now ready to enter the information in the table. However, you will first want to construct the second table to contain the information on Remarks. Close the CINEMA table by choosing **Close** from the **File** menu. You will be returned to the database window and you will see the table CINEMA listed.

To construct the REMARKS table follow these instructions:

1 Click on the **Table** button in the database window and then click on the **New** button. The Table design view appears.
2 Create the four fields in the database as shown earlier in Figure 9.1. The field named Record is again the common field. This field should be set to **Counter**, and the other three fields should be set to Logical data type by selecting the option **Yes/No** from the drop-down selection menu box. In the **Description** column, remember to type a brief summary description of the information contained in the field. Do not worry about setting the field width, as it is

Field Name	Data Type	Description
Record	Counter	record number of each cinema
CMatinee	Yes/No	Yes the cinema provided children's matinees or No it did not
CProgramme	Yes/No	Yes the cinema provided a special programme or No it did not
Sound	Yes/No	Yes the cinema had sound equipment installed or No it did not

Figure 9.14 Completed table design view for REMARKS table

155

automatically set at 3. The completed design view is shown in Figure 9.14.

3   Create a primary key. Select the row that contains the Record field, and click the Primary Key button on the tool bar (see Figure 9.13). A key symbol appears to the left of the field name.

4   Save the database table. From the **File** menu choose **Save As . . .**. The **Save As** dialogue box appears. Type REMARKS in the Table Name box, and then click on **OK**.

5   Close the CINEMA table by choosing **Close** from the **File** menu. You will be returned to the database window and you will see the REMARKS table listed, together with the CINEMA table you created earlier.

You should finally construct the PRICE table. This is a simple design containing the Record field (Number type) and the Price field (Number type). Note that the Record field is now a Number type because you want to enter duplicate numbers into the database. A Counter data type will not allow you to do this. To construct the PRICE table follow these instructions:

1   Type in the two field names and set both to data type Number.

2   From the **File** menu choose **Close**.

3   A **Save** message box appears, click on **Yes** to save the table. Name the table: PRICE.

4   A second message box appears: **There is no primary key defined. Create a primary key?** Click on **No**. A primary key is not relevant to this table because it contains duplicate records.

Once you have constructed this table you can then proceed to Stage 6 and begin to enter the information into the database tables. If, however, you want to break off at this stage then follow these instructions for quitting the Access program:

1   Click on the Access control box located on the top left of the database window.

2   Choose **Close** and the program will end and you will be returned to the Windows Program Manager.

Stage 6
Entry of
Data

Start Windows on your computer and then open Access. Close the **Welcome to Access** box and the Access start-up window will be displayed. You will now need to open the Cinema database file. Follow these instructions:

1   From the **File** menu choose **Open** database. The **Open Database** dialogue box appears.

2   From the **File Name** box choose CINEMA.MDB (MDB is the file suffix allocated to Access database files).

3   Click on **OK** and the database window will open and the two tables you created will be listed.

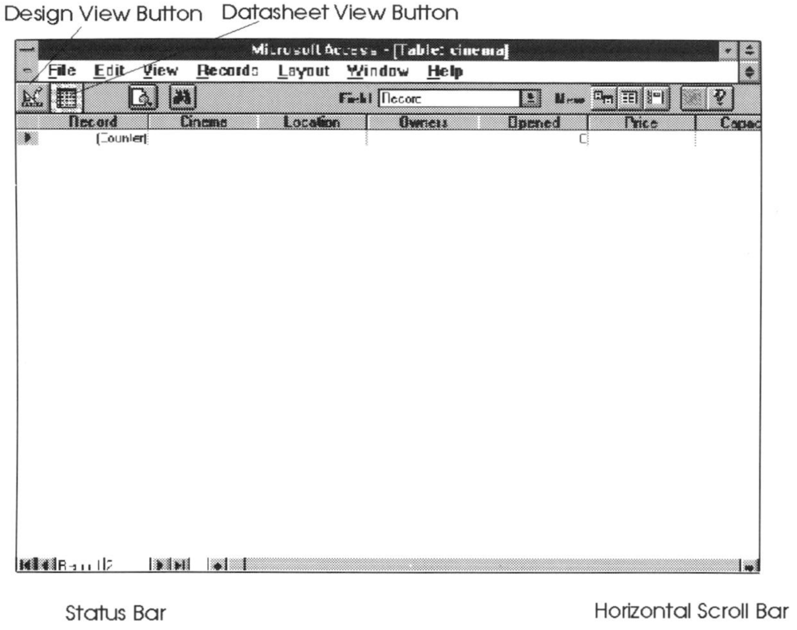

Design View Button   Datasheet View Button

Status Bar   Horizontal Scroll Bar

Figure 9.15 Datasheet view

Entering Information for the CINEMA Table

Select the CINEMA table by clicking on it, the table name will be highlighted. Now click on the **Open** button and the datasheet view, shown in Figure 9.15, appears on the screen. The fields you created in the database are listed across the columns of the database table. You will not be able to see all the fields in the table because the width of the table is too great. To move across the table use the horizontal scroll bars shown in Figure 9.15. There are two views in an Access database: the datasheet view, where you enter and view the information in the table, and the design view which you used earlier to produce the structure of the database table. Figure 9.15 shows the Datasheet View and Design View buttons on the tool bar. You use these to move between the two views. Click on the Design View button and the table's design view will appear. To move back to the Datasheet View click on the datasheet view button on the tool bar.

To enter the first record in the database follow these instructions:

1   The insertion point, the flashing black line, is located in the Record field. The description of the information contained in the field is shown in the status bar (see Figure 9.15). The word **Counter** is automatically placed in this field: the record will automatically be given a number as you enter information. Note that the current record is indicated in the table by a black

triangle. To move to the next field, Cinema, press the Tab key on the keyboard.

2 Type: Globe Picture Palace. When you type do not place any punctuation in the text as this may affect the processing of the data. Note that the text you enter is truncated. Do not worry about this at present, you can easily expand the width of the column to display all the information in the field. Press Tab to move to the next field: Location.

3 Type: Ecclesall Rd. Press Tab to move to the next field: Owners.

4 Type: Ecclesall Picture Palace Ltd. Note, again, that the text is truncated. Press Tab to move to the next field: Opened.

5 Type: 1914. Press Tab to move to the last field: Capacity.

6 Type: 850. Press Tab and you will move to the next row in the database and be ready to enter the information for the second record. Note that the black triangle moves down to the next row indicating this is the current record. At this stage, if you want to view all the information in the two truncated fields, then move the mouse pointer to the intersection between the Cinema column and the Location column. The mouse pointer turns to a double-headed arrow. Keep the mouse button depressed and drag the column to the right until you are satisfied with the width. Now place the mouse pointer between the intersection of the Owners and Opened columns and drag the column to the right.

7 Having entered the first record in the database table, you should now enter all the records from Data Set A. If at any stage you want to quit the database table then choose **Close** from the **File** menu. A message box appears: **Save Changes to Table 'Cinema'?** Click on the **Yes** button and you will be returned to the database window.

If you make a mistake in your typing then you can easily edit this. Select the field you want to edit by moving the mouse pointer to the field. The mouse pointer turns to an I-shaped bar indicating the insertion point. Click once with the mouse where you want to insert changes. The usual flashing black line appears, prompting you to type in the alteration. For future reference, there are a number of ways to move around a database

Table 9.5 Moving around a database table

Move	Instruction
Up the database table	Press up-arrow key on keyboard
Down the database table	Press down-arrow key on keyboard
Across the row of the database table (i.e. field to field) from left to right	Press tab key on keyboard
Across the row of the database table (i.e. field to field) from right to left	Press shift and tab keys simultaneously on keyboard

table, apart from using the mouse, and these are described in Table 9.5. When you have entered all the records into the CINEMA table you can move on to enter the records into the REMARKS table.

Entering Information for the REMARKS Table

Select the table from the database window and click on the **Open** button. The datasheet view, shown in Figure 9.16, appears. The fields you created are listed across the columns of the database table. You can now enter the information in Data Set A on Remarks, i.e. the information in the final column. To enter the first record follow these instructions:

1 The insertion point, the flashing black line, is located in the Record field, the common field in both database tables. Press the Tab key on the keyboard to move to the CMatinee field.

2 All the remaining fields in the table are Yes/No (Logical) types. Note that the Status Bar records the description of the CMatinee field: Yes, the cinema provided children's matinees, or No, it did not provide them. The first record in Data Set A is for the Globe Picture Palace, and this cinema provides a children's matinee. Therefore, type: Yes. Press Tab to move to the next field: CProgramme. Note that when you typed Yes in the CMatinee field the word No appeared in the remaining two fields of the table. This is the default (automatic) setting for Yes/No fields.

3 The cinema provides no special programme for children. The field already contains the word No and this is highlighted; press Tab to move to the last field: Sound.

4 The cinema has sound equipment installed. Type: Yes, and it will overwrite the word No. Press Tab and you will move to the next row in the database and be ready to enter the information for the second record.

5 Having entered the first record in the database table, you should now enter all the records contained in Data Set A.

Record	CMatinee	CProgramme	Sound
Counter			

Figure 9.16 Datasheet view for REMARKS table

Entering Information for the PRICE Table

This information is contained in Data Set B. Enter all the information exactly as you see it in Data Set B. When you have completed entering the information you should proceed to Stage 7.

Stage 7
**Checking
Data**

Having completed the data entry you should now do two things:

1　Check the database for mistakes in typing and ensure you have entered the correct information.
2　You should also consider if there is any additional information which is important to enter into the database.

In the database we have constructed there is no need to add new fields but the following is a guide to changing the design of a database table:

1　Click on the row in the design view where you want to insert the new field.
2　From the **Edit** menu choose **Insert Row** and a blank row will appear.
3　Type the name of the new field, set the data type, and provide a description of the information contained in the field.
4　Click on the Datasheet View button on the tool bar. A question box appears: **Switching to the datasheet requires saving changes made to the table. Continue?** Click on **OK** and you will be returned to the datasheet. You will see that all the data you entered is still recorded in the table, but you have a new field included in the table.

Your can now proceed to Stage 8 and process the information.

Stage 8
**Data
Processing**

Processing involves interrogating the information contained in the database. Data processing uses the functions of a database management system as discussed in Chapter 8 to selectively retrieve, group, order and count information. You perform these operations by designing queries. A query allows you to ask questions of the records in the database and provides an answer. You therefore need to think through a set of questions which you are going to ask of the data. There are numerous questions you could ask and queries you could perform, and to illustrate some of these you should complete the exercises below.

Exercise 1
**Doing
select
queries**

A select query allows you to ask a question and then select the records you want. Let us assume that you are interested in two companies in Sheffield which owned cinemas: Heeley & Amalgamated Cinemas Limited and Sheffield District Cinemas Limited. You will want to see how many cinemas each of these companies owned in the city. The first query is for Heeley & Amalgamated Cinemas, and to perform this query follow these instructions:

1　From the database window click on the **Query** button, and then click on **New**. The Query window opens and the **Add Table** dialogue box is displayed. The title bar of the Query window displays the title: **[Select Query: Query1]**.
2　The **Add Table** dialogue box allows you to select tables you wish to include in the query and the two tables you have created are listed. Select the CINEMA

table and then click on **Add** to include the table in the query. Finally click on **Close** and the Query window appears.

3   The Query window is shown in Figure 9.17. The menu bar contains the selection menus for **File**, **Edit**, **View**, **Query**, **Window**, **Help**, some of which you will use in these exercises. The top part of the window contains the fields list for the CINEMA table. The bottom part contains the QBE (Query By Example) grid where you define which fields and records you want to include in the query. When you perform a query you can either add all the fields in a field list to the QBE grid or include a selection of fields. In this example we will include all the fields. To do this, double-click the title bar of the Cinema field list (see Figure 9.17). Click inside the field list and hold down the mouse button. Drag the fields to the first field cell of the QBE grid as shown in Figure 9.18. The field names are now listed across the QBE grid.

4   In the QBE grid select the **Criteria** cell for the Owners field. The **Criteria** defines the selection you want to make. Type: "Heeley & Amalgamated Cinemas Ltd". Note that when you are setting the selection criteria for a Text-type field you must always include the inverted commas.

5   To carry out the query and display the selected data click on the Query View button shown in Figure 9.17. To return to the Query window click on the Datasheet View button shown in Figure 9.17.

6   To save the query choose **Close** from the **File** menu. A question box appears: **Save Changes to Query 'Query 1'?** Click on the **Yes** button. A **Save As . . .**

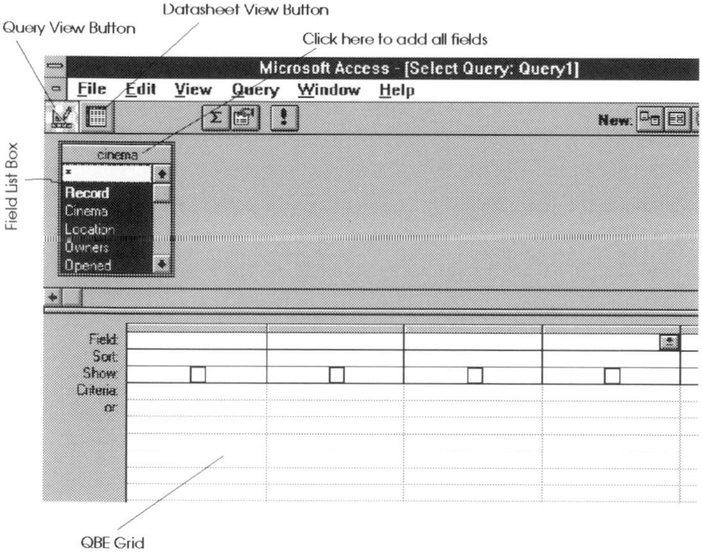

Figure 9.17 Query window

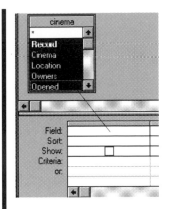

Figure 9.18 Dragging to add all fields to the QBE grid

dialogue box appears. Give the file a name, e.g. Heeley, and then click on **OK**. You are returned to the database window and the query file is listed.

Query files are permanent stores of selected records, and you can alter the query at any time. For example, assume you wanted the selected records in the Heeley query to be ordered alphabetically by cinema name, and to only display the fields for Cinema, Owner and Capacity. To do this follow these instructions:

1 Select Heeley from the database window and click on **Open**. The query datasheet view, listing the selected records, appears.
2 Click on the Query View button.
3 Select the **Sort** cell for the Cinema field. A drop-down selection arrow appears in the right-hand corner of the cell. Click on the arrow and the selection box appears as shown in Figure 9.19. Click on **Ascending** to order the records.
4 The **Show** cell of the QBE grid contains a box with a cross in it. When the cross is displayed then that field is included in the datasheet view. To remove a field from the view click on the **Show** box and the cross will disappear. Do this for all fields except Cinema, Owner and Capacity. Note

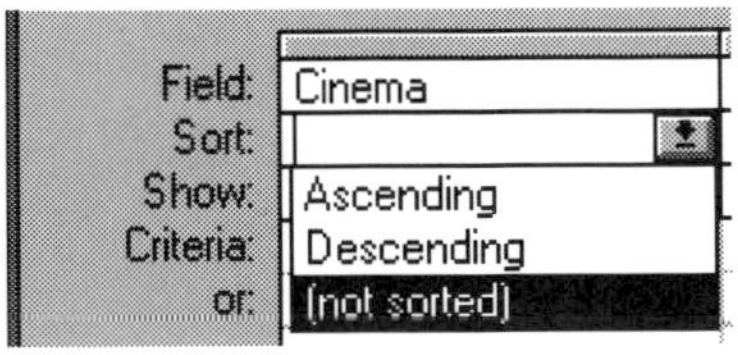

Figure 9.19 Selection box for sorting data in a field

that if you again want to show a field then you simply click on the empty box until the cross appears.

5   To display the sorted data click on the Datasheet View button.

6   Choose **Close** from the **File** menu. A message box appears: **Save Changes to Query 'Heeley'?** Click the **Yes** button.

You can now perform the second query and select the cinemas owned by Sheffield District Cinemas Limited. The procedures are the same as for the query explained above. Note when you open the **Add Table** dialogue box that the Heeley query is included. You can thus perform queries on queries. In this second query, however, do not include all the fields in the query, but just those for Cinema, Owner and Capacity. You do this by dragging a selected field from the Field List box and placing it in the QBE grid. Click inside the Field List box and select Cinema. Hold down the mouse button and drag the field to the first **Field** cell of the QBE grid as shown in Figure 9.20. Perform the same operation for the Owner and Capacity fields. When you have finished the query save it as: District.

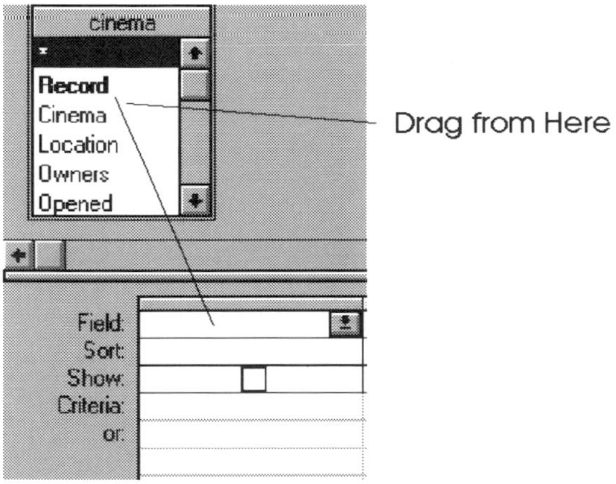

Figure 9.20 Dragging to add selected fields to the QBE grid

To demonstrate what you have learnt above, perform the following query: is there a concentration of cinemas in working-class districts in Sheffield? In this query you would want to select key words in the Location field of the database. To perform this query you would of course have to do further research to identify the working-class areas of the city. We can, however, give you a clue so you can perform a preliminary examination of this question. The district of Attercliffe was associated with the heavy steel industry of Sheffield and contained a concentration of working-class housing. Open a new query, add the CINEMA table, and include the Cinema and Location fields in the QBE grid. Now follow these instructions:

1 In the QBE grid select the **Criteria** cell for the Location field. Type: "Attercliffe".

2 Often, when you are selecting, you are unsure of the exact criteria to use. For example, if you simply type "Attercliffe" then the records displayed will only match this criterion but not display records for other locations containing this keyword, e.g. "Attercliffe Common". To increase the accuracy of your selection click on the **or** cell of the QBE grid and type: "Attercliffe *". The asterisk is a symbol which substitutes for a word and is known as a 'wild card'. You are now selecting any record that contains the word 'Attercliffe'.

3 Click on the Datasheet View button to display the selected records.

4 Close the file and name it Attercliffe.

Before moving on to the next exercise, you should think of more questions to ask of the CINEMA table and perform the appropriate queries.

Exercise 2
Grouping records and counting

Assume you want to know if cinema companies owned more than one cinema? You can easily perform this task by grouping the records and using the count function to count the cinemas owned by each company. To do this follow these instructions:

1 From the database window click on the Query button, and then click on **New**.

2 From the **Add Table** dialogue box select the CINEMA table and then click on **Add** to include the table in the query. Click on **Close** and the Query window appears.

3 Include in the query the Record field and the Owners field. Drag the selected fields from the Field List box and place them in the QBE grid as shown in Figure 9.21.

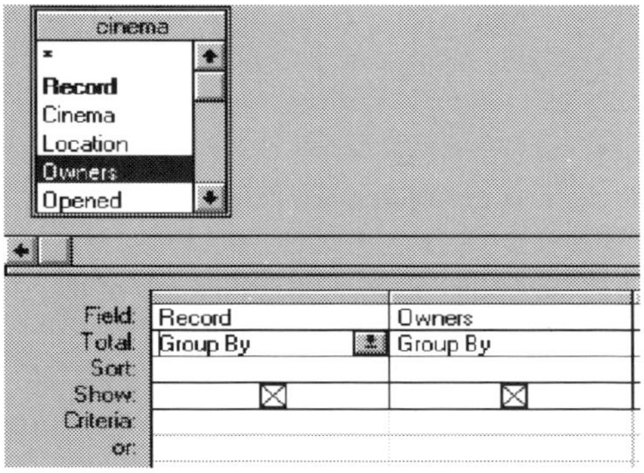

Figure 9.21 Performing a group query for Owners

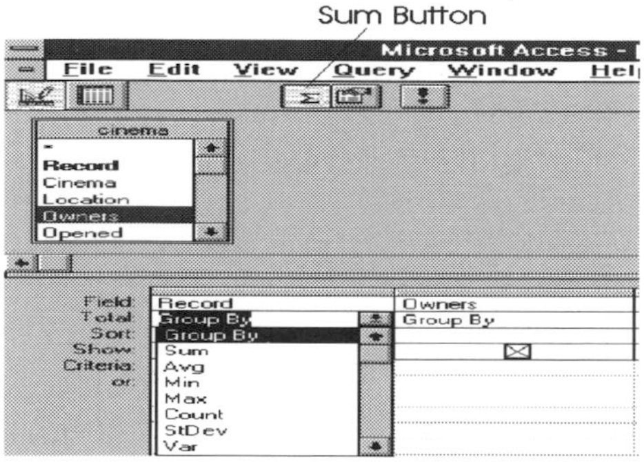

Sum Button

Figure 9.22 Drop-down selection box for totals

4   You now want to group together all the names of owners and count their record numbers. Click the Sum button on the tool bar (see Figure 9.22). The **Total** row in the QBE grid displays the words **Group By** as shown in Figure 9.21.

5   Click the **Total** cell below the Record field, and then click the arrow. From the drop-down list shown in Figure 9.22 select **Count**. Since there is one record number for each cinema, you are counting the number of cinemas grouped by owner.

6   To display the data click on the Datasheet View button. Each cinema owner is now grouped in alphabetical order and the number of cinemas owned by each is displayed in the column headed CountofRecord. For example, the Heeley & Amalgamated Cinemas Ltd will display a count of 4.

7   Now close the query and give the file a name, i.e. Owners.

| *Exercise 3* **Doing queries on number fields** | A key field in your database is Capacity: this gives us a proxy of the size of cinemas by seating capacity. Assume you wanted to know how many cinemas had a seating capacity greater than 1,000. To perform this query follow these instructions: |

1   Open a new query and add the CINEMA table.

2   Include in the QBE grid the Cinema field and the Capacity field.

3   In the **Criteria** cell for the Capacity field type: >1000. The symbol > is the mathematical operator for 'greater than', and the range of mathematical operators you can use is shown in Table 9.6.

4   Click on the **Sort** cell and click on the arrow. Select **Ascending** to order the data from lowest to highest number.

5   Click on the Datasheet View button to display the data. All cinemas with a capacity above 1,000 are included and listed in ascending order.

Table 9.6 Mathematical operators

Operator	Function
<	Less than
>	Greater than
<=	Less than or equal to
>=	Greater than or equal to

Return to the QBE grid by clicking on the Query View button. Delete the selection you made earlier and now perform these queries using the mathematical operators shown in Table 9.6:

- Select all cinemas with a capacity less than 1,000.
- Select all cinemas with a capacity equal to or greater than 1,000.
- Select all cinemas with a capacity less than or equal to 1,000.

> **Exercise 4**
> **Doing simple summary calculations**

You can make a number of calculations to summarise the information in Number-type fields in your database. For example, you might want to sum the total capacity of all cinemas in the CINEMA table. To do this follow these instructions:

1 Create a new query and add the CINEMA table.
2 Add the Capacity field from the Field List box.
3 Click the Sum button on the tool bar. The **Total** row in the QBE grid displays the word **Group**.
4 Click the **Total** cell below the Record field, and then click the arrow. From the drop-down list select **Sum**.
5 To display the summary calculation click on the Datasheet View button. The total is displayed in a column labelled SumofCapacity. The answer is 45,623.

Now use the same procedures to calculate:

- The average of the capacity field.
- The Min (minimum) and Max (maximum) capacity.

You can also do these calculations for selected records in the database table. For example, perform this exercise:

1 Add the Owners field to the QBE grid and type "Heeley & Amalgamated Cinemas Ltd" in the **Criteria** cell.
2 In the **Total** cell underneath the Capacity field select **Sum** from the drop-down list box.
3 To display the summary calculation click on the Datasheet View button. The total is 3,550.

Now perform a calculation for the capacity of all cinemas in Attercliffe. Having familiarised yourself with these procedures you should now experiment and work out your own calculations.

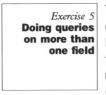

Exercise 5
Doing queries on more than one field

You can do queries on more than one field in the database. For example, perform this query: select the cinema in Attercliffe owned by Scala Cinemas. To do this simply add the Location and Owners field to the QBE grid, type: "Attercliffe" for the Location in the **Criteria** cell, and type: "Scala Cinemas" in the **Criteria** cell for Owners.

Finally perform this query: select all the records of cinemas opened before 1914 with a capacity greater than 1,000.

Exercise 6
Joining two tables to see related data

In this exercise you can join the CINEMA and REMARKS tables to examine the cultural impact of the cinema. The influence of the cinema on children was a key area of investigation for the Social Survey Committee. Children, they concluded,

go to be amused and excited, or at least escape from dullness, overcrowded homes, or bad weather, but incidentally and insensibly their experience of life is extended, prejudices are rooted, moral standards are acquired, and strong notions find a habitation in growing minds.

(Sheffield Social Survey 1931: 9)

Certainly, the investigators were critical of the profit motive of cinema owners who screened adult material at children's matinees. In a scathing attack, they claimed that this was,

The easy thing to do . . . from a purely business point of view . . . The entertainment needs of the once-a-week audience of children can hardly enter into it.

(Sheffield Social Survey 1931: 10)

To examine these observations, you can join the CINEMA table with the REMARKS table and address the following questions:

- How many cinemas provided children's matinees?
- How many cinemas which provided children's matinees also screened a special programme for children?

To join the tables and construct queries to answer these questions follow these instructions:

1 From the database window click on the Query button, and then click on **New**.
2 From the **Add Tables** dialogue box select the CINEMA table and then click on **Add**. Now select the REMARKS table and click on **Add**. Both tables are now added to your query. Finally click on **Close**.

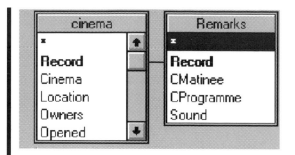

Figure 9.23 Joining database tables

3   The common field in both tables is the Record field, so you will want to join these fields to create a link. Select the Record field from the CINEMA Field List box and then drag the field to the REMARKS Field List box. When you release the mouse button, you will see that the link is identified by the joining line shown in Figure 9.23.

4   Drag the Record field and Cinema field from the Cinema Field List box and place them in the QBE grid.

5   Drag the CMatinee and CProgramme fields from the Remarks Field List box to the QBE grid.

6   In the **Criteria** cell for CMatinee type: Yes (note that you should not include inverted commas for selections on Logical fields).

7   To display the data click on the Datasheet View button.

8   Return to the query design and complete the query showing the number of cinemas which provided children's matinees and also provided a special programme for children. You will now have to set the criteria for both these fields.

You should now think through other queries you want to construct from these related tables. Note also that you can join as many tables as you wish by adding the tables to the query and dragging the common field from the Field List boxes.

Exercise 7
More examples of joining tables

In this example you will join the CINEMA table to the PRICE table and examine the pricing policy of cinemas. Did cinemas charge variable prices, i.e. did they offer customers higher-quality seating? This is an important question because the implication is that consumers go to the cinema not simply to consume the film but also to consume entertainment which includes the comfort in which the show was viewed. Thus, cinemas were not simply competing by the type of film shown but also they had to provide variable options for comfort. To create the link follow these instructions:

1 Create a new query and add the CINEMA and PRICE tables.
2 In the CINEMA table Field List box click on Record and, keeping the mouse button depressed, drag to the Record field in the Price box. Release the mouse button and a line will appear showing the link has been created.
3 Add the Record and Cinema fields (CINEMA table) and the Price field (PRICE table) to the QBE grid.
4 You now want to group together all the different prices charged by cinemas. Click the Sum button on the tool bar. The words **Group By** are displayed.
5 Click the **Total** cell below the Record field, and then click the arrow. From the drop-down list select **Count**.
6 Click on the **Sort** cell and click on the arrow. Select **Ascending** to sort the data from lowest to highest number.
7 To display the data click on the Datasheet View button. Each cinema is now grouped in ascending order and the number of prices charged is listed.

Having completed the above exercises you should now be familiar with the basic functions of a database and should ask your own questions of the data and construct appropriate queries. Here are some examples:

● What is the minimum price charged by cinemas?
● What is the maximum price charged by cinemas?
● Do large cinemas with a capacity over 1,000 charge higher prices than smaller cinemas?
● Do cinemas that have sound equipment installed charge higher prices than cinemas with no sound equipment?

When you are satisfied that you have exhausted the possible queries you can proceed to Exercise 8.

Exercise 8 **Converting queries to make table queries**

Previously, when you have made queries you have stored the selected information in separate query files. The following provides instruction on this:

1 From the **Query** menu, choose **Make Table**. The **Query Properties** dialogue box opens.
2 In the **Table Name** box type the name of the new table. You are adding a table to the current database, and this is automatically selected for you.
3 Click on the **OK** button. The title bar of the Query window changes to **Make Table Query: Query1**.
4 To run the **Make Table Query**, click the Run button (the button marked with an ! mark) on the tool bar. A message appears: **1 row (s) will be copied into new table**.
5 Click on **OK** to continue the **Make Table Query**.

6   From the **File** menu close the table. You will return to the database window. To view the data in the new table click on **Table**, and you will see the table. Open the table by clicking on the **Open** button.

You should now be familiar with using the query function of a database and should proceed to Stage 9.

Stage 9
Producing
Summary
Information

You can print your tables and queries by choosing **Print ...** from the **File** menu in the database window. You can also build customised reports by clicking on the **Report** button in the database window. This function will take you step-by-step through the procedures for designing your printed reports. You can also use **Help** if you lose your way.

Stage 10
Data
Analysis

Having finished the exercises in this chapter we recommend that you write a short report which summarises your main findings from the Sheffield Cinema Database. In the next chapter we will give some further examples of how you can use historical databases in independent study drawn from a range of historical areas.

Databases and Independent Study

10.1 Introduction

This chapter continues to explore the use of databases in independent study. Rather than focusing on one main study we will offer three exercises drawn from different historical areas. These are shown in Table 10.1 together with the names of the appropriate data sets which are located in Appendix 6. For each exercise you will be invited to carry out the following tasks:

1   Design a database from the sources provided.
2   Enter the historical information into the database.
3   Design a list of queries to interrogate the information contained in the database.
4   Present your findings in the form of a short report.

Table 10.1 Exercises in this chapter

Exercise	Topic	Data Sets
1	The small saver in mid-Victorian Sheffield	1A
2	The structure of the cotton industry in the Industrial Revolution	2A, 2B, 2C, 2D
3	Assisted emigration to Australia, 1825–1832	3A

10.2 Three Database Exercises

The exercises reflect the areas of social and demographic history, and economic and business history. If your main interests are in social history, for example, you might be interested in looking at Exercise 1; on the other hand, if you are an economic or business historian you might be interested in engaging with Exercise 2. Finally, Exercise 3 should attract interest from demographic historians. All historians might be interested in Exercise 2 because it provides a useful example of a relational database. Indeed, you should not be deterred from looking at any of the exercises, as they all provide a historical introduction. As you will have already found in this book, the boundaries between the various approaches to historical studies are essentially artificial, and the probability is that in most research projects you will be required to cross over them.

This example uses a local data source to examine the profile of the small saver in mid-Victorian society.

Historical introduction In recent years historians have become interested in the economic life of the working classes: their spending, their income and their savings. For example, John Benson has provided an excellent study of 'penny capitalism' in the nineteenth century; this is a term used to describe the way the working class supplemented their income through self-employment and petty entrepreneurial activity; more recently Paul Johnson has produced a detailed account of working-class savings and spending from 1870 to 1939 (Benson 1983; P. Johnson 1992). Both these studies provide valuable insight into much neglected aspects of working-class life: savings, income and spending. In particular the question of working-class savings is important, because it relates to both economic and cultural issues, i.e. the standard of living of the working class and the cultural ideology of thrift.

The nineteenth century saw the development of institutions which were devoted towards mobilising the savings of the small investor; foremost amongst these were the savings banks. These banks were small-scale financial institutions aimed at managing the savings of the 'industrious classes'. As early as 1828 legislation was passed to provide protection to savings-bank investors and to increase the confidence of the small saver in these institutions. The purpose of the legislation was to expand the number of savers rather than mobilise their savings for wider investment purposes. The money deposited was managed by a board of unpaid trustees who supervised a salaried managerial staff. A maximum of £30 per depositor per annum was allowed under the legal rules of the banks and was re-invested with the Commissioners of the National Debt. These banks were conducive to a culture of saving rather than risk-taking investment. Their stated aim was to create amongst the 'industrious classes' a culture of thrift (Lloyd-Jones and Lewis 1990b: 1–4). But this begs the question, who were the 'industrious classes'? One witness giving evidence to the 1850 Select Committee on Savings Banks claimed that the largest group of depositors were not working men but small tradesmen, masters and gentlemen's servants (Parliamentary Papers 1850: 67). To test this assertion you can explore the pattern of investment in these banks at the local level by examining the Sheffield Savings Bank. This bank was founded in 1817 and the money value of deposits rose rapidly throughout the nineteenth century from £4,056 in 1819 to £215,000 in 1850, and £1,161,000 by 1890. It is worth noting here that the nineteenth century was generally a century of falling prices, and the increase in the value of the deposits in the bank between 1817 and 1890 was not inflated by rising prices. A selection of reading to enhance the study is as follows: Benson J., *The Penny Capitalists: A Study of Nineteenth-Century Working-class Entrepreneurs* (1983); Johnson P., *Saving and Spending: The Working-class Economy in Britain 1870–1939* (1992); Lewis M.J. and Lloyd-Jones R, 'Small Savers in the Mid-Victorian Period', *Sheffield School of Cultural Studies Pamphlet* (1990b); Parliamentary Papers, 9 Geo. Cap. 92, 1828, *The Law Relating to Savings*

Banks in England and Wales, p. 3; Parliamentary Papers, 1850 (508), *Report of the Select Committee on the Savings of the Middle and Working Classes*; see especially the evidence of J. S. Mill; Payne P. L., 'The Savings Bank of Glasgow 1836–1914', in P. L. Payne (ed.), *Studies in Scottish Business History* (1967); Pollard S., *A History of Labour in Sheffield* (1959), p. 27. Smiles S., *Self Help* (1895). Full details can be found in the bibliography.

Data for the exercise The legal parameters governing the operation of savings banks required them to keep a declaration book of depositors. For the Sheffield Savings Bank there is a continuous run of these books from 1861 to 1930. These were deposited in the Sheffield Archives in the 1970s by the Trustee Savings Bank (TSB Records). These provide a mine of information on the profile of depositors and a sample entry in the Declaration Book for 1861 is shown as Table 10.2. This provides biographical details on depositors.

Table 10.2 Sample record from Trustee Savings Bank Declaration Book, 1861

Date	Progressive number	Reference number	Name	Residence	Trade or occupation	Age	Place of birth
5 January	28643	20856	Rachel Naylor	Change Alley	Domestic servant	19	Sheffield

Note that when an infant or married woman was recorded as a depositor, the occupation of the father or husband was recorded. Thus the gender codes used in Data Set 1A reflect the gender of the account holder. The information from the 1861 Declaration Book was sampled, i.e. we took a 1 in 10 sample of depositors. The total number of depositors in the Bank in 1861 was 2,472 and we decided that a 1 in 10 sample would provide an ideal number for a small database, and reflect a representative population of the total number of depositors. The key information from this sample has been conceptualised and is reproduced in Data Set 1A. The conceptualisation of the data was informed by the basic set of aims and objectives of the study. These were to establish a profile of depositors based on the age, gender, and socio-economic background of the small saver in the mid-Victorian period. Further, each record extracted was given a depositor's ID (identification) number. This uniquely identifies the individual records on depositors extracted from the source. Study Data Set 1A and then complete the tasks in the next section.

Tasks	1	Design a database table to capture the information in Data Set 1A.
	2	Enter the information from Data Set 1A into the database table you have designed.
	3	What questions would you ask of the information contained in your database? As a starting point you

might want to examine the information contained in the field for occupation. This is a key field in your database and provides an insight into the type of depositor who invested in the bank. Did depositors come from a particular occupation group? You will need to shape queries to address this broad question. To help you undertake this the following provides some guidelines:

- Create a new table by performing a Make Table Query which groups all the different occupations in alphabetical order and counts the number of depositors relating to each occupational description. You did a similar exercise in Chapter 9 (see Stage 8, Exercises 2 and 8). This will display a wide variety of occupation types, but for purposes of analysis you will want to categorise this data into general occupational categories to reflect the city's economic structure. Here, of course, you have to use your skills as a historian to determine how the occupational data is to be categorised. To help you in this, Table 10.3 provides you with 15 general occupation categories which reflect the city's economic structure (Lloyd-Jones and Lewis 1990b: 12). Codes 3 to 13 reflect well-established categories of information derived from studying the Standard

Table 10.3 General occupation categories for depositors

Code	Occupation description
1	Light trades
2	Heavy trades
3	Domestic service and other services
4	Primary production, e.g. agriculture and mining
5	Small-scale manufacturing
6	Building/construction
7	Hotel and drink trades
8	Wholesale
9	Office workers
10	Management/professional
11	Minor professional
12	Municipal/local government/legal
13	Transport
14	Miscellaneous
15	No occupation

Table 10.4 Occupation descriptions with relationship to light and heavy trades

Occupation description	Occupation description
Light trades	Heavy trades
Chaser	Engine fitter
Cutler	Engine tenter
Edge tool grinder	Engineers tool fitter
File cutter	Furnace man
File smith	Iron moulder
German silver polisher	Plate springer
Metal smith	Sheet roller
Pen blade forger	Steel forger
Razor grinder	Steel melter
Saw handle maker	Steel moulder
Saw maker	Wire cutter
Scale and spring maker	
Scale cutter	
Scissors smith	
Scythe smith	
Sickle grinder	
Silver brusher	
Silver polisher	
Silversmith	
Spring knife cutler	
Spring maker	
Table blade maker	
Table blade striker	
Table knife cutler	
Table knife hafter	
Table knife striker	
White metal maker	

Industrial Classification. Categories 1 and 2, however, are more specific to the industrial structure of the steel city of Sheffield in the nineteenth century. The light trades represent workers in industries such as cutlery, tool making and silver work, while the heavy trades capture those workers in the steel works, heavy engineering and foundry work, and armaments. This distinction has been used in Sidney Pollard's splendid monograph on the history of labour in Sheffield (Pollard 1959). Category 14 is included as a catch-all category for occupation descriptions that do not easily lend themselves to a general definition. The final category, 15, is for those depositors who were recorded in the depositors' lists as having no specific occupation. Coding is a well-established procedure in History and Computing, and at this stage we do not want to get engaged in a long discussion on such issues. If you want more details on the use of coding in building historical databases then see Blumin (1990). For a steel city such as Sheffield, the two key categories are those for the light and heavy metal trades. The light trades, in particular, were characterised by a complex sub-division of labour and the use of skilled artisan labour. To help you classify these general categories the occupation descriptions in your database relating to the light and heavy trades are shown in Table 10.4.

- Add a new field to the new table you created and work through the records entering the codes (1 or 2) for the light and heavy trades shown in Table 10.3 to the new field.
- Now work through the data and determine which occupation descriptions match the other categories in Table 10.3. If you are uncertain of a category then use the miscellaneous category (code 14), and of course if you think it appropriate you can build on the occupation categories shown in Table 10.3 by adding your own classifications.
- You can now perform another grouped query to count the number of depositors in each of the general categories in your database.

After you have completed these tasks you might want to perform queries and address the following questions:

(a) Is there a specific age structure of depositors?
(b) What is the gender balance of depositors, e.g. were there more male than female depositors?
(c) What is the balance of depositors between those born outside the city and those born within the city?

4 Present the findings from your interrogation of the database in the form of a short report, i.e. perhaps between 500 and 1,000 words.

Further study

The queries you performed in this exercise provide an insight into the small saver in a mid-Victorian city and enable you to undertake a small-scale independent project. But the data source used is potentially a rich one, and you could use your expertise to expand the database to include a broader survey of the Victorian small saver. The Depositors Declaration books run annually from 1861 to 1930 and you might want to build relational database tables to explore whether there were changes in the clientele using the Savings Bank in the second half of the nineteenth century. Further, deposit books exist for other cities and therefore you might want to undertake a comparative study. The combination of a rich local source with an understanding of the use of a database management system may allow you to extend a small-scale project to a much wider exercise with the potential for original research.

This exercise uses regional data on the cotton industry and makes an ideal project for students interested in the pattern of regional economic and business development.

Historical introduction

Recent studies of the Industrial Revolution in Britain, notably by N. F. R. Crafts (Crafts 1985), have called into question the whole notion of an Industrial Revolution bringing with it dramatic changes in the economy. This has helped to establish a current view that economic change was gradual and less dramatic than previously believed. However, not all economic historians are convinced by this view. Pat Hudson and Maxine Berg, for example, have emphasised the importance of the regional perspective when exploring the changes associated with the Industrial Revolution (Hudson 1989; Berg and Hudson 1992). At a regional level the impact of industrial change was particularly felt in Lancashire where the rise of cotton textiles, associated with the diffusion of factory-based production, created the notion of the industrial region. Any examination of the economic and business changes associated with the Industrial Revolution in Britain necessitates an understanding of the 'leading sector' of cotton. The cotton industry from the 1780s embarked upon an accelerated growth path which saw it become the dominant manufacturing industry of the Industrial Revolution. In the first three decades of the nineteenth century its growth was 'extraordinary' (Berg 1980: 23).

As an American economic historian, Donald McCloskey, argues: 'ingenuity governed the Industrial Revolution' (McCloskey 1981: 108). Symbolic of this ingenuity were the major innovations associated with cotton textiles (notably Arkwright's water frame, Hargreaves's spinning jenny, Crompton's spinning mule and Cartwright's power loom), and the linking of the cotton factory with the Industrial Revolution. By the end of the Napoleonic Wars in 1815 the spinning branch of the industry was almost entirely a factory-based activity, and the weaving branch was subsequently transformed from the 1820s by the rapid diffusion of the power loom (Berg 1980: 23). Between 1780 and 1840 the cotton trade increased its output at an average rate of 7.4 per cent per annum, six times faster than the growth of population in Britain (Farnie 1979: 7). This growth of output was based on increased labour productivity: the number of operative hours required to process 100 lb of cotton fell from approximately 2,000 in 1780 to less than 200 by the mid-1820s (Chapman 1987: 20).

As productivity increased it brought forth a fall in the price of cotton goods which stimulated growth in both domestic (see Edwards 1967: Chapter 3) and foreign markets. It was in the export sector of the economy that the industry was to experience long-term success. In 1761 cotton goods were Britain's sixth most valuable export, by 1783 they were second, and by 1803 they were the most valuable. Between 1785 and 1830 cotton exports 'expanded in value 50 percent faster than all other domestic exports' and 'undoubtedly increased the role of foreign trade in the national economy' (Farnie 1979: 10). From a commercial perspective cotton was an international industry importing raw cotton and exporting yarn and cloth (Farnie 1979: 10). However, geographically it was highly localised in one region, Lancashire. It was in this region where the industry was to grow and prosper, and by the First World War half of the world's entire cotton factory equipment was in this region. The two great centres of the trade were Liverpool, the port for the import of raw cotton and the export of yarn and cotton goods, and Manchester, the manufacturing 'cottonopolis' of the Industrial Revolution (Farnie 1979: 10; Lloyd-Jones and Lewis 1988: 1, 23; M. Williams with Farnie 1992: 14). Although it would be misleading to suggest that the economic and social history of Britain between 1780 and 1840 could be written in terms of the development of this one industry, nevertheless it had a profound effect on the changes in the economy and society we associate with the period of the Industrial Revolution.

Yet, the impact of the factory cannot be explored independently from the business unit which managed and operated it, i.e. the business firm. Our vision of the cotton industry is clouded by notions of large capitalist firms employing a mass factory workforce and characterised by frequent conflicts between employers and labour. But such an observation requires further examination, and the aim of this exercise is to study the structural aspects of the Lancashire cotton industry in the Industrial Revolution. By structural aspects we mean the size distribution of firms (i.e. was the industry dominated by large firms?), their locational pattern across the Lancashire cotton towns, and the technical processes which defined their firm type (i.e. single-process spinning, single-process weaving, or integrated firms which combined both spinning and weaving). In this exercise you will examine these structural aspects by creating a database from a number of historical sources.

Supplementary reading is provided by the following: Berg M., *The Machinery Question and the Making of Political Economy, 1815–1848* (1980); Berg M. and Hudson P., 'Rehabilitating the Industrial Revolution', *Economic History Review*, vol. 45 (1992); Chapman S. D., 'Financial Constraints on the Growth of Firms in the Cotton Industry, 1790–1850', *Economic History Review*, vol. 32 (1979); Chapman S. D., *The Cotton Industry in the Industrial Revolution* (1987); Crafts N. F. R., *British Economic Growth During the Industrial Revolution* (1985); Edwards M. M., *The Growth of the British Cotton Trade 1780–1815* (1967: Chapter 3); Farnie D. A., *The English Cotton Industry and the World Market, 1815 to 1896* (1979); Gatrell V. A. C., 'Labour, Power, and the Size of Firms in Lancashire Cotton in the Second Quarter of the Nineteenth Century', *Economic History Review*, vol. 30 (1977); Hudson P., *The Industrial Revolution* (1992); Hudson P. (ed.), *Regions and Industries: A Perspective on the Industrial Revolution in Britain* (1989); Lee C. H., *A Cotton Enterprise 1795–1840: A History of McConell and Kennedy, Fine Cotton Spinners* (1972); Lloyd-Jones R. and Le Roux A.A., 'The Size of Firms in the Cotton Industry: Manchester 1815–1841', *Economic History Review*, vol. 33

(1980); Lloyd-Jones R. and Lewis M.J., *Manchester and the Age of the Factory: The Business Structure of Cottonopolis in the Industrial Revolution* (1988); Williams M. with Farnie D. A., *Cotton Mills in Greater Manchester* (1992).

Data for the exercise

Data Set 2A contains conceptualised information collected from an important survey of Lancashire cotton firms of 1833 (see Chapter 8 also). The information was compiled by S. Stanway, a Manchester accountant. Stanway was commissioned by the factory inspectors in 1833 to gather information on Lancashire and Cheshire cotton firms, and his survey comprised 151 firms in total. Detailed though this information was, the Commissioner's Report did not give the names of the firms or their locations. The data was reproduced in full by Dr Andrew Ure in 1836, in his notable investigation: *The Cotton Manufacture of Great Britain Systematically Investigated* (Ure 1836). Ure was a supporter of the factory system, and was interested in the structural features of firms and also the pattern of wages paid in the industry. It is the latter work by Ure which has been used to provide the information in Data Set 2A.

The key information from this sample has been conceptualised. This data includes the name of the firm, the number of factories the firm operated (firms could operate more than one factory), the towns in which they were located, and data on employment. The final category contains codes identifying the type of business activity they were involved in: S for spinning only, W for weaving only, and I for integrated, i.e. combining both types of activity.

Data Set 2B contains information on the important cotton town of Stockport for 1832 extracted from a Parliamentary Select Committee in 1832 (Parliamentary Papers 1832). The information relates to cotton spinning. The name of the firm is provided, as is information on the spinning technology used and the total number of spindles employed by the firm. The information on technology is important because it shows the scale of operations of the firm. The standard technology used in cotton spinning in the first half of the nineteenth century, indeed throughout the nineteenth century, was the mule. This was a steam-driven machine whose size was determined by the number of spindles it operated. In the 1820s some firms began introducing long mules (mules with over 300 spindles per machine), while other firms remained committed to small mules (less than 300 spindles) (Catling 1978: 41–42; Lloyd-Jones and Lewis 1988: 201–203). There were also firms employing throstle spinning, a process largely employing female workers. Although throstle spinning was steam-driven, it was a throwback to Arkwright's water frame. The continued deployment of throstle spinning and the small mule shows the continuation of older forms of technology in the industry. Finally, the size of firm may be determined by the total number of spindles used, a further indicator to that of employment. Although the data set is relatively small, it can be related to the information for Stockport firms in the larger Data Set 2A for 1833.

Data Sets 2C and 2D contain information on Manchester, 'the heart of a system of cities comprising the domain of cottonia' (M. Williams with Farnie 1992: 14). These data sets allow you to study the factory system at the very centre of the Lancashire industry. Both data sets contain information for 1815, and can be used to construct related database tables. The data was extracted from the Poor Law Assessment Books (Manchester Archives) which contain much information on property in the town (Lloyd-Jones and Lewis 1988: Chapter 3; 1990a). Data Set 2C provides information on factories: each factory is given a unique number, and the rateable value of the factory is given. The rateable value is used as an indicator of the size of the factory because it is an approximation of the value of the factory building. The rate book also distinguished between the valuation of the whole building and of parts of the same building. Thus Data Set 2D is concerned with information relating to the firm and not the factory. The factory and the firm are two different entities because while some firms might occupy all of a factory there were cases where different firms shared part of the same factory (Lloyd-Jones and Lewis 1988: 16). Consequently, there could be more firms than actual factories. This is an example of a one-to-many relationship as discussed in Chapter 8. The occurrence of one entity (the factory) in Data Set 2C may have more than one occurrence of an entity (the firm) in Data Set 2D. The data set for firms contains a common category of information (Factory Number). When you have constructed two database tables you can then link the records through the common field. It also contains a Firm Number, uniquely identifying the individual firm, the name of the firm, and the rateable value of the factory or part of factory occupied by the firm. The last therefore provides an estimate of the size of the firm, not simply the factory, because it captures the rateable values of firms that occupied only a part of a factory premise. You can therefore define firms as Wholly Occupied Firms (occupied all of factory) or Shared Part Factory Firms (shared part of factory). Study the data sets and then complete the following tasks.

Tasks

1   Design a database table to capture the information in Data Set 2A.
2   Enter the information from Data Set 2A into the database table you have designed.
3   What queries would you make of the information contained in your database? You might want to develop queries on the following lines:

(a) What is the pattern of firm type by process, i.e. how many firms were single-process spinners (code S), single-process weavers (code W), or integrated firms (code I)?
(b) How many firms in the survey were situated in different locations, e.g. Manchester, Stockport, etc.? Remember the information is only partial, i.e. the survey did not record all firms in Lancashire.
(c) What was the size structure of firms in the survey? One measurement of the size of firms is by employment. An employment estimator for size is

Table 10.5 Size category estimators by employment

Firm size category	Employment scale
Small	1–150
Medium	151–500
Large	501+

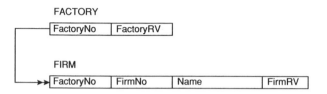

Figure 10.1 Database table design FACTORY and FIRM database tables

shown in Table 10.5 using the categories calculated by Lloyd-Jones and Le Roux (1980) in their study of Manchester cotton firms between 1815 and 1841. Use these estimators to determine the size pattern across the survey.

(d) What other queries can you create from the 1833 database?

4 Select the records for all the firms in Stockport in your database for 1833. Then build a database table from the information in Data Set 2B. You can then link the records from the 1833 database to those from the new database table you have constructed. What does the data tell you about firms in Stockport?

5 Build two database tables from the information in Data Sets 2C and 2D. To help you with the design of the database tables, Figure 10.1 provides a possible structure for the tables. The double-headed arrow illustrates the link between the common field (FactoryNo) in the two tables. Make sure you create the common field in both tables. Link the tables and perform queries. Group the records by factory so that you can compare the number of firms that occupied a whole factory (Wholly Occupied Factory Firms) or shared part of a factory (Shared Part Factory Firms). To allow a comparison of your findings with another time date, Table 10.6 shows the conclusions from the analysis of the data on firms and factories for 1825 (Lloyd-Jones and Lewis

Table 10.6 Factory occupancy by firm, 1825

Total number of factory firms	Shared part factory firms	Wholly occupied factory firms
82	11	57

Note: In addition, 14 firms occupied factories which were recorded as part empty.

1988: 107). It shows quite clearly the predominance of wholly occupied firms. How does this compare with your findings for 1815?

6 Present the findings from your interrogation of the database in the form of a short report. You should also question the extent to which the 1833 sample is sufficiently representative for determining the structural aspects of the industry.

<table>
<tr><td>**Further study**</td><td>There are at least two ways you could extend this study further:</td></tr>
</table>

- By use of a more extensive survey of the Lancashire cotton industry by the Factory Inspector for Lancashire, Leonard Horner, in 1841 (Parliamentary Papers 1841). Using this later evidence, you could examine broad changes in the industry, e.g. the rise of the combined firm and changes in size structure.
- By using the 1833 survey as a basis for focusing in on a particular cotton town to study and build relational database tables. There is a range of material for cotton towns such as Manchester, Stockport, Ashton-under-Lyne and Bolton for the 1830s and 1840s.

**Exercise 3
Assisted
Emigration
to Australia,
1825–1832**

This exercise uses official national data to investigate the type of emigrant who moved to the colony of New South Wales under state-assisted emigration schemes between 1825 and 1832.

<table>
<tr><td>**Historical introduction**</td><td>Following the end of the Napoleonic Wars there was an acceleration of emigration from Britain, and Ireland, both to the USA and the Colonies. The emigration issue became embroiled in debates over the Poor Law and the Malthusian controversy over rising population. As the Under-Secretary for War and the Colonies, John Wilmot Horton, stated in 1823:</td></tr>
</table>

I consider it [colonisation] only as the best and cheapest mode of dispensing of that superfluous population from the general labour market, which I contend to be the main remedy for the distressed condition of the labouring classes in the United Kingdom.

(Cited in Carrothers 1929: 53)

In the 1820s Horton pushed in Parliament for assisted emigration schemes, and, working behind the scenes, he was influential in shaping the conclusions of the 1826 *Select Committee on Emigration* (Parliamentary Papers 1827). He urged a broad programme of emigration, 'financed in Britain by borrowing on the security of the Poor Law, and in Ireland [as yet with no Poor Law] by landlords who would be able to rationalise their estates'. In either case, the aim was identical. to spend money to remove paupers to strengthen the position of the Colonies instead of their being maintained indefinitely at home. Horton, however, found little support from his own government and only managed to persuade Parliament to grant £65,000 on limited schemes between 1823 and 1827. These schemes were considered for Canada, New South Wales and Van Diemen's Land. It is estimated that between 1821 and 1831 some 196,000 emigrants left the United Kingdom (three-fifths from Ireland) (Carrothers 1929: Chapter 2); but who among them were assisted emigrants, and more importantly did they belong to the pauper classes? A clue to which groups took advantage of assisted emigration schemes may be gleaned from the *Second Select Committee Report on Emigration* published in 1827. It reported that,

> In addition to those ordinary causes, which in many parts of the United Kingdom appear to have led to a superabundant population, or rather to a disproportion between the demand and the supply of labour, an important change has been wrought, and is still in gradual but certain progress, in the conditions of some of the manufacturing districts, by the transition from hand loom to power loom weaving.
>
> (Parliamentary Papers 1827)

The implication of this Report suggests that weavers would form a significant proportion of those who received assisted schemes to emigrate. To examine this issue, you will use data on assisted emigrants to New South Wales.

Further reading on emigration is to be found in: Carrothers W. A., *Emigration From the British Isles* (1929); Bythell D., *The Handloom Weavers* (1969); Glass D. V. and Taylor P. A. M., *Population and Emigration* (1976); Johnson H. J. M., *British Emigration Policy 1815–30: Shovelling Out Paupers* (1972); Lloyd T. O., *The British Empire 1558–1983* (1984); Richards E., 'How Did Poor People Emigrate from the British Isles to Australia in the Nineteenth Century?' *Journal of British Studies*, vol. 22 (1993); Shaw A. G., 'British Attitudes to the Colonies 1820–1850', *Journal of British Studies*, vol. 9 (1969).

<table>
<tr><td>

Data for the exercise

</td><td>

Data Set 3A contains conceptualised information on assisted emigrants to New South Wales over the period 1825–1832. This data was extracted from information supplied to the 1833 *Select Committee on Emigration* (Parliamentary Papers 1833) and includes the family ID number identifying the head of household, their previous trade (i.e. occupation) in Britain, the number of persons in

</td></tr>
</table>

each family, and the amount of assistance granted to each family from the Board of Emigration. You should study the data in Data Set 3A and then complete the tasks in the next section.

1   Design a database table to capture the information in Data Set 3A.

2   Enter the information from Data Set 3A into the database table you have designed.

3   What queries would you make of the information contained in your database? For example, create a new table by performing a Make Table Query which groups all the different occupations in alphabetical order and counts the number of different occupation types (see Chapter 9, Stage 8, Exercises 2 and 8). You then might want to test the following propositions:

(a) Can you detect a pattern in the previous occupational backgrounds of assisted emigrants?

(b) Is there a link between the pattern detected and pauperism (see historical introduction to this exercise).

What other queries can you create from the database?

4   Present the findings from your interrogation of the database in the form of a short report.

Further study   You might wish to extend the analysis into the 1830s and 1840s when Australia became an important recipient of British emigrants under the scheme of Edward Gibbon Wakefield. You might also explore a particular region associated with a heavy concentration of hand-loom weavers and examine local evidence concerning the movement of labour out of a declining trade. There is rich detail on the movement of emigrants in Government Blue Books (Parliamentary Papers), and the topic is one that cuts across a number of boundaries in historical studies, i.e. ranging from questions of pauperism and poverty to issues of Colonial policy and reform and the schemes of Edward Gibon Wakefield in the 1830s and 1840s.

Appendices

Data Set for Workshop Exercises in Chapter 4

Data Set A

The British labour force 1841–1931 (males and females)

Date	Male workers (thousands)	Female workers (thousands)	Proportion males (%)	Proportion females (%)
1841	5,093	1,815		
1851	6,545	2,832		
1861	7,266	3,254		
1871	8,220	3,650		
1881	8,852	3,887		
1891	10,010	4,489		
1901	11,548	4,751		
1911	12,927	5,413		
1921	13,656	5,699		
1931	14,790	6,265		

Source: Mitchell and Deane 1962: 60–63

Data Sets for Workshop Exercises in Chapter 5

Data Set A

The political parties in the House of Commons, 1900 and 1910

Party	Seats 1900	Seats 1906	Seats Jan 1910	Seats Dec 1910
Conservative	402	157	273	272
Liberal	184	400	275	272
Labour	2	30	40	42
Home Rule	82	83	82	84

Source: A.R. Ball 1987: 15–16

Note: The number of seats for the Conservatives in 1900 includes 68 seats held by the Liberal Unionists

Data Set B

Gross public expenditure on defence and education, art and science, 1870–1914

Date	Defence £ million	Education, art, science £ million
1870	21.5	1.6
1871	21.1	1.8
1872	24.2	1.9
1873	23.1	2.2
1874	23.6	2.4
1875	24.5	2.6
1876	25.0	2.9
1877	25.5	3.2
1878	25.1	3.6
1879	28.7	4.0
1880	25.2	4.0
1881	25.2	4.3
1882	26.3	4.4
1883	25.4	4.6

Data Set B cont'd

Date	Defence £ million	Education, art, science £ million
1884	26.8	4.8
1885	30.0	5.1
1886	29.7	5.3
1887	31.7	5.5
1888	30.5	5.6
1889	29.0	5.7
1890	32.7	5.8
1891	33.4	6.1
1892	34.2	7.0
1893	33.2	8.9
1894	33.4	9.4
1895	35.4	9.8
1896	38.2	10.3
1897	40.5	10.7
1898	40.2	11.5
1899	44.1	12.0
1900	69.6	12.2
1901	121.0	12.5
1902	123.3	12.8
1903	100.6	13.3
1904	72.2	14.6
1905	66.0	15.6
1906	63.2	16.4
1907	59.2	16.9
1908	58.2	17.4
1909	59.0	17.4
1910	63.0	17.9
1911	67.8	18.7
1912	70.5	19.0
1913	72.5	19.5
1914	77.1	19.5

Source: Mitchell and Deane 1962: 397–398

Data Sets for Workshop Exercises in Chapter 6

Data Set A

Index of cost of living and money earnings: Sheffield light and heavy trades, 1851–1911 (1900=100)

Year	Cost of living	Money earnings Light trades	Money earnings Heavy trades
1851	100.5	78	71
1861	115.9	75	73
1871	116.4	100	89
1881	110.8	86	87
1891	101.5	96	83
1901	101.0	95	94
1911	105.9	98	109

Source: Pollard 1959: 339–340

Data Set B

Wages and earnings in the Sheffield light trades, 1851–1911 (index, 1900 = 100)

Date	Cost of living	Money earnings Light trades	Money earnings Heavy trades
1851	100.5	78	71
1852	100.5	79	73
1853	107.6	82	77
1854	121.5	82	72
1855	125.1	80	72
1856	124.6	89	68
1857	119.0	88	75
1858	110.8	82	65
1859	109.7	82	65
1860	113.3	83	68
1861	115.9	75	73

Data Set B cont'd

Date	Cost of living	Money earnings Light trades	Money earnings Heavy trades
1862	113.3	74	75
1863	110.3	75	79
1864	109.2	81	77
1865	110.3	89	84
1866	116.4	97	82
1867	122.6	91	75
1868	120.5	82	70
1869	115.9	83	78
1870	115.9	86	83
1871	116.4	100	89
1872	122.6	104	97
1873	123.6	100	104
1874	120.0	93	91
1875	116.4	87	86
1876	114.4	83	82
1877	116.4	83	83
1878	114.4	83	72
1879	109.2	82	68
1880	112.3	83	79
1881	110.8	86	87
1882	111.3	92	93
1883	109.2	92	92
1884	107.2	81	85
1885	103.6	77	76
1886	100.5	76	68
1887	98.5	79	74
1888	98.5	83	77
1889	100.5	91	86
1890	100.5	93	90
1891	101.5	96	83
1892	101.5	88	72
1893	99.0	84	68
1894	97.4	86	73
1895	95.4	89	79
1896	94.9	98	86
1897	96.9	103	90
1898	98.5	98	94
1899	97.4	101	101
1900	100.0	100	100

Data Set B cont'd

Date	Cost of living	Money earnings Light trades	Money earnings Heavy trades
1901	101.0	95	94
1902	102.0	93	86
1903	101.2	88	92
1904	101.2	85	87
1905	101.4	83	90
1906	101.2	90	97
1907	103.4	88	104
1908	104.6	84	90
1909	104.9	86	90
1910	105.7	93	101
1911	105.9	98	109

Source: Pollard 1959: 339–340

Data Set C

Real earnings in coal, shipbuilding and engineering, and cotton (1891=100)

Date	Real earnings Coal	Real earnings Shipbuilding/engineering	Real earnings Cotton
1851		74	55
1852		75	56
1853		77	59
1854		82	58
1855		82	59
1856		82	62
1857		82	62
1858		80	62
1859		80	64
1860		79	68
1861		80	68
1862		81	67
1863		81	66
1864		82	66
1865		84	71
1866		85	77
1867		83	77
1868		83	79
1869		83	78
1870		84	81
1871		85	85

Data Set C cont'd

Date	Real earnings Coal	Real earnings Shipbuilding/engineering	Real earnings Cotton
1872		89	87
1873		92	89
1874		94	90
1875		94	90
1876		94	92
1877		95	94
1878		94	88
1879		89	84
1880	71	90	87
1881	73	92	90
1882	78	95	90
1883	79	95	91
1884	76	94	91
1885	73	92	90
1886	70	90	89
1887	70	91	90
1888	74	95	94
1889	87	98	95
1890	99	100	96
1891	100	100	100
1892	91	99	101
1893	93	98	101
1894	88	98	101
1895	84	98	101
1896	83	101	102
1897	84	103	102
1898	91	105	103
1899	96	108	104
1900	116	108	107
1901	109	100	108
1902	101	108	107
1903	98	106	107
1904	95	106	108
1905	94	106	110
1906	96		115
1907	111		
1908	108		
1909	103		
1910	104		
1911	102		

Source: Mitchell and Deane 1962: 349–351

Data Set D

Real earnings in the UK, 1851–1902, adjusted for unemployment

Date	Real earnings adjusted for unemployment
1851	102
1852	100
1853	107
1854	97
1855	94
1856	95
1857	94
1858	94
1859	104
1860	105
1861	99
1862	100
1863	107
1864	118
1865	120
1866	117
1867	105
1868	105
1869	111
1870	118
1871	125
1872	126
1873	132
1874	136
1875	138
1876	136
1877	132
1878	128
1879	126
1880	132
1881	136
1882	138
1883	142
1884	138
1885	140
1886	142

Data Set D cont'd

Date	Real earnings adjusted for unemployment
1887	149
1888	155
1889	161
1890	169
1891	166
1892	159
1893	161
1894	165
1895	170
1896	177
1897	176
1898	176
1899	183
1900	184
1901	181
1902	176

Source: Mitchell and Deane 1962: 347–348

Appendix 4

Data Sets for Chapter 7

Data Sets for Historical Theme 1

Data Set 1A

General Election results 1900–1910: total votes

Party	1900	1906	Jan 1910	Dec 1910
Conservative	1,797,444	2,451,454	3,127,887	2,420,566
Liberal	1,568,141	2,757,883	2,880,581	2,295,888
Labour	63,304	329,748	505,657	371,772
Home Rule	90,076	35,031	124,586	131,375
Others	544	52,387	28,693	8,768
Total				

Source: Butler 1972: 235

Data Set 1B

The economic composition of the House of Commons elected in 1906 and January and December 1910

Economic category	1906	Jan 1910	Dec 1910
Landowners	129	171	164
Heavy industry	100	95	90
Transport	121	107	99
Public utilities	19	20	19
Publishing	37	40	30
Misc. manufactures	20	18	19
Finance	229	226	227
Merchants	82	70	76
Mining and oil	51	50	47
Construction	12	13	16
Plantation owners	27	21	20
Food and drink	33	35	34
Textiles	34	24	25

Source: Compiled from J. A. Thomas 1958: 14–16

Data Set 1C

The economic composition of the House of Commons by party elected in 1906 and January and December 1910

Economic category	1906		Jan 1910		Dec 1910	
	Liberal	Conservative	Liberal	Conservative	Liberal	Conservative
Landowners	62	64	39	130	38	123
Heavy industry	70	30	44	51	47	43
Transport	66	49	51	52	45	48
Public Utilities	16	3	13	7	10	7
Publishing	27	6	23	11	18	8
Misc. manufactures	12	8	13	5	15	4
Finance	134	88	91	126	92	124
Merchants	54	12	38	19	40	20
Mining and oil	32	16	25	23	26	19
Construction	12	0	9	4	11	5
Plantation owners	20	5	12	6	12	5
Food and drink	15	13	10	21	10	20
Textiles	31	3	20	4	20	5

Source: Compiled from J. A. Thomas 1958: 14–16

Data Sets for Historical Theme 2

Data Set 2A

GNP 1929–1940 at 1929 prices

Date	Total GNP (billion $)	Civilian population (millions)
1929	104.4	121.8
1930	91.1	123.1
1931	76.3	124.0
1932	58.5	124.8
1933	56.0	125.6
1934	65.0	126.4
1935	72.5	127.2
1936	82.7	128.1
1937	90.8	128.8
1938	85.2	129.8
1939	91.1	130.9
1940	100.6	131.9

Source: Compiled from *Historical Statistics of the United States* 1960: Series D1–D12

Data Set 2B

Labour force 1929–1940, thousands of persons aged 14+

Year	Total civilian labour force (millions)	Unemployed (millions)
1929	49,180	1,550
1930	49,820	4,340
1931	50,420	8,020
1932	51,000	12,060
1933	51,590	12,830
1934	52,230	11,340
1935	52,870	10,610
1936	53,440	9,030
1937	54,000	7,700
1938	54,610	10,390
1939	55,230	9,480
1940	55,640	8,120

Source: Compiled from *Historical Statistics of the United States* 1960: Series A1–A3, F1–F5

Data Set 2C

Indicators of aggregate demand contributions to GNP

Date	Durable goods (billion $)	Non-durable goods (billion $)	Services (billion $)	Total investment (billion $)
1929	9.2	37.7	32.1	16.2
1930	7.2	34.0	29.8	10.3
1931	5.5	28.9	26.9	5.5
1932	3.6	22.8	22.9	0.9
1933	3.5	22.3	20.7	1.4
1934	4.2	26.7	21.0	2.9
1935	5.1	29.3	21.9	6.3
1936	6.3	32.8	23.5	8.4
1937	6.9	35.2	25.1	11.7
1938	5.7	34.0	25.0	6.7
1939	6.7	35.1	25.8	9.3
1940	7.8	37.2	26.9	13.2

Source: Compiled from *Historical Statistics of the United States* 1960: Series F67–F86

Data Set 2D

Indicators of manufacturing

	Manufacturing production index (1929=100)	Car production (millions)
1929	100	4.5
1930	83	2.8
1931	67	1.9
1932	52	1.1
1933	63	1.6
1934	71	2.2
1935	82	3.3
1936	95	3.7
1937	105	3.9
1938	82	2.0
1939	100	2.9

Source: Manufacturing index compiled from Potter 1985: 95, Table 20, 137, Table 23; car production compiled from *Historical Statistics of the United States* 1960: Series Q310–Q320.

Data Set 2E

Economic indicators in Germany

Date	Actual GNP (BM)	Potential GNP (BM)	Unemployment (millions)	Private consumption (% of national income)	Private investment (BM)	Industrial production (1928=100)	Production per employed worker all industry (1932=100)	Car production
1928	89.5	89.5	1.4	71.0	9.7	100.0		71,960
1929	89.7	92.4	1.8			100.1		58,774
1930	83.9	95.2	3.1			87.0		43,430
1931	70.4	98.1	4.5			70.1		92,160
1932	57.6	101.0	5.6	83.0	0.3	58.0	100.0	147,050
1933	59.1	104.0	4.8	81.0	3.2	66.0	101.0	205,092
1934	66.5	107.1	2.7	76.0	4.7	83.0	102.0	244,289
1935	74.4	110.3	2.2	71.0	7.2	96.0	107.0	269,005
1936	82.6	113.6	1.6	64.0	9.2	107.0	110.0	276,592
1937	93.2	116.0	0.9	62.0	10.5	117.0	111.0	143,602
1938	104.5	119.5	0.4	59.0	12.2	122.0		

Source: Compiled from Overy 1982: 20, 29,36; Overy 1975: 438

Note: BM = billion marks

The potential GNP is calculated from a hypothetical growth rate of GNP of 2.9% per annum, the figure achieved on average by the German economy, 1870–1913.

Data Sets for Historical Theme 3

Data Set 3A

Total emigration from the British Isles, 1820–1899

Year	Thousands of emigrants				
	North American Colonies	United States	Australia & NZ	Cape of Good Hope & Natal	Others
1820	17.9	6.7			1.1
1821	13.0	5.0	0.3		0.4
1822	16.0	4.1	0.9		0.3
1823	11.4	5.1	0.5		0.2
1824	8.8	5.1	0.8		0.1
1825	8.7	5.5	0.5		0.1
1826	12.8	7.1	0.9		0.1
1827	12.6	14.5	0.7		0.1
1828	12.1	12.8	1.1		0.1
1829	13.3	15.7	2.0		0.2
1830	30.6	24.9	1.2		0.2
1831	58.1	23.4	1.6		0.1
1832	66.3	32.9	3.7		0.2
1833	28.8	29.1	4.1		0.5
1834	40.1	33.1	2.8		0.3
1835	15.6	26.7	1.9		0.3
1836	34.2	37.8	3.1		0.3
1837	29.9	36.8	5.1		0.3
1838	4.6	14.3	14.0		0.3
1839	12.7	33.5	15.8		0.2
1840	32.3	40.6	15.8		2.0
1841	38.2	45.0	32.6		2.8
1842	54.1	63.8	8.5		1.8
1843	23.5	28.3	3.5		1.9
1844	22.9	43.7	2.2		1.9
1845	31.8	58.5	0.8		2.3
1846	43.4	82.2	2.3		1.8
1847	109.7	142.2	4.9		1.5
1848	31.1	188.2	23.9		4.9
1849	41.4	219.4	32.2		6.5
1850	33.0	223.1	16.0		8.8
1851	42.6	267.4	21.5		4.5
1852	32.9	244.3	87.9		3.7

Data Set 3A cont'd

Year	North American Colonies	United States	Australia & NZ	Cape of Good Hope & Natal	Others
1853	34.5	230.9	61.4		3.1
1854	43.8	193.1	83.2		3.4
1855	18.0	103.4	52.3		3.1
1856	16.4	111.8	44.6		3.8
1857	21.0	126.9	61.2		3.7
1858	9.7	59.7	39.3		5.3
1859	6.7	70.3	31.0		12.4
1860	9.8	87.5	24.3		6.9
1861	12.7	49.8	23.7		5.6
1862	15.5	58.7	41.8		5.1
1863	18.1	146.8	53.1		5.8
1864	12.7	147.0	40.9		8.2
1865	17.2	147.3	37.3		8.0
1866	13.3	161.0	24.1		6.5
1867	15.5	159.3	14.5		6.7
1868	21.1	155.5	12.8		6.9
1869	33.9	203.0	14.9		6.2
1870	35.3	196.1	17.1		8.5
1871	32.7	198.8	12.2		8.7
1872	32.2	233.7	15.9		13.4
1873	37.2	233.1	26.4		13.9
1874	25.4	148.2	54.0		13.4
1875	17.4	105.0	35.5		15.9
1876	12.3	75.5	33.2		17.2
1877	9.3	64.0	31.1		15.6
1878	13.8	81.6	37.2		15.1
1879	22.5	134.6	42.2		17.9
1880	29.3	257.3	25.4	9.8	10.4
1881	34.6	307.0	24.1	14.2	11.7
1882	53.5	295.5	38.6	13.6	12.1
1883	53.6	252.2	73.0	6.7	11.6
1884	37.0	203.5	45.9	4.7	12.7
1885	22.9	184.5	40.7	4.0	12.3
1886	30.1	238.4	44.1	4.7	13.6
1887	44.4	296.9	35.2	5.7	14.3
1888	49.1	293.1	31.7	7.7	18.9
1889	38.1	240.4	28.8	15.7	19.7
1890	31.9	233.5	21.6	12.1	16.9

Data Set 3A cont'd

| Year | Thousands of emigrants | | | | |
	North American Colonies	United States	Australia & NZ	Cape of Good Hope & Natal	Others
1891	33.7	252.0	20.0	10.7	18.1
1892	41.9	235.2	16.2	11.6	16.5
1893	50.4	213.2	11.4	16.2	16.5
1894	23.6	159.4	11.1	16.8	15.8
1895	22.4	195.6	10.8	26.0	17.0
1896	22.6	154.5	10.7	35.8	18.3
1897	22.7	132.0	12.4	28.8	17.4
1898	27.5	123.7	11.0	25.6	17.3
1899	33.7	159.1	12.3	18.9	16.8

Source: Compiled from Carrothers 1929: Appendix 1, 305–307

Data Set 3B

Emigration and economic indicators, 1820–1899

Year	United States emigrants (thousands)	Exports by value (£ thousands)	Real earnings (Index 1850=100)	Number of outdoor paupers (thousands)	% in unions unemployed
1820	6.7	3.9			
1821	5.0	6.2			
1822	4.1	6.9			
1823	5.1	5.5			
1824	5.1	6.1			
1825	5.5	7			
1826	7.1	4.7			
1827	14.5	7			
1828	12.8	5.8			
1829	15.7	4.8			
1830	24.9	6.1			
1831	23.4	9.1			
1832	32.9	5.5			
1833	29.1	7.6			
1834	33.1	6.8			
1835	26.7	10.6			
1836	37.8	12.4			
1837	36.8	4.7			
1838	14.3	7.6			
1839	33.5	8.8			

Data Set 3B cont'd

Year	United States emigrants (thousands)	Exports by value (£ thousands)	Real earnings (Index 1850=100)	Number of outdoor paupers (thousands)	% in Unions unemployed
1840	40.6	5.3		1,030	
1841	45.0	7.1		1,107	
1842	63.8	3.5		1,205	
1843	28.3	5.0		1,301	
1844	43.7	7.9		1,247	
1845	58.5	7.1		1,256	
1846	82.2	6.8		1,132	
1847	142.2	11.0		1,456	
1848	188.2	9.6		1,571	
1849	219.4	12.0		955	
1850	223.1	14.9		886	
1851	267.4	14.4	102	827	3.9
1852	244.3	16.6	100	804	6.0
1853	230.9	23.7	107	776	1.7
1854	193.1	21.4	97	753	2.9
1855	103.4	17.3	94	776	5.4
1856	111.8	21.9	95	792	4.7
1857	126.9	19.0	94	762	6.0
1858	59.7	14.5	94	786	11.9
1859	70.3	22.6	104	744	3.8
1860	87.5	21.7	105	695	1.9
1861	49.8	9.1	99	709	5.2
1862	58.7	14.3	100	743	8.4
1863	146.8	15.3	107	872	6.0
1864	147.0	16.7	118	844	2.7
1865	147.3	21.2	120	783	2.1
1866	161.0	28.5	117	746	3.3
1867	159.3	21.8	105	755	7.4
1868	155.5	21.4	105	801	7.9
1869	203.0	24.6	111	817	6.7
1870	196.1	28.3	118	838	3.9
1871	198.8	34.2	125	843	1.6
1872	233.7	40.7	126	791	0.9
1873	233.1	33.6	132	702	1.2
1874	148.2	28.2	136	646	1.7
1875	105.0	21.9	138	616	2.4
1876	75.5	16.8	136	657	3.7
1877	64.0	16.4	132	530	4.7

Data Set 3B cont'd

Year	United States emigrants (thousands)	Exports by value (£ thousands)	Real earnings (Index 1850=100)	Number of outdoor paupers (thousands)	% in unions unemployed
1878	81.6	14.6	128	527	6.8
1879	134.6	20.3	126	555	11.4
1880	257.3	30.9	132	582	5.5
1881	307.0	29.8	136	561	3.5
1882	295.5	31.0	138	557	2.3
1883	252.2	27.4	142	551	2.6
1884	203.5	24.4	138	534	8.1
1885	184.5	2.0	140	533	9.3
1886	238.4	26.8	142	542	10.2
1887	296.9	29.5	149	555	7.6
1888	293.1	28.9	155	554	4.6
1889	240.4	30.3	161	548	2.1
1890	233.5	32.1	169	530	2.1
1891	252.0	27.5	166	515	3.2
1892	235.2	26.5	159	499	5.8
1893	213.2	24.0	161	505	7.5
1894	159.4	18.8	165	519	6.9
1895	195.6	27.9	170	523	5.8
1896	154.5	20.4	177	535	3.3
1897	132.0	21.0	176	530	3.3
1898	123.7	14.7	176	525	2.8
1899	159.1	18.1	183	538	2.0

Source: The data for the value of exports, real earnings and the percentage of unemployed in the unions is compiled from Mitchell and Dean 1962: 64–65, 313–319, 343–345. The number of outdoor paupers is compiled from an excellent statistical series compiled by K. Williams 1983: Statistical Appendix, Section B, Table 4.5.

Data Sets for Chapter 9

Data Set A

Survey of Sheffield cinemas in 1931: data for entry into CINEMA and REMARKS database tables

Record number	Cinema	Address	Financial control	Date of opening	Seating	Remarks
1	Globe Picture Palace	Ecclesall Rd	Ecclesall Picture Palace Ltd	1914	850	Children's matinee: Yes special programme: No Sound: Yes
2	Theatre Royal	Attercliffe	Bryan W	1920	950	Children's matinee: No special programme: No Sound: No
3	Unity Picture Palace	Langsett Rd	Upperthorpe Picture Palace Co Ltd	1913	960	Children's matinee: Yes special programme: Yes Sound: Yes
4	Norfolk Picture Palace	Duke St	Norfolk Picture House Co Ltd	1914	1000	Children's matinee: Yes special programme: No Sound: Yes
5	Abbeydale Picture House	Abbeydale Rd	Abbeydale Picture Co	1920	1100	Children's matinee: No special programme: No Sound: No
6	Electra Palace	Fitzalan Sq	Sheffield District Cinemas Ltd	1912	800	Children's matinee: No special programme: No Sound: No
7	Heeley Green Picture Palace	Gleadless Rd	Heeley Green Picture House Ltd	1914	900	Children's matinee: Yes special programme: No Sound: Yes
8	Page Hall Cinema	Firth Park	Page Hall Cinema Ltd	1921	750	Children's matinee: No special programme: No Sound: No
9	Woodseats Picture Palace	Chesterfield Rd	Heeley & Amalgamated Cinemas Ltd	1926	800	Children's matinee: Yes special programme: No Sound: Yes
10	Regent Theatre	Upwell St	Bronson J	1927	2300	Children's matinee: No special programme: No Sound: Yes
11	Picture Palace	High Green	G Woffender	1920	600	Children's matinee: No special programme: No Sound: Yes
12	Attercliffe Pavilion	Attercliffe	Attercliffe Picture Co	1916	1000	Children's matinee: Yes special programme: Yes Sound: Yes
13	Heeley Colisium	London Rd	Heeley Colisium Ltd	1911	800	Children's matinee: No special programme: No Sound: Yes

Data Set A cont'd

Record number	Cinema	Address	Financial control	Date of opening	Seating	Remarks
14	Park Picture Palace	South Road	Sheffield Park Pictures Ltd	1924	900	Children's matinee: Yes special programme: Yes Sound· Yes
15	Kinema House	Crookes Place	Grosvenor Estate Co Ltd	1926	1100	Children's matinee: Yes special programme: No Sound: Yes
16	Tinsley Picture Palace	Tinsley	Wincobank Picture Co Ltd	1911	650	Children's matinee: No special programme: No Sound: No
17	Woodhouse Picture Palace	Market Place	Scala Cinemas	1914	650	Children's matinee: No special programme:No Sound: No
18	Cinema House	Fargate	Sheffield District Cinemas Ltd	1913	800	Children's matinee: Yes special programme: Yes Sound: Yes
19	Landsdowne Picture Palace	London Rd	Landsdowne Pictures Ltd	1913	1200	Children's matinee: No special programme: No Sound: Yes
20	Crookes Picture Palace	Crookes	Hallamshire Cinemas Ltd	1912	800	Children's matinee: No special programme: No Sound: Yes
21	Attercliffe Theatre Royal	Attercliffe	Scala Cinemas	1904	950	Children's matinee: No special programme: No Sound: Yes
22	Rosco Picture Palace	Infirmary Rd	Sheffield Amusements Ltd	1928	700	Children's matinee: Yes special programme: No Sound: No
23	Hilsborough Park Cinema	Middlewood Rd	Sheffield District Cinemas Ltd	1911	600	Children's matinee: Yes special programme: Yes Sound: No
24	Don Picture Palace	West Bar	Don Palace Picture Co	1921	550	Children's matinee: No special programme: No Sound: Yes
25	Coliseum	Spital Hill	Coliseum Ltd	1912	1050	Children's matinee: No special programme: No Sound: Yes
26	Manor Picture Palace	Ridgeway Rd Intake	Manor Picture Co Ltd	1920	700	Children's matinee: No special programme: No Sound: No
27	Regent Picture House	Barkers Pool	Regent Picture Co	1926	900	Children's matinee: No special programme: No Sound: Yes
28	Victory Picture Palace	Grimesthorpe	Bickler N	1922	800	Children's matinee: Yes special programme: No Sound: Yes
29	Scala Picture Palace	Winter St	Scala Cinemas	1921	1020	Children's matinee: Yes special programme: Yes Sound: Yes
30	Tivoli Picture Palace	Norfolk St	Tivoli Ltd	1920	1000	Children's matinee: No special programme: No Sound: Yes
31	Albert Hall	Barkers Pool	Sheffield District Cinemas Ltd	1902	1200	Children's matinee: No special programme: No Sound: Yes
32	Oxford Picture House	Upperthorpe	Heeley & Amalgamated Cinemas Ltd	1913	800	Children's matinee: Yes special programme: No Sound: Yes

Data Set A cont'd

Record number	Cinema	Address	Financial control	Date of opening	Seating	Remarks
33	Pavillion	Attercliffe Common	Heeley & Amalgamated Cinemas Ltd	1912	750	Children's matinee: Yes special programme: Yes Sound: Yes
34	Darnall Cinema	Darnall	Brindley W C	1912	531	Children's matinee: No special programme: No Sound: No
35	Darnall Picture House	Staniforth Rd	Hallamshire Cinemas Ltd	1912	1000	Children's matinee: Yes special programme: No Sound: Yes
36	Heeley Picture Palace	London Rd	Heeley & Amalgamated Cinemas Ltd	1911	1200	Children's matinee: Yes special programme: No Sound: Yes
37	Lyric Picture House	Main Rd Darnall	Lyric Picture House Ltd	1922	1000	Children's matinee: Yes special programme: Yes Sound: Yes
38	Phoenix Theatre	Hilsborough	Adelphi Ltd	1911	702	Children's matinee: No special programme: No Sound: Yes
39	Palace Theatre	Attercliffe	Palace Theatre Ltd	1914	650	Children's matinee: No special programme: No Sound: No
40	Wicker Picture Palace	Wicker	Wicker Picture House Syndicate	1923	900	Children's matinee: Yes special programme: No Sound: Yes
41	Star Picture House	Ecclesall Rd	Sheffield Premier Pictures Ltd	1924	800	Children's matinee: No special programme: No Sound: Yes
42	Union Street Picture Palace	Union St	Union Pictures Ltd	1910	1000	Children's matinee: No special programme: No Sound: Yes
43	Western Picture Palace	Saint Phillips Rd	Hallamshire Cinemas Ltd	1920	1100	Children's matinee: No special programme: No Sound: Yes
44	Sunbeam Picture House	Barnsley Rd	Sunbeam Pictures Ltd	1925	1200	Children's matinee: Yes special programme: No Sound: Yes
45	Rutland Picture House	Rutland Rd	Rutland Pictures Ltd	1915	890	Children's matinee: Yes special programme: Yes Sound: Yes
46	Central Picture House	The Moor	Central Picture House Ltd	1920	800	Children's matinee: No special programme: No Sound: No
47	Walkley Palladium	South Rd Walkley	Walkley Palladium Ltd	1916	670	Children's matinee: No special programme: No Sound: Yes
48	Chantrey Picture House	Chesterfield Rd	Chantrey Pictures Ltd	1925	700	Children's matinee: Yes special programme: No Sound: Yes
49	Wincobank Picture Palace	Wincobank	Wincobank Picture Palace Ltd	1910	1200	Children's matinee: Yes special programme: No Sound: Yes
50	Adelphi	Vicarage Rd	Adelphi Sheffield Ltd	1920	1350	Children's matinee: No special programme: No Sound: Yes

Data Set B

Survey of Sheffield cinemas: data for entry into PRICE database table

Record	Price	Record	Price	Record	Price
1	3	18	18	34	9
1	9	19	3	35	3
2	4	19	4	35	6
2	9	19	6	36	3
3	4	20	3	36	6
3	8	20	5	37	4
4	2	20	6	37	15
4	6	21	3	38	4
5	4	21	4	38	12
5	9	21	6	39	12
6	6	22	3	40	8
6	12	22	6	40	12
7	5	23	8	41	4
7	8	24	3	41	12
8	6	24	9	42	6
8	12	25	4	43	6
9	3	25	6	43	8
9	8	25	9	44	3
10	8	26	4	44	6
10	28	26	12	45	3
11	5	27	8	45	6
11	9	27	28	46	3
12	2	28	3	46	6
12	6	28	9	47	6
13	4	29	6	47	24
13	6	29	12	48	4
13	12	30	4	48	8
14	6	30	18	48	12
15	4	31	6	49	3
15	12	31	28	49	11
16	4	32	4	50	3
17	4	33	4	50	9
17	6	33	12		
18	6	34	4		

Data Sets for Chapter 10

Data Set 1A

Depositors to the Sheffield Savings Bank, 1861

Depositor's ID	Gender	Occupation	Age	Place of birth
1	F	Spring knife Cutler	1	Sheffield
2	F	Silversmith	1	Sheffield
3	M	Miller	7	Sheffield
4	F	Domestic servant	24	London
5	M	Farmer	10	Hathersage
6	F	Shoemaker	65	London
7	F	Domestic servant	19	Sheffield
8	M	Silver brusher	25	Sheffield
9	F	Single	57	Oswestry
10	M	Sheet Roller	16	Sheffield
11	M	Miner	17	Sheffield
12	F	Silver polisher	5	Skelton
13	M	Miner	35	Devonshire
14	M	Sheet roller	16	Sheffield
15	F	Joiner	1	Sheffield
16	M	Spring maker	27	Sheffield
17	F	Spring knife cutler	9	Sheffield
18	M	Joiner	23	Wakefield
19	M	Hotelier	8	Sheffield
20	F	Warehouseman	20	Edale
21	M	Steel melter	17	Sheffield
22	F	Druggist	24	Sheffield
23	F	Boot and shoe maker	6	Sheffield
24	F	Grocer	25	Huddersfield
25	M	Steel melter	20	Cleveland
26	M	Tinner	20	County Mayo
27	M	Spring knife cutler	24	Sheffield
28	M	Tailor	12	Sheffield

Data Set 1A cont'd

Depositor's ID	Gender	Occupation	Age	Place of birth
29	M	Chaser	16	Sheffield
30	M	Saw maker	14	Portmahon
31	F	Single	20	Sheffield
32	M	Labourer	32	Sheffield
33	F	Publican	3	Sheffield
34	M	Spring knife cutler	37	Sheffield
35	M	Engraver	21	Sheffield
36	M	File Smith	17	Sheffield
37	M	Publican	8	Sheffield
38	F	Butcher	20	Sheffield
39	M	Apprentice grocer	16	Sheffield
40	M	Shoe maker	14	Sheffield
41	F	Publican	6	Sheffield
42	M	Clerk	33	Sheffield
43	M	Mill manager	36	Sheffield
44	F	Single	16	Sheffield
45	F	Single	23	Sheffield
54	M	Forge man	26	Sheffield
55	M	Iron moulder	50	Sheffield
56	M	Butcher	45	Rotherham
57	M	Carrier	21	Selby
58	F	Minister	2	Birmingham
59	M	Saw maker	25	Sheffield
60	M	Merchant	28	Sheffield
61	F	Domestic servant	19	Sheffield
62	M	Pupil teacher	17	Sheffield
63	M	Publican	2	Sheffield
64	F	Domestic servant	17	Wadsley
65	M	Farmer	24	Sheffield
66	M	Ivory carver	27	Sheffield
67	F	Widow	44	Thurlstone
68	F	Domestic servant	20	Sheffield
69	F	Forge man	35	Sheffield
70	F	Domestic servant	21	Sheffield
71	F	File smith	29	Sheffield
72	M	File cutter	26	Sheffield
73	M	File cutter	27	Sheffield
74	M	Cutler	42	Sheffield
75	M	Joiner	23	Ouston Ferry
76	M	Farmer	46	Sheffield

Data Set 1A cont'd

Depositor's ID	Gender	Occupation	Age	Place of birth
77	M	Cabinet maker	19	Sheffield
78	F	Plate springer	35	Sheffield
79	M	Blacksmith	4	Sheffield
80	F	Saw maker	30	Howden
81	F	Joiner	35	Sheffield
82	M	Pen blade forger	24	Sheffield
83	F	Publican	12	Sheffield
84	F	Domestic servant	21	Sheffield
85	F	Forge man	44	Sheffield
86	M	Engineers tool fitter	23	Sheffield
87	F	Draper	3	Sheffield
88	M	Saw handle maker	22	Treeton
89	F	Single	17	Bilston
90	M	Farm labourer	17	Deepcar
91	M	Engineer	19	Kent
92	M	Engine tenter	22	Wakefield
93	M	Labourer	25	Sheffield
94	F	Widow	41	Sheffield
95	F	Domestic servant	14	Sheffield
96	F	Domestic servant	19	Sheffield
97	M	Steel melter	30	Derby
98	F	Domestic servant	27	Manchester
99	F	Foreman	38	Sheffield
100	M	Silversmith	1	Rivelin
101	M	Spring knife cutter	39	Sheffield
102	F	Labourer	51	Sheffield
103	M	Razor grinder	21	Sheffield
104	M	Labourer	45	Mansfield
105	M	Millwright	48	Sheffield
106	M	Nail maker	34	Sheffield
107	F	Domestic servant	19	Derby
108	M	Sawmaker	19	Sheffield
109	F	Painter	3	Ripon
110	M	Scale cutter	42	Sheffield
111	M	Stock keeper	13	Shropshire
112	F	Domestic servant	20	Sheffield
113	F	Single	29	Sheffield
114	F	House keeper	37	Stockport
115	F	Shoe manufacturer	20	Sheffield
116	M	Blacksmith	1	Sheffield

Data Set 1A cont'd

Depositor's ID	Gender	Occupation	Age	Place of birth
117	F	Widow	30	Sheffield
118	F	Domestic servant	14	Sheffield
119	M	Brick maker	23	Sheffield
120	M	Grocer	29	Sheffield
121	M	Clergyman	7	Sheffield
122	M	Steel melter	19	Sheffield
123	M	Steel melter	21	Sheffield
124	M	Farmer	72	Sheffield
125	F	Domestic servant	17	Sheffield
126	M	Engine tenter	66	Londonderry
127	M	Store dealer	26	Nottingham
128	M	Table knife hafter	24	Sheffield
129	M	Table knife striker	62	Sheffield
130	F	Widow	55	Wentworth
131	M	Coke burner	33	Sheffield
132	M	Baker	47	Sheffield
133	F	Carter	25	County Roscannin
134	M	Shoe maker	49	Anston
135	F	Single	19	Sheffield
136	F	Domestic servant	50	Rotherham
137	M	Table knife hafter	1	Sheffield
138	M	White metal maker	25	Sheffield
139	M	Scissors smith	19	Sheffield
140	M	Tinner	21	Pontefract
141	M	Labourer	26	Wyburton
142	M	Merchants clerk	18	Sheffield
143	M	Steel moulder	22	Sheffield
144	M	Brick layer	23	Chesterfield
145	F	Scythe smith	48	Somerset
146	F	Domestic servant	14	Sheffield
147	M	Table knife hafter	30	Sheffield
148	M	Table knife grinder	36	Chesterfield
149	F	Single	32	Sheffield
150	F	Domestic servant	15	Nottingham
151	M	File cutter	25	Sheffield
152	F	Carrier	36	Nottingham
153	M	Glass grinder	23	Manchester
154	F	Single	57	Sheffield
155	F	Single	26	Sheffield
156	M	Watchman	34	Sheffield

Data Set 1A cont'd

Depositor's ID	Gender	Occupation	Age	Place of birth
157	M	Table knife cutter	60	Sheffield
158	M	Millwright	20	Rotherham
159	M	Book keeper	30	Sheffield
160	M	Blacksmith	38	Derby
161	F	Single	26	Sheffield
162	M	Photographer	32	Liverpool
163	F	Mason	22	Brighouse
164	M	Engine fitter	44	Sheffield
165	M	Sickle maker	66	Sheffield
166	F	Butcher	38	Sheffield
167	M	File cutter	28	Sheffield
168	M	Painter	38	Brighouse
169	F	Single	31	Sheffield
170	M	Apprentice grocer	18	Sheffield
171	M	Labourer	22	Arlington
172	M	Wire cutter	24	Sheffield
173	M	Optician	1	Sheffield
174	M	Furnace man	45	Buckinghamshire
175	M	Time keeper	52	Chesterfield
176	M	Miner	16	Hounsfield
177	F	Blacksmith	37	Sheffield
178	F	Domestic servant	47	Barnsley
179	F	Domestic servant	26	Aston
180	F	File cutter	42	Sheffield
181	M	Painter	15	Manchester
182	M	Spring maker	32	Lincolnshire
183	F	Domestic servant	14	Sheffield
184	F	Labourer	24	Sheffield
185	F	Blacksmith	39	Sheffield
186	F	Table blade maker	42	Sheffield
187	M	Grocer	21	Sheffield
188	M	Merchant	26	Sheffield
189	F	Domestic servant	21	Rawmarsh
190	F	Widow	48	Farnley
191	M	Steel forger	28	Haddon
192	F	Widow	65	Bentley
193	F	Joiner	38	Sheffield
194	F	Razor smith	9	Sheffield
195	F	Table blade striker	27	Sheffield
196	M	Blacksmith	39	Lincoln

Data Set 1A cont'd

Depositor's ID	Gender	Occupation	Age	Place of birth
197	F	Cheese agent	25	Sheffield
198	F	Spring knife cutter	24	Sheffield
199	F	Single	24	Sheffield
200	M	Out of business	49	Derby
201	F	Manager	49	Manchester
202	F	Engine fitter	43	Sheffield
203	F	Domestic servant	26	Sheffield
204	M	German silver polisher	49	Aston
205	F	Single	17	Sheffield
206	M	Tailor	30	Sheffield
207	M	Steel melter	30	Sheffield
208	F	Single	18	Liverpool
209	F	Single	29	Liverpool
210	F	Musician	20	Sheffield
211	M	Shoe maker	51	Batley
212	M	Spindle turner	32	Sheffield
213	M	Labourer	36	Stannington
214	M	Joiner	21	Cambridgeshire
215	M	Gas man	40	Sutton
216	M	Cutler	17	Sheffield
217	F	Single	19	Sheffield
218	M	Labourer	27	Armagh County
219	M	Blacksmith	22	Manchester
220	M	Cutler	17	Cambridgeshire
221	F	Waiter	26	Sheffield
222	M	Scale and spring maker	19	Sheffield
223	F	Single	23	Sheffield
224	F	Miner	30	Bolsover
225	F	Gas fitter	31	Rotherham
226	F	Schoolmaster	26	Sheffield
227	F	Razor grinder	33	London
228	F	Razor grinder	4	Sheffield
229	M	Miner	40	Derby
230	M	Labourer	56	Sheffield
231	M	Engraver	27	Birmingham
232	M	Sickle grinder	26	Sheffield
233	F	Farm servant	36	Eaden
234	M	Farm servant	26	Sheffield
235	F	Metal smith	46	Sheffield
236	M	Butcher	5	Sheffield

Data Set 1A cont'd

Depositor's ID	Gender	Occupation	Age	Place of birth
237	M	Clerk	16	Sheffield
238	M	Sickle grinder	21	Sheffield
239	M	Gas fitter	31	Loxley
240	F	Single	25	London
241	M	Table knife hafter	19	Sheffield
242	M	Edge tool grinder	42	London
243	M	Clerk	29	Denmark
244	F	Labourer	28	Winterton
245	M	Blacksmith	31	Cawthorne
246	M	Chaplain	1	Sheffield
247	M	Tailor	36	Scotland
248	M	Farmer	18	Sheffield
249	M	Priest	29	Waterford
250	M	Porter	21	Lincoln
251	F	Bookbinder	28	Sheffield
252	F	Labourer	27	Sheffield
253	M	Cooper	36	London
254	M	File cutter	25	Sheffield

Notes: Age and Gender relate to the account holder, the occupation may relate to a relative, i.e. a husband or father.

If you are particularly interested in those depositors whose place of birth was outside Sheffield you might wish to construct an additional field providing more specific information on location, e.g. most people know that Lincoln is in Lincolnshire but they may not know that Winterton is also in Lincolnshire. Similarly, there are a number of depositors whose birthplace was in Ireland, eg. Waterford..

Data Set 2A

Lancashire cotton firms, 1833

Name of firm	No. of factories	Location	Spinners employed	Weavers employed	Others employed	Total employed	Firm type by process
Birley & Kirk	2	Manchester	1,173	471	114	1,692	I
Ormrod & Hardcastle	1	Bolton	1,255	295	26	1,576	I
Mconnell & Co.	1	Manchester	1,493	0	52	1,545	S
Bolling E & W	4	Bolton	1,324	0	32	1,356	S
Houldsworth T	1	Manchester	1,155	0	46	1,201	S
Horsefield Joseph	1	Dhs	475	705	3	1,183	I
Ashton Thomas	1	Dhs	386	762	1	1,149	I
Marsland T	1	Stockport	347	566	34	947	I
Taylor Hindle & Co.	1	Bolton	860	40	24	924	I
Collinge & Lancashire	1	Oldham	338	444	71	853	I

Data Set 2A cont'd

Name of firm	No. of factories	Location	Spinners employed	Weavers employed	Others employed	Total employed	Firm type by process
Murray A & G	1	Manchester	805	0	36	841	S
Stirling & Beckton	1	Manchester	343	432	66	873	I
Lees J & Sons	1	Stockport	305	542	26	796	I
Oxford Road Twist Co.	1	Manchester	306	427	41	774	I
Smith William	1	Stockport	267	490	4	761	I
Lambert Hoole & Co.	1	Manchester	725	0	27	752	S
Ogden T R & T	1	Manchester	709	0	3	712	S
Guest James	1	Manchester	323	326	3	712	I
Howard I & T	1	Dhs	224	403	21	648	I
Sampson Lloyd & Co.	3	Stockport	223	408	1	632	I
Howard John	1	Dhs	241	358	29	628	I
Kennedy James	1	Manchester	594	0	5	599	S
Beaver Hugh	1	Manchester	201	301	23	525	I
Ashworth H & E	1	Bolton	515	0	2	517	S
Pooley & Son	1	Manchester	475	0	39	514	S
Cheetham George & Sons	1	Dhs	454	0	6	560	S
Howard Jesse	1	Stockport	292	153	5	450	I
New Bridge Mills Twist Co.	1	Manchester	444	0	6	450	S
Howard Apples	1	Stockport	176	268	2	446	I
N/D	1	Manchester	238	173	33	444	I
Gee James & R	1	Stockport	211	208	14	433	I
Axon Charles	1	Stockport	189	213	17	419	I
Harbottle Thomas	1	Manchester	126	267	8	401	I
Fernley Thomas	1	Stockport	116	279	5	400	I
Ashton J & R	1	Dhs	155	240	2	397	I
Gray Benjamin	1	Manchester	388	0	3	391	S
Orrell Ralph	1	Stockport	194	190	4	388	I
Knowles G T	1	Stockport	143	243	1	387	I
Sandford Benjamin	1	Manchester	365	0	17	382	S
Robinson Thomas	1	Stockport	123	219	7	349	I
Decca Twist Co.	1	Manchester	180	155	13	348	I
Ogden Thos & Sons	1	Manchester	344	0	2	346	S
Plant Thomas	1	Manchester	342	0	1	343	S
Ratcliffe Samuel	1	Oldham	186	153	3	342	I
Hardy & Andrew	1	Stockport	310	6	3	319	I
Brown John	1	Stockport	156	154	2	312	I

Data Set 2A cont'd

Name of firm	No. of factories	Location	Spinners employed	Weavers employed	Others employed	Total employed	Firm type by process
Tattersall John	1	Oldham	116	188	0	304	I
Holland Roger & Co	1	Bolton	277	3	18	298	I
Rooth & Mayer	1	Stockport	112	176	1	289	I
Steel T & Son	1	Stockport	140	122	22	284	I
Sidebottom John	1	Dhs	107	169	0	276	I
Lord James	1	Manchester	0	253	20	273	W
Dronsfield D	1	Oldham	177	92	0	269	I
Higson W	1	Stockport	99	166	0	265	I
Ainsworth I & Co.	1	Bolton	235	13	3	251	I
Ewart Peter	1	Manchester	250	0	1	251	S
Garside John	1	Stockport	112	132	1	245	I
Thompson Richard	1	Oldham	211	23	7	241	I
Barton T & Co.	1	Manchester	105	135	0	240	I
Bellhouse J & W	1	Manchester	208	0	3	211	S
Haigh Abraham	1	Bolton	209	0	1	210	S
Adshead & Brothers	1	Dhs	204	0	5	209	S
Dodgshon E & T	1	Manchester	79	119	5	203	I
Hague J & T	1	Oldham	149	51	3	203	I
Wagstaff & Sidebottom	1	Dhs	196	0	6	202	S
Taylor Weston & Co.	1	Manchester	180	10	8	198	I
Higgins William	1	Manchester	180	0	16	196	S
Moore S M	1	Manchester	186	0	3	189	S
Bayley Brothers	1	Dhs	243	322	20	585	I
Hall James & Son	1	Dhs	185	0	2	187	S
Mcool Alexander	1	Bolton	185	0	1	186	S
Ogden & Walmsley	1	Oldham	82	104	0	186	S
Shaw Hugh & Co.	1	Manchester	181	0	1	182	S
Thorniley A W & Brothers	1	Dhs	121	60	1	182	I
Pin Mill Twist Co.	1	Manchester	76	105	0	181	I
Robinson & Armitage	1	Dhs	76	94	3	173	I
Seville & Wright	1	Oldham	166	2	4	172	I
Clayton F S	1	Stockport	0	155	0	155	W
Rothwell J	1	Bolton	150	0	1	151	S
Marsland H & Co.	1	Stockport	43	102	1	148	I
Gleadhill James Assignees of	1	Oldham	142	0	4	146	S
Gough Nathan	1	Manchester	139	0	5	144	S
Carruthers William	1	Manchester	143	0	0	143	S
Smith & Rawson	1	Manchester	128	0	5	133	S

Data Set 2A cont'd

Name of firm	No. of factories	Location	Spinners employed	Weavers employed	Others employed	Total employed	Firm type by process
Welsh & Sells	1	Manchester	46	86	0	132	I
Gould & Cooper	1	Oldham	82	48	0	130	I
France & Boardman	1	Manchester	0	122	2	124	W
Forster S & Co.	1	Manchester	42	75	4	121	I
Howard J & R	1	Dhs	114	0	1	115	S
Wimpenny & Swindells	1	Dhs	110	0	3	113	S
Haywood & Sons	1	Manchester	109	0	3	112	S
Broadbent & Sons	1	Oldham	104	0	2	106	S
Johnson & Brookes	1	Manchester	42	60	3	105	I
Wilkinson James	1	Dhs	104	0	0	104	S
Clegg John	1	Oldham	49	48	2	99	I
Brideoak Edward	1	Oldham	95	2	0	97	I
Bradbury I	1	Oldham	94	0	1	95	S
Ogden & Walmsley	1	Oldham	10	80	0	90	I
Wilde Edmund	1	Oldham	90	0	0	90	S
Clegg Abraham	1	Oldham	88	0	0	88	S
Schofield Robert	1	Manchester	87	0	0	87	S
Buckley & Howard	1	Dhs	82	0	0	82	S
Islington Twist Co.	1	Manchester	76	0	1	77	S
Nield Daniel Jnr	1	Oldham	48	2	0	74	I
Shaw Hugh	1	Dhs	23	50	0	73	W
Hope T & R	1	Manchester	0	73	0	73	W
Rigg Sibson	1	Manchester	66	0	0	66	S
Duncuff John	1	Oldham	60	0	0	60	S
Nield James Jnr	1	Oldham	53	0	0	53	S
Waring & Sons	1	Oldham	49	0	0	49	S
Parrott & Weston	1	Stockport	47	0	0	47	S
Cheetham & Hill	1	Dhs	44	0	1	45	S
Cheetham John	1	Stockport	36	2	1	39	I
Moss & Howard	1	Oldham	28	0	0	28	S
Graeves J	1	Stockport	26	0	0	26	S
Lamb Joseph	1	Stockport	25	1	0	26	I
Lane Joseph & Sons	1	Stockport	305	542	26	873	I
Stocks Samuel	1	Stockport	177	259	2	438	I

Note: The abbreviation Dhs in the Location column represents the cotton towns of Duckinfield, Staleybridge and Styal.

Data Set 2B

Stockport cotton firms, 1832

Name of firm	Mule technology used	Number of spindles employed
Marsland T	Long mule	36,544
Lane J	Long mule	34,392
Smith W	Small mule	23,942
Howard James	Small mule	23,168
Lloyd S	Long mule	20,300
Howard John	Small mule	19,348
Howard A P	Long mule	16,206
Axon I	Long mule	15,654
Brown J	Long mule	15,582
Stocks S	Long mule	10,804
Mayor & Booth	Small mule	10,608
Robinson T	Long mule	10,192
Oriell R	Throstle spinning	8,000
Garside	Long mule	7,348
Steel T	Long mule	7,232
Higson W	Small mule	4,816
Fearnley T	Small mule	4,752
Marsland H	Long mule	4,512
Knowles G T	Throstle spinning	2,520

Data Set 2C

Manchester cotton factory data, 1815

Factory number	Rateable value of factory (£)	Factory number	Rateable value of factory (£)
1	59	25	101
2	147	26	45
3	118	27	217
4	84	28	336
5	114	29	54
6	216	30	199
7	519	31	154
8	244	32	15
9	449	33	14
10	478	34	18
11	89	35	111
12	933	36	199
13	924	37	166
14	41	38	191
15	74	39	389
16	64	40	118
17	322	41	79
18	83	42	59
19	57	43	117
20	29	44	116
21	522	45	81
22	150	46	58
23	240	47	478
24	63		

Data Set 2D

Information on Manchester cotton factory firms, 1815

Factory number	Firm number	Name of firm	Rateable value of firm (£)
30	A1	Appleton & Ogden	199
27	A2	Appleton P	217
40	A3	Austin J	47
46	A4	Barton	3
19	A5	Bennett J & C	57
18	A6	Bigger W	5
43	A7	Birch J & Co.	21
22	A8	Bland I	5
22	A9	Blomley	10
32	A10	Bowler J	15
42	A11	Bowman R & Co.	59
18	A12	Braddock J	74
15	A13	Bury & Wrigley	32
14	A14	Carruthers A	41
35	A15	Chadwick & Clogg	111
45	A16	Dean Twist & Co.	81
41	A17	Dunkerley J	79
28	A18	Edwards Lewis & Co.	336
37	A19	Ewart P	166
22	A20	Figgen	10
16	A21	Firth J	64
15	A22	Fitton J	17
31	A23	Fogg & Hughes	154
18	A24	Freer W	2
44	A25	Frost J	40
6	A26	Galimore & Johnson	85
22	A27	Gerrard	30
20	A28	Gore H	29
39	A29	Gough Clowes & Lloyd	240
8	A30	Gray & Kirby (Ancoats Twist Co.)	244
26	A31	Green T	5
39	A32	Hackey W	79
26	A33	Haigh J	5
11	A34	Halliday	89
24	A35	Harrison Bros	63
15	A36	Harsden	4

Data Set 2D cont'd

Factory number	Firm number	Name of firm	Rateable value of firm (£)
26	A37	Hattersall J	20
23	A38	Hencroft G	30
6	A39	Holt & Firth	65
46	A40	Houghton & Leeming	52
21	A41	Houldsworth D	522
25	A42	Howarth K	13
23	A43	Hughes T	15
46	A44	Jones H	3
9	A45	Kennedy John	449
22	A46	Lamb J	30
36	A47	Latham J	199
39	A48	Lonsdale & Green	67
6	A49	Luke C	25
47	A50	Marriott T	478
39	A51	Mathie P	3
12	A52	McConnel & Kennedy	933
34	A53	McNiven & Green	18
38	A54	Milner	32
25	A55	Milner J	31
7	A56	Mitchell W	519
13	A57	Murray G & A	924
18	A58	Naboth J	2
25	A59	Nicholls B	25
44	A60	Nixon I & Brown J N	56
22	A61	Ogden	10
22	A62	Ogden R	15
26	A63	Ogden S	5
43	A64	Oxley Sutcliffe & Gough	20
4	A65	Parker H	20
10	A66	Pollard J	478
22	A67	Potter A	10
29	A68	Ramsbottom T & J	54
1	A69	Robinson E	59
22	A70	Salthorse I	30
5	A71	Sandford B & W	114
23	A72	Schofield R	195
44	A73	Scholar J	20
17	A74	Simpson Executors of	322
2	A75	Smith & Townley	147

Data Set 2D cont'd

Factory number	Firm number	Name of firm	Rateable value of firm (£)
6	A76	Smith & Welsh	41
3	A77	Smith Alex	118
43	A78	Stone C	25
38	A79	Stonehouse	64
15	A80	Storey J	11
43	A81	Stubbs & Mayer	51
25	A82	Taylor & Heathcoat	7
25	A83	Taylor E	25
33	A84	Thackery J	14
26	A85	Waddle D	10
40	A86	Walker & Marsden	47
4	A87	Walker Bros	64
38	A88	Wilson & Fairweather	95
40	A89	Wooley & Co	24
15	A90	Yates John	10

Data Set 3A

Assisted emigrants to New South Wales, 1825–1832

Family ID	Trade	Number of persons in each family	Amount granted to each (£)
1	Shoemaker	5	10
2	Painter	8	20
3	Weaver	5	20
4	Engineer	4	15
5	Sawyer	2	16
6	Cartwright	2	13
7	Wheelwright	6	20
8	Blacksmith	2	16
9	Sawyer	2	20
10	Nailor	4	10
11	Farrier	2	20
12	Engineer	8	20
13	Tanner	4	20
14	Upholsterer	2	20
15	Weaver	7	20
16	Plasterer	5	20
17	Brick maker	2	10
18	Engineer	7	20

Data Set 3A cont'd

Family ID	Trade	Number of persons in each family	Amount granted to each (£)
19	Shoemaker	2	10
20	Bricklayer	6	20
21	Whitesmith	5	15
22	Farrier	5	20
23	Gardener	8	20
24	Shoemaker	5	20
25	Shoemaker	4	20
26	Painter	2	18
27	Sawyer	2	20
28	Stone mason	2	20
29	Sawyer	2	20
30	Painter	3	20
31	Weaver	5	20
32	Tailor	5	20
33	Quarryman	7	20
34	Cabinet maker	2	20
35	Shoemaker	6	20
36	Weaver	2	20
37	Butcher	2	16
38	Farmer	6	20
39	Engineer	6	20
40	Engineer	7	20
41	Sawyer	2	20
42	Baker	5	20
43	Painter	3	20
44	Blacksmith	2	20
45	Slater	5	20
46	Butcher	4	20
47	Stone mason	2	20
48	Brick maker	2	15
49	Cutler	2	20
50	Brick maker	2	20
51	Harness maker	6	20
52	Carpenter	2	20
53	Weaver	5	20
54	Coach painter	5	20
55	Bricklayer	3	20
56	Sawyer	4	20
57	Shoemaker	3	20

Data Set 3A cont'd

Family ID	Trade	Number of persons in each family	Amount granted to each (£)
58	Weaver	5	20
59	Sawyer	3	20
60	N/A	3	20
61	Weaver	3	20
62	Shoemaker	2	20
63	Weaver	4	20
64	Carpenter	2	20
65	Sailor	3	11
66	Shipwright	5	20
67	Shoemaker	2	20
68	Tin plate worker	2	20
69	Carpenter	2	20
70	Bricklayer	2	20
71	Farrier	7	20
72	Watch maker	2	20
73	Coach painter	2	20
74	Schoolmaster	4	20
75	Painter	6	20
76	Collar maker	2	20
77	Shipwright	3	20
78	Carpenter	2	20
79	Cooper	6	20
80	Blacksmith	4	20
81	Smith	5	20
82	Caulker	2	20
83	Carpenter	5	20
84	Glazier	4	20
85	Tailor	2	20
86	Wheelwright	3	20
87	Joiner	5	20
88	Candle maker	2	20
89	Chair maker	2	20
90	Butcher	2	20
91	Weaver	8	20
92	Weaver	6	20
93	Weaver	7	20
94	Shoemaker	2	20
95	Coppersmith	2	20
96	Engineer	2	20

Data Set 3A cont'd

Family ID	Trade	Number of persons in each family	Amount granted to each (£)
97	Engineer	4	20
98	Tailor	6	20
99	Shoemaker	3	20
100	Nailor	4	20
101	Printer	2	20
102	Harness maker	2	20
103	Weaver	2	20
104	Coach maker	2	20
105	Joiner	2	20
106	Harness maker	3	20
107	Sawyer	2	20
108	Joiner	2	20
109	Weaver	2	20
110	Blacksmith	2	20
111	Stone cutter	3	20
112	Carpenter	2	20
113	Baker	3	20
114	Joiner	4	20
115	Shipwright	5	20
116	Caulker	8	20
117	Boat builder	3	20
118	Stone mason	4	20
119	Cooper	3	20
120	Saddler	3	20
121	Brick maker	6	20
122	Piano maker	4	20
123	Schoolmaster	3	20
124	Cabinet maker	2	20
125	Locksmith	5	20
126	Stone cutter	4	20
127	Blacksmith	3	20
128	Gardener	5	20
129	Weaver	4	20
130	Wool sorter	5	20
131	Carpenter	6	20
132	Carpenter	5	20
133	Baker	2	20
134	Brass worker	3	20
135	Carpenter	3	20

Data Set 3A cont'd

Family ID	Trade	Number of persons in each family	Amount granted to each (£)
136	Gardener	4	20
137	Weaver	3	20
138	Blacksmith	2	20
139	Wheelwright	4	20
140	Butcher	9	20
141	Joiner	2	20
142	Tailor	2	20
143	Weaver	6	20
144	Bricklayer	3	20
145	Cooper	2	16
146	Cooper	6	20
147	Cooper	4	20
148	Carpenter	2	20
149	Shipwright	4	20
150	Carpenter	6	20
151	Cabinet maker	2	20
152	Cutler	3	20
153	Stone mason	5	20
154	Shoemaker	5	20
155	Cooper	6	20
156	Engineer	6	20
157	Cooper	6	20
158	Tailor	7	20
159	Carpenter	2	20
160	Carpenter	2	20
161	Carpenter	2	20
162	Blacksmith	4	20
163	Baker	2	20
164	Wheelwright	2	20
165	Silk dyer	2	20
166	Shoemaker	4	20
167	Sawyer	4	20
168	Smith	2	20
169	Butcher	3	20
170	Dyer	6	20
171	Shoemaker	3	20
172	Blacksmith	7	20
173	Brass founder	3	20
174	Rope maker	6	20

Data Set 3A cont'd

Family ID	Trade	Number of persons in each family	Amount granted to each (£)
175	Stone mason	2	20
176	Carpenter	2	20
177	Cabinet maker	2	20
178	Cooper	6	20
179	Shipwright	5	20
180	Plasterer	3	20
181	Dyer	2	20
182	Bricklayer	3	20
183	Bookbinder	3	20
184	Bricklayer	2	20
185	Baker	4	20
186	Hatter	5	20
187	Butcher	4	20
188	Carpenter	2	20
189	Dyer	6	20
190	Joiner	8	20
191	Blacksmith	4	20
192	Weaver	6	20
193	Slater	5	20
194	Joiner	3	20
195	Millwright	5	20
196	Cooper	3	20
197	Hatter	5	20
198	Baker	6	20
199	Stone mason	3	20
200	Stone mason	7	20
201	Stone mason	3	20
202	Herdsman	2	20
203	Comb maker	4	20
204	Tailor	6	20
205	Cooper	4	20
206	Tanner	2	20
207	Engineer	2	20
208	Carpenter	3	20
209	Smith	2	10
210	Smith	3	20
211	Plasterer	6	20
212	Gun maker	2	20
213	Smith	3	20

Data Set 3A cont'd

Family ID	Trade	Number of persons in each family	Amount granted to each (£)
214	Shoemaker	4	20
215	Tailor	5	20
216	Painter	2	20
217	Blacksmith	8	20
218	Weaver	2	20
219	Mason	4	20
220	N/A	2	20
221	Glazier	2	20
222	Baker	3	20
223	Stone mason	2	20
224	Stone mason	2	20
225	Painter	2	20
226	Carpenter	2	20
227	Carpenter	2	20
228	Shoemaker	2	20
229	Sawyer	4	20
230	Carpenter	3	20
231	Shoemaker	7	20
232	Tailor	8	20
233	Butcher	2	20
234	Painter	4	20
235	Shoemaker	5	20
236	Saddler	2	20
237	Harness maker	4	20
238	Tailor	2	20
239	Cabinet maker	2	15
240	Engineer	2	15
241	Stone mason	3	20
242	Saddler	4	20
243	Sawyer	2	20
244	Sawyer	8	20
245	Blacksmith	3	20
246	Carpenter	2	20
247	Varnish maker	4	20
248	Tailor	2	20
249	Carpenter	2	20
250	Painter	2	20
251	Weaver	3	20
252	Cabinet maker	6	20

Data Set 3A cont'd

Family ID	Trade	Number of persons in each family	Amount granted to each (£)
253	Blacksmith	8	20
254	Cooper	9	20
255	Dyer	2	20
256	Carpenter	4	20
257	Iron founder	5	20
258	Blacksmith	5	20
259	Cabinet maker	4	20
260	Cooper	8	20
261	Dyer	2	20
262	Mason	3	20
263	Cabinet maker	3	20
264	Tailor	5	20
265	Glazier	4	20
266	Sone mason	6	20
267	Brick maker	3	20
268	Painter	2	20
269	Joiner	5	20
270	Weaver	2	20
271	Slater	2	20
272	Carpenter	6	20
273	Cooper	10	20
274	Painter	5	20
275	Gilder	4	20
276	Carpenter	4	20
277	Plasterer	2	20
278	Plasterer	8	20
279	Brick maker	3	20
280	Weaver	2	20
281	Baker	4	20
282	Rope spinner	3	20
283	Shoemaker	3	20
284	Cooper	6	20
285	Mason	5	20
286	Cooper	5	20
287	Blacksmith	2	20
288	Bricklayer	6	20
289	Smith	2	20
290	Carpenter	6	20
291	Tailor	6	20

Data Set 3A cont'd

Family ID	Trade	Number of persons in each family	Amount granted to each (£)
292	N/A	5	20
293	Carpenter	4	20
294	Coachmaker	8	20
295	Shoemaker	5	20
296	Mason	4	20
297	Weaver	2	20
298	Bricklayer	4	20
299	Gunsmith	8	20
300	Tailor	4	20
301	Plasterer	8	20
302	Waterman	5	20
303	Tailor	5	20
304	Carpenter	3	20
305	Shipwright	2	20
306	Bricklayer	3	20
307	Glazier	5	20
308	Tailor	4	20
309	N/A	5	20
310	Hatter	6	20
311	N/A	4	20
312	Builder	2	20
313	Tailor	5	20
314	Wire worker	2	20
315	Carpenter	5	20
316	Shoemaker	4	20
317	Dyer	8	20
318	Engineer	5	20
319	Spinner	3	20
320	Spinner	2	20
321	Weaver	2	20
322	Painter	2	20
323	Carpenter	2	20
324	Shoemaker	6	20
325	Painter	2	20
326	Coppersmith	3	20
327	Saddler	2	20
328	Plasterer	7	20
329	Plasterer	3	20
330	Cooper	3	20

Data Set 3A cont'd

Family ID	Trade	Number of persons in each family	Amount granted to each (£)
331	Smith	2	20
332	Baker	2	20
333	Plumber	2	20
334	Cooper	3	20
335	Cabinet maker	3	20
336	Brick maker	2	20
337	Blacksmith	4	20
338	Tailor	7	20
339	Mason	3	20
340	Stone mason	2	20
341	Brush maker	9	20
342	Joiner	6	20
343	Carpenter	3	20
344	Cooper	3	20
345	Cooper	5	20
346	Printer	4	20
347	Currier	3	20
348	Tanner	2	20
349	Turner	3	20
350	Cabinet maker	8	20
351	Weaver	10	20
352	Carpenter	5	20
353	Cabinet maker	3	20
354	Tailor	2	20
355	Weaver	4	20
356	Plasterer	4	20
357	Tailor	8	20
358	Bookbinder	5	20
359	Baker	3	20
360	Miner	3	20
361	Tailor	2	20
362	Shoemaker	7	20
363	Shipwright	4	20
364	Slater	2	20
365	Carpenter	2	20
366	Blacksmith	3	20
367	Cooper	3	20
368	Carpenter	2	20
369	Bricklayer	2	20

Data Set 3A cont'd

Family ID	Trade	Number of persons in each family	Amount granted to each (£)
370	Stone mason	5	20
371	Slater	5	20
372	Mason	7	20
373	Weaver	4	20
374	Hatter	5	20
375	Mason	3	20
376	Mason	2	20
377	Slater	12	20
378	Mason	3	20
379	Baker	3	20
380	Farmer	8	20
381	Cooper	5	20
382	Sawyer	2	20
383	Butcher	7	20
384	Joiner	5	20
385	Cooper	8	20
386	Tin plate worker	6	20
387	Tyler	3	20
388	Hatter	2	20
389	Butcher	2	20
390	Pipe maker	4	20
391	Weaver	3	20
392	Smith	3	20

Glossary

This glossary contains definitions of technical computer terms, explanations of terms explicitly used in the Microsoft Excel and Access software which are used as exemplers in this book, and explanations of basic statistical concepts. When you see the term worksheet used in the glossary it is the name given by the designers of the Microsoft Excel software for a spreadsheet.

active cell Where you type information into a worksheet. The cell is made active by clicking on it with the mouse.

aggregate data Information about a group which produces a total.

aligning In Excel to position text or numbers in cells, i.e. centre, left or right align.

annotation In Excel to add titles, text, legends and arrows to a chart.

application The particular program to be used on the computer, e.g. Microsoft Excel is a program for producing worksheets and charts.

area chart Shows the magnitude of change over time and is particularly useful when several components are changing and you are interested in the sum of these components.

bar chart A series of horizontal bars, useful for showing the comparative size of two or more items at a point in time, e.g. the number of seats held by the parties in the House of Commons in 1906.

button A common method of performing an action with a mouse, e.g. use the mouse to click on the bold button on the tool bar. Also the buttons on the mouse you use to carry out a command.

calculated data Statistical data which is calculated, e.g. on a worksheet you enter a formula to perform calculations.

categorisation To arrange information according to a set of criteria.

cell The box where you enter text and numbers into a worksheet, the intersection of a row and a column.

cell address A unique label to identify each cell in a worksheet: thus the address A3 locates information in the third row of the first column.

cell ranges A group of adjacent cells in a worksheet.

chart A common word for a graph. Used as such in Excel

chart 3-D A three dimensional graph.

chart screen window In Excel the window that appears on the screen when you create a new chart.

click on To use the mouse to point to an item.

coding A standardised abbreviation which is assigned to a particular piece of information, e.g. M for male, F for female.

column Information in a table which is divided vertically, i.e. a column in a worksheet table or a field in a database table.

column chart A series of vertical columns that allow comparison of the relative size of two or more items, often over time, e.g. output of cotton and output of coal 1815–1840.

column width The horizontal size of a column in a worksheet or database which can be adjusted.

combination chart Combines a column chart and a line chart to compare two types of data, e.g. expenditure on education and defence 1870–1914.

comparative data Information which allows a comparison of trends, e.g. output of steel in Britain compared to output of steel in the USA.

conceptualisation of data Defining the information to be entered into a database.

control box A button commonly used to exit from a window.

correlation coefficient A measurement of the statistical relationship between two variables. The nearer the correlation coefficient is to 1, the greater is the strength of the relationship between the two variables.

CPU (central processing unit) Contains the silicon chip of the personal computer.

CTI Computers in Teaching Initiative.

cursor A symbol, usually flashing, which tells you where you are on the screen.

customise In Excel to design a chart to your own requirements.

data entry Using the keyboard to type historical information into a computer.

data processing Producing results using a computer.

data series A range of numbers on a worksheet which can be plotted to create a chart.

data set A selection of information relevant to a specific historical theme.

data sheet view In Access a screen view which allows you to view the database in a tabular form.

data type In a database the definition of the data contained in a field, e.g. textual, numerical, counter and logical (Yes/No).

database A collection of historical records which contains discreet categories of information called fields.

database management system (DBMS) A computer application which allows the user to build electronic database tables, select, order and count records. Access is a DBMS and most modern versions have relational capabilities. See relational database management system. Other commercial DBMS programs are Paradox and Dbase.

database table Another name for a database, i.e. a series of records organised in fields. For example a table might contain a number of records about business firms, each of which gives the name of firm, the number employed and their date of origin.

database window The window which is displayed when you open a Microsoft Access database.

desk top The background against which a window appears on the screen.

dialogue box A means of providing information or answering questions about an option you have chosen from a menu when using the Excel worksheet or Access database.

disaggregated data Information broken down from aggregate data into categories, e.g. the breakdown of the total British workforce by occupation categories for 1841. This data is often displayed as a proportion of the aggregate or total data.

DISH Design and Implementation of Software for Historians.

disk drive A slot in the computer which holds a floppy disk.

disks Magnetic disk on which you store your information. See also floppy disk and hard disk.

DOS Disk Operating System. A standard operating system compatible with IBM computers. It is a program which manages the communication between other programs and the computer itself and handles the filing of documents and data.

drag and drop Using the mouse to drag an object on the screen onto another, e.g. using the Access database you can drag a field from the field list box and position it (drop it) in the QBE grid. You drag an object by positioning the mouse pointer over the object, holding down the mouse button, and then releasing the mouse button when the object is where you want it to be. You can also drag the mouse to highlight text on which you want to perform an action.

Drive see disk drive and hard disk.

edit Changing/correcting information which has been entered into a computer.

edit area In Excel the area on the screen in which you make changes/corrections to information.

enhancing In Excel to enhance a worksheet, i.e. to change column width, to include borders and patterns, to change fonts and to align information.

Excel Window A view on the screen which allows you to work with a worksheet.

exit To exit a program. Same as quit.

field Identical categories of information contained in a database, e.g. the attributes of an individual: age, gender, marital status, etc.

field name A name given to a field of information in a database, e.g. age, gender, marital status.

field properties In Access a menu which allows you to set the parameters for information contained in a field, e.g. set the width of a field.

field width the size of a field measured by the number of characters (text or numbers) it contains.

file name The name given to a computer file.

fill handle In Excel in the lower right corner of the active cell which you can drag with the mouse to copy information and formulas.

filter In a database to apply a set of criteria to show a subset of the records or to sort the records, e.g. in a census database to show all householders with an age greater than 30. You filter out the records which do not meet this criteria.

floppy disk A removable flexible disk encased in a hard cover which you insert into a computer drive to store information.

fonts Size and style of typeface, e.g. characters per inch (CPI), bold and italics.

formatting To change the appearance of a document you are working with e.g. in an Excel worksheet to change column width, set decimal points, align information. Also refers to the preparation of a floppy disk so that it can be read by a computer.

formula Standard algebraic notation which you type in to a worksheet or database to perform a calculation.

formula bar In Excel a bar on the screen where you type in formulas.

gallery menu In Excel a menu which you use to change chart type, e.g. from a column to a line chart.

graphical user interface (GUI) Common to Microsoft Windows it allows you to perform actions by clicking on a graphical image called an icon.

graphs Another name for charts.

group icon A collection of associated programs. See icon.

group query An action you perform in a database. A request for a particular collection of records which are grouped together.

hard copy A paper print-out from a printer.

hard disk A fixed disk which permanently stores information.

hardware The actual computer itself.

HiDES Historical Document Expert System.

icon A graphical symbol which represents a program or an action. It is selected by using the mouse.

index numbers A common method of representing statistical data to show change. An index number is a multiple of 100 calculated from a base year.

insertion point A flashing line on the screen prompting you to enter information.

joining (linking) A database operation that links data in two tables on the basis of matching values so that the combined data can be used in a query. You thus create relationships between tables.

keyboard Used for entering text and numbers into a computer.

keys The individual keys on a keyboard.

line chart A chart used to show trends over time.

linking database tables See joining.

mainframe computer Large central computer accessed by a number of individual terminals.

make table query A query in a database that creates a new table from selected data.

matrix A grid containing columns and rows where you enter data.

menu A list of options which you choose from.

menu bar In Excel the part of the window which contains the drop-down menus from which you select options.

Microsoft Access for Windows A standard commercial database program for Microsoft Windows.

Microsoft Excel A standard commercial spreadsheet program for Microsoft Windows. In the terminology of this package a spreadsheet is referred to as a worksheet.

Microsoft Windows A graphical user interface produced by Microsoft. It allows you to run software programs such as word processors, spreadsheets and databases.

mouse A peripheral device used to move a pointer on the screen and to select options and perform actions.

mouse pointer A white arrow which moves around the screen when you use the mouse.

multi-table database A database containing a number of tables which can be joined together to perform queries.

network Several computers joined together.

numerical data A term for statistical information.

one to many relationship Defines the relationship between information in database tables. The occurrence of entity A in one table can be associated with many occurrences of entity B in another table.

one to one relationship Defines the relationship between information in database tables. The occurrence of entity A in one table can be related to only one occurrence of an entity B in another table.

open To open a computer application or a file of information.

PC Personal computer, IBM and compatibles.

pie chart Used for comparing the percentages of a total and displaying as a chart, e.g. each slice of a pie chart shows male and female workers as a percentage of total workers.

primary key Defines one or more fields in a database table whose value or values uniquely identify each record in a table.

print preview A screen view which shows how text will look on the printed page.

printer Used to produce a paper copy of what is displayed on screen.

program A set of instructions for the computer.

program manager In Microsoft Windows a graphical user interface which contains icons which you access by using a mouse.

proportional data Data recorded as a percentage of the total.

pull down menus A feature graphical user interfaces. Microsoft Excel and Access use these menus: you make a menu appear by pointing and dragging the mouse.

QBE grid In Access the Query By Example Grid. You add fields to the grid by using the mouse to drop and drag. It is a portion of the screen where you perform queries.

qualitative evidence Historical documents and text, both primary and secondary sources.

quantification Use of statistical information to measure.

query A method of processing information in a database. You can think of it as a request for a particular collection of records, it is a question you ask of the database. For example, in a database containing records of emigrants to Canada in the nineteenth century how many emigrants were aged over 30? By performing this query you can view only those records which meet this criteria. See also filter.

query window In Access the area where you provide instructions to perform queries.

question box An option box which appears on the screen when you perform an action, e.g. when you close a file in Excel a question box appears asking you if you want to SAVE CHANGES? You use the mouse to select an option: YES NO, CANCEL.

RAM Random Access Memory. The computer's memory which holds the operating system, software, and files in use while you work.

record A set of information that belongs together. A database is made up of individual records, e.g. a medical history database could contain information on the records of patients: name, place of birth, age, sex, occupation. Thus a record contains discreet fields (categories) of information about a certain object of study.

relational data Data arranged to show the relationship between two or more variables.

relational database A database compiled from two or more database tables. By creating joins between the tables using information contained in common fields you can cross-reference information in the various tables and establish relationships between the data.

relational database management system (RDMS) A program which allows you to associate data in two or more tables on the basis of common fields. Access is a RDMS.

retrieve An operation performed with a database management system. By performing queries you can select particular records, e.g. in a census database the name of a particular householder.

row Information in a table which is divided horizontally, i.e. a row in a worksheet table or a record in a database table.

save as In Excel a method of saving and naming files.

save changes Saving information on file after alterations have been made.

scatter chart Shows the relationship between pairs of numbers and the trends they present. For each pair, one of the numbers is plotted on the X-axis and the other number is plotted on the Y-axis. Where the two meet a symbol is placed on the chart and when a number of such points is plotted a pattern may emerge.

scroll bars A method of moving around a document quickly. You use the mouse to operate the scroll bars.

select An operation performed with a database management system to select records which meet certain criteria.

select query A query which allows you to ask a question and select the records you want from a database table.

software A computer program.

sort An operation to organise information, i.e. in a database. Text can be arranged alphabetically (ascending and descending) and numbers arranged from highest to lowest or vice versa.

spreadsheet A type of software ideal for organising numerical data in a table. It is made up of rows or columns and where these intersect it is called a cell. Microsoft Excel is a commercial spreadsheet program and is referred to as a worksheet. Other commercial software are Lotus 1-2-3 and Quattro Pro.

status bar In Excel the part of the window which displays messages.

structured data A source of historical information which is organised into clearly defined categories.

table design view In Access the window you operate in to design a database table.

textual data Letters and words.

time series A set of information which measures change over time.

title bar In Excel the part of the window which shows the name of the worksheet.

tool bar In Excel the part of the window from which you use the mouse pointer to click on buttons (tools) to perform actions.

transferable skills Computer skills which you learn and can then apply in your future careers.

undo A menu option you use to cancel an action you have performed.

unstructured data Historical information which does not come in a structured format, i.e. not organised in clearly defined categories.

variable In a database the same as a field of information.

VDU (visual display unit) The monitor attached to the computer.

WIMP (windows, icons, mouse, pull-down menus); a description of a program such as Microsoft Windows which uses a graphical user interface.

windows A name given to the area where you work on screen using icons and menus to operate a program.

word processor Program used for typing and formatting text.

worksheet window In Excel the area on the screen where you enter information into a worksheet. It is also called the active window.

worksheet In Excel the name given to a spreadsheet.

x-axis The horizontal line on a chart.

y-axis The vertical line on a chart.

Bibliography

Aldcroft, D. H. (1983) *The British Economy between the Wars*, London: Philip Allen.

Ayrton, A. (1989) 'Reflex Revisited. A Database Package for Undergraduate History Teaching: Borland's Reflex', *History and Computing*, 1, 1.

Badger, A. J. (1989) *The New Deal: The Depression Years, 1933–40*, London: Macmillan.

Bagwell, P. S. and Mingay, G. E. (1987) *Britain and America. A Study of Economic Change 1850–1939*, London: Routledge and Kegan Paul.

Balio, T. (1985) *The American Film Industry*, Madison, Wisconsin: University of Wisconsin Press.

Ball, A. R. (1987) *British Political Parties: The Emergence of a Modern Party System*, Basingstoke: Macmillan Education.

Ball, S. (1991) 'Parliament and Politics in Britain 1900–1951', *Parliamentary History*, 10, part 2.

Barnsby, G. J. (1971) 'The Standard of Living in the Black Country during the Nineteenth Century', *Economic History Review*, 24, 2.

Beddoe, D. (1988) 'Women between the Wars', in T. Herbert and Gareth Elwyn Jones (eds) *Wales between the Wars*, Cardiff: University of Wales Press.

Benson, J. (1983) *The Penny Capitalists: A Study of Nineteenth Century Working-class Entrepreneurs*, London: Gill and Macmillan.

—— (1989) *The Working Class in Britain 1850–1939*, London: Longman.

Berg, M. (1980) *The Machinery Question and the Making of Political Economy, 1815–1848*, Cambridge: Cambridge University Press.

Berg, M. and Hudson, P. (1992) 'Rehabilitating the Industrial Revolution', *Economic History Review*, 45.

Blewett, N. (1968) 'Free Fooders, Balfourites, Whole Hoggers, Factionalism within the Unionist Party 1906–10', *Historical Journal*, 11, 1.

Blumin, S. (1990) 'The Classification of Occupations in Past Times: Problems of Fission and Fusion', in E. Mawdsley *et al.* (eds) *History and Computing III: Historians, Computers and Data*, Manchester: Manchester University Press.

Bowley, A. L. (1937) *Wages and Income in the United Kingdom since 1860*, Cambridge: Cambridge University Press.

Broadberry, S. N. (1991) 'Unemployment', in N. F. R. Crafts and N. Woodward (eds) *The British Economy since 1945*, Oxford: Clarendon Press.

Butler, D. (1972) 'Electors and Elected', in D. Butler and D. Stokes (eds) *Political Change in Britain*, London: Penguin.

Bythell, D. (1969) *The Handloom Weavers: A Study in the English Cotton Industry during the Industrial Revolution*, Cambridge: Cambridge University Press.

Cain, P. J. (1979) 'Political Economy in Edwardian England: The Tariff Reform Controversy', in A. O'Day (ed.) *The Edwardian Age: Conflict and Stability*, London: Macmillan.

Carr, E. H. (1990 edition) *What is History?*, London: Penguin.

Carrothers, W. A. (1929) *Emigration from the British Isles*, London: reprinted by Frank Cass, 1965.

Catling, H. (1978) 'The Development of the Spinning Mule', *Textile History*, 9.

Chandler, L. V. (1970) *America's Greatest Depression 1929–41*, New York: Harper and Row.

Chapman, S. D. (1979) 'Financial Constraints on the Growth of Firms in the Cotton Industry, 1790–1850', *Economic History Review*, 32.

—— (1987) *The Cotton Industry in the Industrial Revolution*, London: Macmillan.

Crafts, N. F. R. (1985) *British Economic Growth during the Industrial Revolution*, Oxford: Oxford University Press.

Craven, J. (1984) *Introduction to Economics*, Oxford: Basil Blackwell.

Cronin, M. J. (1994a) 'The Blueshirts in Ireland: The Movement and its Members 1932–5', unpublished D.Phil. thesis, University of Oxford.

—— (1994b) 'The Socio-economic Background and Membership of the Blueshirt Movement 1932–5', *Irish Historical Studies*, 29, 114.

Edwards, M. M. (1967) *The Growth of the British Cotton Trade 1780–1815*, Manchester: Manchester University Press.

Eichengreen, B. (1992) 'The Origins of the Great Slump Revisited', *Economic History Review*, 45, 2.

Englander, D. (1983) *Landlord and Tenant in Urban Britain 1838–1918*, Oxford: Clarendon Press.

Fair, J. D. (1986) 'Party Voting Behaviour in the British House of Commons, 1886–1918', *Parliamentary History*, 5.

Farnie, D. A. (1979) *The English Cotton Industry and the World Market, 1815 to 1896*, Oxford: Clarendon.

Fearon, P. (1983) *War, Prosperity and Depression: The US Economy 1917–45*, London: Philip Allan.

Feinstein, C. H. (1990a) 'What Really Happened to Real Wages?: Trends in Wages, Prices, and Productivity in the United Kingdom, 1880–1913', *Economic History Review*, 43, 3.

—— (1990b) 'New Estimates of Average Earnings in the United Kingdom, 1880–1913', *Economic History Review*, 43, 4.

Floud, R. (1977) *An Introduction to Quantitative Methods for Historians*, London: Methuen.

Fraser, W. H. (1981) *The Coming of the Mass Market 1850–1914*, London: Macmillan.

Gatrell, V. A. C. (1977) 'Labour, Power, and the Size of Firms in Lancashire Cotton in the Second Quarter of the Nineteenth Century', *Economic History Review*, 30.

Gazeley, I. (1989) 'The Cost of Living for Urban Workers in Late Victorian and Edwardian Britain', *Economic History Review*, 42, 2.

Glass, D. V. and Taylor, P. A. M. (1976) *Population and Emigration*, Dublin: Irish University Press.

Gourvish, T. R. (1979) 'The Standard of Living, 1890–1914', in A. O'Day (ed.) *The Edwardian Age: Conflict and Stability*, London: Macmillan.

Greenstein, D. I. (1989) 'A Source Orientated Approach to History and Computing: The Relational Database', *Historical Science Research*, 14.

—— (1994) *A Historian's Guide to History and Computing*, Oxford: Oxford University Press.

Harvey, C. and Press, J. (1991) 'The Business Elite of Bristol: A Case Study in Database Design', *History and Computing*, 3, 1.

Hay, J. R. (1986) *The Origins and Impact of the Liberal Welfare Reforms 1906–1914*, London: Macmillan.

Higgs, E. (1990) 'Structuring the Past: The Occupational and Household Classification of Nineteenth Century Census Data' in E. Mawdsley *et al.* (eds) *History and Computing III: Historians, Computers and Data*, Manchester: Manchester University Press.

Historical Statistics of the United States (1960) *Historical Statistics of the United States From Colonial Times to 1970*, 2 volumes, Washington DC: US Bureau of the Census.

Hitchcock, T. (1993) '"She's Gotta Have IT": Teaching Information Technology to Undergraduate History Students', *History and Computing*, 5, 3.

Hudson, P. (ed.) (1989) *Regions and Industries: A Perspective on the Industrial Revolution in Britain*, Cambridge: Cambridge University Press.

—— (1992) *The Industrial Revolution*, London: Edward Arnold.

Hunt, E. H. (1973) *Regional Wage Variations in Britain, 1850–1914*, Oxford: Oxford University Press.

—— (1986) 'Industrialisation and Regional Inequality in Britain, 1760–1914', *Journal of Economic History*, 46, 4.

Igartua, J. E. (1991) 'The Computer and the Historian's Work', *History and Computing*, 3, 2.

Johnson, H. J. M. (1972) *British Emigration Policy 1815–30: Shovelling out Paupers*, Oxford: Clarenden Press.

Johnson, P (1992) *Saving and Spending: The Working-class Economy in Britain 1870–1939*, Oxford: Clarendon Press.

Lee, C. H. (1972) *A Cotton Enterprise 1795–1840: A History of McConell and Kennedy: Fine Cotton Spinners*, Manchester: Manchester University Press.

Lewis, E. D. (1959) *The Rhondda Valleys*, London: Phoenix House.

Lewis, M. J. (1990) 'The Growth and Development of Sheffield's Industrial Structure 1880–1930', unpublished Ph.D. thesis, Sheffield Hallam University.

Lloyd, T. O. (1984) *The British Empire 1558–1983*, Oxford: Oxford University Press.

Lloyd-Jones, R. and Le Roux, A. A. (1980) 'The Size of Firms in the Cotton Industry: Manchester 1815–1841', *Economic History Review*, 33, 1.

Lloyd-Jones, R. and Lewis, M. J. (1988) *Manchester and the Age of the Factory: The Business Structure of Cottonopolis in the Industrial Revolution*, London: Croom Helm.

—— (1990a) 'A Database for Historical Reconstruction: Manchester in the Industrial Revolution', in E. Mawdsley *et al.* (eds) *History and Computing III: Historians, Computers and Data*, Manchester: Manchester University Press.

—— (1990b) *Small Savers in the Mid-Victorian Period*, Sheffield Hallam University: School of Cultural Studies Pamphlet.

—— (1993a) 'Housing Factory Workers: Ancoats in the Early Nineteenth Century', *Manchester Region History Review*, Special Edition.

—— (1993b) 'Business Structure and Political Economy in Sheffield: The Metal Trades 1880–1920s', in C. Binfield, R. Childs, R. Harper, D. Hey, D. Martin and G. Tweedale (eds), *The History of the City of Sheffield*, 2, Sheffield: Sheffield Academic Press.

—— (1994a) 'Personal Capitalism and British Industrial Decline: The Personally Managed Firm and Business Strategy in Sheffield, 1880–1920', *Business History Review*, 68, 3.

—— (1994b) 'What Can We Do with Historical Databases?: Applications in Teaching and Research', *History Microcomputer Review*, 10, 2.

McCloskey, D. N. (1981) 'The Industrial Revolution, 1780–1860: A Survey', in R. Floud and D. N. McCloskey (eds), *The Economic History of Britain since 1700*, Cambridge: Cambridge University Press

Mackerness, E. D. (1993) 'Sheffield's Cultural Life' in C. Binfield, R. Childs, R. Harper, D. Hey, D. Martin and G. Tweedale (eds), *The History of the City of Sheffield*, 2, Sheffield: Sheffield Academic Press.

Marrison, A. J. (1977) 'The Development of a Tariff Reform Policy during Joseph Chamberlain's First Campaign, May 1903 – February 1904', in W. H. Chaloner and B. M. Ratcliffe (eds), *Trade and Transport*, Manchester: Manchester University Press.

Mathias, P. (1969) *The First Industrial Nation*, London: Methuen.

Mawdsley, E. and Munck, T. (1993) *Computing for Historians. An Introductory Guide*, Manchester: Manchester University Press.

Mawdsley, E., Morgan, N., Richmond, L. and Trainor, R. (eds) (1990) *History and Computing III: Historians, Computers and Data*, Manchester: Manchester University Press.

Middleton, R. (1989) 'Computer Techniques and Economic Theory in Historical Analysis', *History and Computing*, 1, 1.

Mitchell, B. R. and Deane, P. (1962) *Abstract of British Historical Statistics*, Cambridge: Cambridge University Press.

Morris, R. J. (1989) 'Editorial', *History and Computing*, 1, 1.

—— (1991) *Class, Sect and Party: The Making of the Middle Class, 1800–1850*, Cambridge: Cambridge University Press.

Munck, T. (1990) 'Counting Heads: Using Small Data Sets from English and Danish Census-type Sources', in E. Mawdsley *et al.* (eds) *History and Computing III: Historians, Computers and Data*, Manchester: Manchester University Press.

Oddy, D. J. (1970) 'Working-class Diets in Late Nineteenth Century Britain', *Economic History Review*, 23.

Oram, A. (1995) *Women Teachers and Feminist Politics 1900–1939*, Manchester: Manchester University Press.

Overy, R. J. (1975) 'Cars, Roads and Economic Recovery in Germany, 1932–8', *Economic History Review*, 38.

—— (1982) *The Nazi Economic Recovery 1932–1938*, London: Macmillan.

Parliamentary Papers (1827) *Report of the Select Committee on Emigration*.

—— (1828) *The Law Relating to Savings Banks in England and Wales*.

—— (1832) *Factory Inspectors' Report*.

—— (1833) *Report of Emigration Commissioners*.

—— (1841) *Factory Inspectors' Report*.

—— (1850) *Report of the Select Committee on the Savings of the Middle and Working Classes*.

—— (1886) *Second Report of the Royal Commission on the Depression of Trade and Industry*.

—— (1889) *Report of the Select Committee on Colonisation*.

Payne, P. L. (1967) 'The Savings Bank of Glasgow 1836–1914', in P. L. Payne (ed.) *Studies in Scottish Business History*, London: Cass.

Pollard, S. (1954) 'Wages and Earnings in the Sheffield Trades, 1851–1914', *Yorkshire Bulletin*.

—— (1959) *A History of Labour in Sheffield*, Liverpool: Liverpool University Press.

—— (1990) *Britain's Prime and Britain's Decline: The British Economy 1870–1914*, London: Edward Arnold.

Potter, J. (1985) *The American Economy between the World Wars*, Basingstoke: Macmillan Education.

Renshaw, P. (1993) 'Aspects of Sport and Recreation', in C. Binfield *et al.* (eds), *The History of the City of Sheffield*, 2, Sheffield: Sheffield Academic Press.

Richards, E. (1993) 'How Did Poor People Emigrate from the British Isles to Australia in the Nineteenth Century?', *Journal of British Studies*, 22.

Ridley, J. (1992) 'The Unionist Opposition and the House of Lords 1906–1910', *Parliamentary History*, 11, part 2.

Rodgers (1989) *Housing in Urban Britain 1870–1914: Class, Capitalism and Construction*, Basingstoke: Macmillan Education.

Rowntree, D. (1991) *Statistics without Tears*, London: Penguin.

Ryall, T. (1986) *Alfred Hitchcock and the British Cinema*, London: Croom Helm.

Schweitzer, A. (1964) *Big Business in the Third Reich*, London: Eyre and Spottiswood.

Schurer, K. (1990) 'The Historical Researcher and Codes: Master or Slave or Slave and Master?' in E. Mawdsley *et al.* (eds) *History and Computing III: Historians, Computers and Data*, Manchester: Manchester University Press.

Searle, G. R. (1993) 'The Edwardian Liberal Party and Business', *English Historical Review*, 98.

Shaw, A. G. (1969) 'British Attitudes to the Colonies 1820–1950', *Journal of British Studies*, 9.

Sheffield Social Survey (1931) Sheffield: Sheffield Archives.

Shuttleworth, J. P. K. (1832) *The Moral and Physical Condition of the Working Classes Employed in the Cotton Manufacture of Manchester*, London: reprinted by Frank Cass, 1970.

Smiles, S. (1895) *Self Help*, London: John Murray.

Spaeth, D. M. (1989) 'The IBM Compatible Anatomised', *History and Computing*, 1, 1.

Speck, W. A. (1994) 'History and Computing: Some Reflections on the Past Decade', *History and Computing*, 6, 1.

Taylor, S. (1993) 'The Industrial Structure of the Sheffield Cutlery Trades, 1870–1914', in C. Binfield *et al.* (eds), *The History of the City of Sheffield*, 2, Sheffield: Sheffield Academic Press.

Temin, P. (1971) *Did Monetary Factors Cause the Great Depression?*, New York: Norton.

Thaler, M. (1989) 'The Need for a Theory of Historical Computing', in P. Denley *et al.*, *History and Computing II*, Manchester: Manchester University Press.

Thane, P. (1982) *The Foundations of the Welfare State*, London: Longman.

Thomas, B. (1954) *Migration and Economic Growth*, Cambridge: Cambridge University Press.

Thomas, D. (1988) 'Economic Decline', in T. Herbert and Gareth Elwyn Jones (eds) *Wales between the Wars*, Cardiff: University of Wales Press.

Thomas, J. A. (1958) *The House of Commons 1906–1911. An Analysis of its Economic and Social Character*, Cardiff: University of Wales Press.

Trainor, R. (1990) 'Improving and Expanding Computer Based Teaching for Undergraduates', in E. Mawdsley *et al.* (eds) *History and Computing III: Historians, Computers and Data*, Manchester: Manchester University Press.

Treble, J. H. (1979) *Urban Poverty in Britain 1830–1914*, London: Batsford.

TSB Records, Deposit Books of the Sheffield Savings Bank, Sheffield: Sheffield Archives.

Turner, H. A. (1969) 'Big Business and the Rise of Hitler', *American Historical Review*, 25.

Tweedale, G. (1993) 'The Business and Technology of Steelmaking', in C. Binfield *et al.* (eds), *The History of the City of Sheffield*, 2, Sheffield: Sheffield Academic Press.

Ure, A. (1836) *The Cotton Manufacture of Great Britain Systematically Investigated*, 1, London: reprinted by H. G. Bohn.

Wakefield Admission Records, Registers of Admissions, Wakefield: Wakefield Public Archives Office.

Ward, R. (1988) *In Memory of Sheffield Cinemas*, Sheffield: Sheffield City Libraries.

Wardley, P. (1990) 'Information Technology in Economic and Social History: The Computer as Philospher's Stone or Pandora's Box', *Economic History Review*, 43, 4.

—— (1994) 'Edwardian Britain: Empire, Income and Political Discontent', in P. Johnson (ed.) *Twentieth Century Britain*, London: Longman.

Williams, K. (1983) *From Pauperism to Poverty*, London: Routledge and Kegan Paul.

Williams, M. with Farnie, D. A. (1992) *Cotton Mills in Greater Manchester*, Manchester: Manchester University Press.

Index